To Sa

Paul Wojdak.

Escape from Siberia,
Escape from Memory

"The story of the orphaned Polish children saved by the Polish Rescue Committee and the Japanese Red Cross continues to gain a growing audience and ever greater currency with every retelling, largely through the efforts of such institutions as the Manghaa Museum of Japanese Art and Technology in Poland, the Social Welfare Corporation Fukudenkai of Tokyo, and the Port of Humanity Tsuruga Museum in Japan, but also through the direct engagement of the Siberian Children's descendants. One of the latter is Paul Wojdak... [He] create[d] a fascinating book, a narrative about a rescued Siberian Child, against the background of Polish exiles and refugees, the search for one's origins, and ultimately a sense of fulfilled duty towards one's father."

— KATARZYNA NOWAK
Director, Manghaa Museum of Japanese Art and Technology, Krakow, Poland

"Paul's new book details his father's life and his own experiences tracing his father's footsteps, and is an epic that connects Russia, Poland, Japan, and North America. It also contributes to comprehensive study of the history and geography of various countries, packed with valuable information based on his vigorous and in-depth research, and is an essential text for us museum staff. A must-read book without difficult technical terms, but with a gentle and comfortable narrative that is consistent throughout the text and reminds us of Paul's personality."

— AKINORI NISHIKAWA
Director, Port of Humanity Tsuruga Museum, Japan

◆ FriesenPress

One Printers Way
Altona, MB R0G 0B0
Canada

www.friesenpress.com

ISBN
978-1-03-919687-2 (Hardcover)
978-1-03-919686-5 (Paperback)
978-1-03-919688-9 (eBook)

1. BIOGRAPHY & AUTOBIOGRAPHY, HISTORICAL

Distributed to the trade by The Ingram Book Company

Escape from Siberia,

Escape from Memory

AN ODYSSEY ACROSS TWO OCEANS &
NINE COUNTRIES TO ARRIVE HOME

PAUL WOJDAK

Contents

To Teresa for her support and inspiration,
To my children for their heritage,
To Descendants of Sybiraks everywhere,
known and unrevealed—they deserve to be remembered

1.

My Father and Family Beginnings

My father, Pawel Wojdak, was a Polish orphan. He was born in 1912 and died in 1984. Pawel Wojdak's life was greatly disrupted by two world wars and other world events. His traumatic youth included the death of his parents. His mind blocked the memory of those events; only fragments of his early life were preserved. As a child, I assumed my father was born in Poland because he was Polish. Beginning my research from his fragmentary memories, I discovered he was born in Asia not Europe, specifically Siberia. The beginning of my father's life story is wrapped up in a tale of survival by 765 Polish children from Siberia.

There were many tens of thousands of Poles in Siberia, an unknown number, but the few children and adults who escaped Siberia were a small portion. Most Polish people—adults and children—died or were stranded and not heard from again. The tale of these Poles, those who escaped and those who were lost, was poorly known for decades, as it was suppressed by Russia and forgotten elsewhere in the world.

For my father, his journey of escape was both physical and emotional because he consigned his memories to a hidden place in his mind to leave them behind. Now, there is an international network of descendants of survivors of Siberian children, which brings their story and memories back to life.

The Siberian children were brought to Poland in 1920–1922, with the crucial help of the Japanese government and the Red Cross. For nearly all the children, it was not a case of "returning to Poland" because they had never lived there. After his arrival, Pawel Wojdak, still an orphan, grew up under difficult circumstances. He was a young man when World War II began, and his life changed irrevocably once more. He made very difficult choices in order to survive. His emotions about his choices and decisions were probably so raw, they became a different type of lost memory, one that was hidden. Here, too, research—in this case, research of war records—gave insight.

Pawel Wojdak was a member of the British Eighth Army's Polish II Corps, also known informally as the Polish Army. The Polish II Corps played an important role in the liberation of Italy and were critical in the pivotal Battle of Monte Cassino. They fought in the British Army to ultimately liberate Poland and return to their homeland. But Russia had occupied Poland and was not about to restore its pre-war borders. For a great many of the Polish soldiers, their homes were now in Belarus, Lithuania, or Ukraine. Nonetheless, they were invited to return to Poland and, eventually, pressured to do so, but virtually every Polish soldier refused because they distrusted Russian motives. Britain recast the Polish Army as the Polish Resettlement Corps and transferred them from Italy to camps scattered across the United Kingdom. Pawel Wojdak came to a resettlement camp near Amersham, England, in 1946.

There, Pawel Wojdak met Ricky Versteeg, a woman who moved from Amsterdam, Netherlands, the same year. She had endured deprivation and emotional upset during the war and came to England in search of a better life. Despite different backgrounds, they had an important connection: they were both lonely and in a foreign land. Pawel spoke Polish, German, and a smattering of Italian. Ricky spoke Dutch, German, English, and a little French. Their first conversations were in German, but in the immediate post-war years, that language was unpopular. Pawel learned English. I was born in a hospital near Amersham on January 4, 1948 (photo 1.1). From the beginning, my father was devoted to me (photo 1.2)

Photo 1.1: Pawel, Ricky, and Paul Wojdak in England, 1948

Photo 1.2: Pawel and Paul Wojdak, about 1950

My name is Paul Wojdak—Paul is the English equivalent of Pawel. In Polish, Wojdak is pronounced Voy-dak. *W* in Polish sounds as *V*, and *j* is pronounced as *i* or, in some words, as *y* like yes. For all people, our family name lies at the core of who we are: it is a key piece of our identity. An important theme of this work is memory and identity, both individual and national. What we remember shapes how we see ourselves and who we are. My searching found some of what Pawel Wojdak could not remember and some of what he wanted to forget.

This story is also about Pawel Wojdak finding his home—his journey from Siberia. In the first forty years of his life, he was in nine countries on three continents as a refugee, an orphan, a fostered farmworker, and a young man in the army. Most of his countless moves were beyond his control. Finally, in Canada, he achieved a home and a settled life, one he would never give up. I cannot determine why Pawel Wojdak's parents were in Siberia, and because he shared part of his young life with other Siberian children, I will track a number of other children, knowing that my father's origins will be somewhere among their stories.

On November 7, 1952, my mother, father, and I boarded a Cunard-line ship to Canada (photo 1.3). I was allowed to bring two prized possessions, five slim "Noddy" books, and a small blue tin of conkers. Dad used significant savings to buy a sheepskin-lined coat because it would be very cold in Canada.

Photo 1.3: Crossing the Atlantic on SS Scythia

The ship log records some variation of stormy weather throughout the trip, but one day stands out for me. My father held me in his arms on the deck near the stern to see monstrous rolling waves heading toward us. From the trough of one, we seemed to look above our heads at the next crest. As that wave rolled ominously toward us, the ship's stern rose sharply and I looked out to the horizon at a succession of giant rollers as far as I could see. Exhilarating—but in an instant, the stern sank into the next trough as the bow rose—frightening again! An alternating feeling of fear and exhilaration continued. A second vivid memory is a shipboard view of snowy Levis, Quebec: colourful houses subdued by a sullen, overcast day. The date of our arrival in Canada was November 15, 1952.

Photo 1.4: The Hogsback overlooking the Credit River

Our first home in Canada was a large, wooded property in Port Credit, west of Toronto, where my mother and father took care of the house and grounds for the affluent owners (photo 1.4). The Credit River below the house was where Dad and I spent many hours fishing. For bait, we dug for worms. Dad would turn the soil with a shovel while I spotted the worms and added each to a jar with a little soil. We caught suckers, catfish, carp, and occasionally bass (photo 1.5). At first, we ate everything because every penny was saved toward a home of our own. I liked catfish best because they had no bones. Gradually, our taste became more selective. Dad planted a large vegetable garden in the rich soil near the river, but deer ate everything before we did! Dad and I were close; I knew he loved me very much. I often sat on his lap as a young child, and we wrestled on the living room floor (photo 1.6). In five years, Pawel and Ricky saved enough for the down payment on a newly built house in a small town named Streetsville.

A home of our own was hugely important to each of us but in different ways. For me, it meant freedom to go anywhere in our house and not be mindful of being silent—though I was quiet, regardless. My mother was free to pursue a career outside the home. It took many years before I appreciated what my father most valued: a home that was truly his and from which he would never be required to move.

Photo 1.5. Carp from Credit River

Photo 1.6. Wojdak family at The Hogsback

In my first few years of school, I learned Wojdak is an awkward name for English-speaking people to pronounce and spell. They are strongly inclined to pronounce *j* as in "jam" or "jack." We became known as the "Wojack" family—at least, that was how it was pronounced and it was commonly misspelled as "Wodjak." I knew what was correct, but as my parents yielded, so did I. We reluctantly accepted a mispronounced name, but we were adamant about a proper spelling. Perhaps because Mom and Dad tired of correcting the spelling, or perhaps because I was teased occasionally at school about our unusual name, they asked one day if I would like to change our name to Woods. Immediately, I vetoed the idea. Decades later, it took the unexpected leadership of my grown children to restore the correct pronunciation of Wojdak. My son, a teacher, has gone full-Polish: his students call him "*Voy-dak.*" After most of my life, it was difficult to make the change, so I am more lenient and use "Woy-dak," pronouncing *W* as it is in English. It gratifies me to know my father would be pleased.

Summer vacations involved camping, and one of Dad's favourite pastimes: fishing. He was an accomplished fisherman; from northern lakes, we ate trout and pickerel (photo 1.7). Gardening was another of his passions. Our home was built on red clay: slimy and slippery when wet; hard as concrete when dry. He worked hard to enrich the soil by repeated applications of topsoil, manure, and fish fertilizer. We no longer ate fish from the Credit River; they were used to supplement the soil. Dad was proud to have the best flowers in the neighbourhood; his roses were remarkable (photo 1.8). He regularly bought flowers for my mother—yellow chrysanthemums in a pot because they last longer than cut flowers. Sometimes when Dad and I were together in the car and we passed a flower market, Dad would say, "We should get some flowers." We would look over the selection and I would make suggestions, but when we came to pay, it was always a pot of yellow chrysanthemums.

Photo 1.7. Fishing success

Photo 1.8. Pawel Wojdak's roses

We enjoyed camping holidays in Algonquin Park or at Lake Temagami; a boat enhanced our enjoyment and was a great advantage for fishing (photo 1.9). Initially, we rented a boat, but in my early teens, Mom and Dad purchased one and an outboard motor. I listened with excitement as they discussed if the proposed purchase was wise, and to prod them, I blurted that I would buy the trailer to tow it, using my savings from a year-long paper delivery route.

With our own motorboat, I learned to water-ski. Dad would use his day off from work in the summer to take several of my friends and I out for a day of fun on the water. One of my friends was particularly slow to control getting out of the water on skis. Dad was patient during his learning process, encouraging him to try over and over again. And then he drove the boat around and around the small lake as four of us took repeated turns.

My mother's holiday meals (birthdays, Easter, Christmas, New Year's) were a special event (photo 1.10), as it was an occasion to celebrate family and abundance in our life in Canada. Unlike my father's, my childhood was idyllic.

Photo 1.9. Lake Temagami, 1960

Photo 1.10. A special dinner

2.

A Boy's Questions

As a young child, I asked each of my parents about their past. There was a great contrast in what each told me. Mom spoke readily about her mother and father, her brother and four sisters, and their happy life as she grew up. On many Sunday afternoons, we looked at photographs as she spoke about the people in them: my aunts and uncles, countless cousins, my oma and opa, and even their parents. Dad spoke almost nothing about his family. I knew, of course, he was an orphan, but there were no photos from Poland at all, just a few from the war, which he did not speak about, so I never discovered who any of the other people in them were.

Ricky was not my mother's proper name; it was Maria, but she did not like that name. When required to use her formal name, she used to say, "If you want to be friends, call me Ricky, not Maria." It is a Dutch custom to modify first names into the diminutive form, so Maria was called Marietje as a youngster, and that was soon shortened to Rietje. In England and later in Canada, she chose to modify Rietje to Ricky.

She was born in Amsterdam on April 23, 1920, into a loving working-class family, the fifth of six children. They lived in a tenement building, in four rooms on the second floor with a shared bathroom down the hall. An aunt and uncle with their children lived on the ground floor. Oom (Uncle)

Kase was in the merchant navy; his uniform, handsome features, and stories of world travels made him a romantic figure to the Versteeg children. All the neighbourhood children played in the street.

Ricky's father worked at a government plant where anthracite coal was converted to coke and gas for cooking in homes. The coke (coal) heated government buildings, including schools. He also rented a plot of land outside the city to grow vegetables. Young Rietje would ride with him on his bike, sitting on a small seat on the crossbar; they were teased as "Pa and Pietje." Ricky's mother took in laundry to supplement the family's income.

Photo 2.1. *The Versteeg children: Nellie, Annie, Wim, Ricky, Jopie, and Tony*

A professional portrait of the six Versteeg children in 1925 serves as a family reference point (photo 2.1). It shows Ricky's oldest sister, Nellie, at seventeen years of age; Tony at sixteen; Wim at thirteen; Annie at eleven; my mother five years old; and Jopie at one-and-a-half—all are abbreviations of their proper names. Nellie and Tony were already working; Nellie started at fourteen as the apprentice of a tailor, making coats and suits. Tony, at the same age, became an apprentice dressmaker; she was so proficient that she was quickly promoted to making sample dresses, which were then reproduced in quantity for marketing. She could make a dress directly from a picture in a fashion magazine without a pattern. Sadly, Tony died of cancer in 1956. With her husband accompanying her, Nellie was the first of my mother's siblings to visit us in Canada. I was a shy teenager, totally unprepared for her powerful bearhug—I remember feeling my lungs nearly collapse in her embrace.

Mom's only brother, Wim, became an apprentice electrician not long after the family portrait was taken. All the children in the photo show perfect posture except Annie, who is slouched and with feet apart, not crossed as all the other girls were coached to do, in the proper style for young ladies. When Ricky began school at about the age in the photo, Annie was responsible for escorting her there. Annie was assertive and "marched to her own drum," in my mother's words, so they commonly arrived late for school. Ricky would say, "It's not my fault; I was with Annie!" The teacher would reply, "Why can't you be more like your sister Tony?" (Tony had been a model student.)

In 1934, at fourteen years of age, Ricky began work in the office of a retail shoe business that had five stores in Amsterdam, one in Arnhem, one in Haarlem, and one in Den Haag (The Hague). She earned fifteen guilders per month and worked 8:30 a.m. to 6:00 p.m., five days per week and a half day on Saturday. Her earnings were turned in to her mother, and she received an allowance, as was customary in European families. She attended night school on weeknights from 7:00 p.m. to 10:00 p.m. to learn accounting, German, and shorthand.

Mom's mother fell gravely ill with pneumonia and pleurisy in 1935 and spent six months in hospital. Mom went to live with Nellie, while Annie quit her job to stay at home and look after youngest sister Jopie, and Wim postponed his marriage. There was a sense of impending war, but people thought the Netherlands could be neutral, as it had been in World War I. When Germany invaded, Nellie, Tony, and Wim were married and had young families. Annie was married too and pregnant with her first child; her husband, Piet, was away from home in the army. The war years were very difficult for the Dutch, perhaps more so for city-dwellers due to food shortages. I will describe that period in a future chapter.

After World War II, Ricky's sister Nellie, Wim, and their large family lived in Amsterdam. Sister Tony, her husband, and their daughter moved to Utrecht. In 1954, Ricky's only brother Wim, his wife, and their four children immigrated to Adelaide, Australia. Sister Annie, Piet, and their large family moved to Castricum, a town close to sand dunes along the North Sea coast. My network of Dutch relatives was distant, but they were part of my life.

This rich detail of the Versteeg family, with their pranks, teasing, and songs, was a stark contrast to my father's barren life. All the places on the map of Poland were difficult combinations of letters, but if he would point out his "hometown" to me or where he lived, I would learn to pronounce it. He was in an orphanage, but he did not say its name. Somehow, from the orphanage, he went to live on a farm, but the farmers seemed not to have a role as parents, not even as foster parents, because there was no affection and he slept in the barn.

When I asked him what happened to his mother, he told me that she had died in a train accident when he was six. "And your father?" I asked, and he replied that he had died in a train accident too, a year later. I didn't know what to make of such an unfortunate coincidence, and Dad said no more. From several other inquiries, I saw that my questions caused him great distress. His jaw became tightly set, all his muscles tensed, and his eyes focused somewhere in the distance. He also said he was in Japan and America as a child—how could that be, I wondered? And there was not a single photograph.

I could not understand why Dad could not tell me more about his life. Once, when I had asked how he got to America and Japan, he said his father brought him. I tried to imagine the circumstances. Could it be that his father was a businessman and they went to America after his mother died? But businessmen are rich, right? So, why was he poor? It was murky and confusing. I began to wonder, was he really in Japan and America? When I sensed his mood was particularly good, I asked again about his childhood, and I hoped he could tell me more of his mysterious past. He added a few words: he was in Chicago and Milwaukee and was amazed to see a tractor for the first time and other machines. Later, in Poland, he wondered why there were no machines there. While in America, he said the children were asked one day, "Who wants to go home?" They all answered yes because, as Dad said, what child does not want to go home? Later, he thought this was a trick to persuade the children, as "home" in Poland was a poor orphanage, not the family home he expected. This is the only comment from my father that indicated he was one of a group of children, a comment that I was not alert to recognize at the time.

I was never aware of any Polish nationalism in my father. He did not make friends easily, but of the ones he did make, none were Polish. He was cautious to be himself, unlike my outgoing mother, who made friends easily. Friends of my mother became Dad's friends too. Some were Dutch couples but not many because my mother did not want to isolate my dad in a Dutch conversation. Their friends became a diverse group of Canadians.

In my early years, there was an unpredictable side to Dad's nature. He could be withdrawn, and a minor event could provoke a great rage; it was intense and the uncertainty meant being around him could be like walking on eggshells. There was never violence, but I was afraid there could be. The target of his rage was not clear, usually something minor. My mother was a strong person; she never cowered or backed down. Gradually, over a twenty-year period, his angry outbursts ended and he enjoyed a good life together with my mother. And importantly, there were two instances of his growing ability to recall early events in his life.

It was many years after Dad died that my mother and I were surprised to learn that we knew so many different slivers of his early life. Perhaps if he had been less secretive, we might have "joined the dots" sooner. Mom asked where he was born; Novo-Mikolajewsk was his answer. I asked where he lived and thought he answered "near Gneizno," but my mother said she never heard him say that, so perhaps I misheard. My mother learned that a small scar on his back was from hospital treatment in Japan. Another time, he mentioned to her that a German boy shared his school lunch because Dad did not have enough to eat. My mother learned the farm he lived on was owned by a German-Polish man and wife named Schulz. I learned that he slept in the barn and had shoes only in the winter, and sometimes, they went to Breslau to sell farm produce. Breslau was in Germany then but in Poland after 1945 and renamed Wroclaw. I searched maps of Poland for

Novo-Mikolajewsk without success. Most significantly, Mom related that when they met, Dad did not speak English, yet he could recite a child's rhyme: *"Come, little sister, and sit by me, and I will teach you A-B-C."*

As a teenager, Pawel Wojdak was placed in a trade school to learn to be a blacksmith. He and another boy ran away but were returned. Dad told me there were no ill feelings between German and Polish people before the war, that animosity was created by propaganda. He told my mother that he went to Germany before the war to find work because there was none in Poland, and that he had been married. Not long after they met, she asked Dad what his mother's name was; she had been reading a newspaper at the same time. Dad leapt to his feet, eager to know what was written in the paper about his mother. He misunderstood; he was still looking for his parents. When my mother and I compared notes, we were surprised we had different fragments of his early life. They were vague and disconnected, not contradictory but difficult to assemble into a historical sequence.

The first and most important clue about my father's past occurred when I was about ten years old. There was a problem with the gas furnace in our house. The repairman was Japanese, and Dad worked closely with him, to see what needed to be repaired or adjusted. I played close by, not listening to their conversation, but when the repairman was about to leave, Dad stood at attention and began to sing in Japanese Japan's national anthem! After the man left, Dad said proudly, "He said I sang it perfectly! And I counted to ten in Japanese too." I was amazed; my dad had never burst into song before in any language. I was to learn after his death about his experience in Japan, which left such a strong impression he remembered the Japanese anthem after forty years! I believe now that it was the Japanese repairman's character, the innate attributes of a Japanese person, that unlocked a long-ago memory in my father's mind. This was a pivotal event for me; any doubt of his being in Japan was erased. However difficult it was to imagine how a young Polish boy came to be in Japan, I was certain he had been there.

On another occasion, after I was no longer living at home, he and my mother were watching a television documentary. The Catholic charity "Caritas" was mentioned. My father jumped to his feet and said, "That's who brought us to America!" I believe the name of the Caritas organization triggered another fact to emerge from his subconscious. But still, most of Dad's childhood remained a mystery both to me and largely to himself. I completed school, began a career as a geologist, married, had children, and moved to Vancouver, far from my parents in Ontario. The puzzle of my father's origins never vanished, but it became a lower priority in a busy life.

As an adult, I recognize that my father's memory was deeply suppressed. My questions about his parents triggered flashbacks that his mind strained to prevent from surfacing. I also recognize that my father was hypersensitive, and the minor incidents that provoked a disproportionate outburst of temper are symptoms of post-traumatic stress disorder (PTSD). PTSD was not a recognized condition at that time, but it is now.

From what I have now learned, I am certain he was present when his mother and father died from hardship or violence. Wieslaw Theiss is a professor at the University of Warsaw and a lecturer at Maria Grzegorzewska University. Theiss investigated Polish child-survivors of World War II who experienced dehumanizing treatment and close experiences with death to determine the impact on their future personality and physical development—a phenomenon known as the "war complex."[1] The study is relevant to Siberian children affected by the Russian Revolution and Civil War in 1917–1920. The effects on a child depend on their age, individual disposition, and childcare. Theiss states, in a translation, that the "deepest traumas arose among younger children and those deprived of a family home . . . and the strongest mental shocks were caused by the death of a loved one, arrests and observation of public executions."[2] Observed behaviours include guilt toward those who died, a tendency to cry, general irritability, language

---

1 Wieslaw Theiss, "Help, Care and Rescue of Children in Poland in the War and Occupation Period (1939–1945): An Outline," *Social Work in Poland* 1 (2018): 8, https://www. academia. edu/42758361/W_Theiss_Help_care_and_rescue_of_children_in_Poland_in_the_ war_and_occupation_period_1939_1945_An_outline.

2 Wieslaw Theiss, "Sieroctwo Wojenne Polskich Dzieci (1939–1945). Zarys Problematyki" ["The War Orphanhood of Polish Children (1939–1945). An Outline"], *Przeglad Pedagogiczny* 1 (2012): 84, https://przegladpedagogiczny.ukw.edu.pl/archive/article/322/ sieroctwo-wojenne-polskich-dzieci-1939-1945-zarys-problematyki/.

disorder[3], nightmares, anxiety, timidity, and suspicion of strangers. In this context, language disorder refers to children who have difficulty to understand what is said to them and struggle to articulate their ideas and feelings. War orphans require a combination of medical, emotional, educational, and social assistance to aid in their recovery.

3 "What is Language Disorder?" Language Disorder Australia, https://languagedisorder.org.au/what-is-language-disorder/?gad=1&gclid=CjwKCAiA3aeqBhBzEiwAxFiOBg5CMINnyHhZJvFMQby72tWcsK2ldVRh7xmWOK9bXXWkuS7TtF_ULRoCUHYQAvD_BwE

3.

Discovery of Pawel Wojdak's Origin

Today, an internet search is a standard and sophisticated tool. In 2001, before Google became predominant, internet searches were comparatively primitive; research was mainly from printed words on paper. My first research campaign took place from March to May 2001, seventeen years after my father's death in 1984. I began by learning about the formation and actions of the 3rd Carpathian Rifle Division,[4] the unit Pawel Wojdak belonged to in the Polish II Corps of the British Army. The aim of my research was to correlate my father's description with movements of the Polish Army during the war and, thereby, trace his steps.

Pawel Wojdak was twenty-seven years old when Germany initiated World War II on September 1, 1939, by invading Poland. Wladyslaw Sikorski, a former military commander and prime minister of Poland (1922–1923), escaped to England and formed the Polish government-in-exile. The United Kingdom declared war against Germany, and Poland expected immediate action to resist the Germans. Instead, sixteen days later, Russia invaded

---

4 Wikipedia, s.v. "Polish Independent Carpathian Rifle Brigade," last modified December 15, 2022, https://en.wikipedia.org/wiki/Polish_Independent_Carpathian_Rifle_Brigade.

Poland from the east. There was a secret agreement between Germany and Russia: the nefarious Molotov-Ribbentrop Pact.[5] The Polish Army was trapped between the Russians and Germans, and most of the Polish soldiers were captured. From those captured by Russia, the majority of Polish soldiers were deported to Russia.

My father was imprecise about his location and participation at the beginning of the war, but he said he was in the Polish Army and had escaped to Palestine in the Middle East with the assistance of partisans. This matches historic accounts.

Remnants of the Polish Army who were not captured by either the Germans or the Russians made their way to France or French-controlled territory in Syria and Lebanon. France was the major patron of Poland's exiled forces through 1939–1940. Several thousand Poles escaped through the Balkans to Syria and Lebanon. I considered that my father was among them. Lebanon was the birthplace of the Carpathian Brigade in 1940—the predecessor of Pawel Wojdak's unit, the 3rd Carpathian Rifles. The cedar of Lebanon superficially resembles a Christmas tree and is featured on the flag of Lebanon. It became the emblem of the Carpathian Brigade. The origin is Biblical; Psalms 92: 13 states, "The righteous shall flourish like the palm tree, he shall grow like a cedar in Lebanon." This emblem and that of the Polish II Corps were on Pawel Wojdak's army jacket that hung on a peg in our basement when I was a boy (photos 3.1 and 3.2). He scarcely ever wore the jacket, but it was there for years; it must have reminded him of his past or perhaps been a validation of his journey.

The Carpathian Brigade comprised 3 500 officers and men when it formed in March 1940 and soon expanded to 5 000. When France capitulated to Nazi Germany in the summer of 1940, the French governor in Lebanon opted to support the French Vichy regime, a Nazi puppet. This was not acceptable to the Polish government-in-exile in England, who then ordered the Carpathian Brigade to relocate to adjacent British-ruled Palestine. Consequently, the Carpathian Brigade and, later, the whole Polish Army came under British command.

---

5 Wikipedia, s.v. "Molotov-Ribbentrop Pact," last modified October 30, 2023, https://en.wikipedia.org/wiki/Molotov%E2%80%93Ribbentrop_Pact.

| Photo 3.1. Emblem of | Photo 3.2. Emblem of |
| *3rd Carpathian Rifle Division* | *Polish II Corps* |

The unit was renamed the Independent Polish Carpathian Brigade and became part of the British Eighth Army, which was hastily formed to repel the combined forces of Italy and Germany in North Africa. Italy had opened hostilities by invading British-ruled Egypt from its territory in Libya. The Eighth Army was an extraordinary amalgamation of British, Polish, South African, Czech, Indian, New Zealand, and Australian divisions and brigades. The Polish Carpathian Brigade was deployed to Tobruk in Libya to support trapped and outnumbered Australian forces. The Siege of Tobruk lasted 241 days, and casualties were heavy, mainly Australians. Pawel Wojdak spoke about the Battle of Tobruk and how intense the fighting was. It was one of his war experiences that he told many times if the topic was brought up in conversation. His experience in the Battle of Monte Cassino in Italy was the other war action he spoke about. I learned it was the pivotal battle of the Italian campaign, one that broke Germany's defensive line, enabling the liberation of Rome. The assault by the Polish II Corps at Monte Cassino was their greatest military distinction.

Another artifact from a pocket of Pawel Wojdak's army jacket was a bracelet with inscriptions on each side and a perforation line (photos 3.3 and 3.4). Dad explained to me that it was a false identity tag in case he was captured by the enemy; the only correct information was his blood type. Such bracelets are more commonly called dog tags nowadays and worn around the neck. They identify the soldier by name, army number, and birthplace or hometown, in addition to blood type. If the soldier is killed, the tag can be separated along the perforations: one half to remain with the body and the other half to be passed up the chain of command so that the family can be notified.

Photos 3.3 and 3.4. Polish Army identity bracelet in the name of Konstanty Mlotek of Wilno, born 1917, NE 3787, blood type A positive

While learning about Russian deportation of Polish soldiers and their families in World War II, I chanced, in 2001, on a brief account of Polish children, many of them orphans arriving in Japan from Siberia in 1920–1921. The children were repatriated to Poland, some by way of America. The years corresponded to when my father was a boy. My father did not talk about Russia or Siberia, but what does a young child know about countries? The link of Polish children with Japan and America was compelling. I was amazed. My heart leapt! I was sure this must be my father's story, and there must be a way to learn more!

Intuitively, I was certain this was his story. It seemed reasonable that the University of Hokkaido in Sapporo, close to Siberia, would focus on the history of Japanese-Soviet relations. The website of the Slavic Research Center at the university enabled contact with two faculty members (Teruyuki Hara and Tadayuki Hayashi) whose areas of specialty were Russian history and East European politics. They confirmed the historic event and facilitated contact with a Japanese journalist living in Warsaw: Teruo Matsumoto.

Teruo Matsumoto replied to my inquiry in June 2001; my gratitude to him is beyond measure. Teruo sent me detailed accounts of the rescue of Polish children in a photocopy from an issue of the periodical written by the Polish Rescue Committee and published in *Echo z Dalekiego Wschodu*

(1924).[6] Herein, this publication will be referred by its English translation, *Echo of the Far East* or simply as *Echo*. Some articles are in Polish; others are in English. Matsumoto also sent his own research paper, written in Japanese, for which I would obtain a translation. The *Echo* articles include photographs of Siberian children in Japan and a list of all the children in Polish. The list includes their age, the place in Siberia where they were found, whether their parents were alive, and their destination in the United States. I examined the list and there, number 186 of boys in the first mission (1920–21), was the following:

> Wojdak, Wladyslaw, 7 years old, Charbin, no parents,
> Milwaukee, Wisconsin

Four of five data match my father: Wojdak was his surname; he was seven years old in 1920 until his birthday in July; his parents were dead; and I knew he was in Milwaukee. Why was he called "Wladyslaw"? That first name does not match—a mystery to be considered deeper in this story. But I am completely convinced this is my father. Charbin was the name of a city in Manchuria, China, in 1920, that is known now as Harbin. Some years later, I obtained a digital copy of an original of a large group of children (photo 3.5).

Photo 3.5. Polish Siberian children at Fukudenkai, Tokyo—is Pawel Wojdak present?

6 Polish Rescue Committee, "Wrocily dzieci polskie z Syberji do Ojczyzny" ["Polish Children From Siberia Returned to Their Homeland"], *Echo z Dalekiego Wschodu* (1924): 7–44, https://polona.pl/preview/6c031f0c-1939-4649-8877-692b0db7e30b.

Teruo Matsumoto arrived in Poland in 1966 as a graduate student in journalism. As he states himself, a two-year stay in Poland soon turned into twenty—and more as he married and raised a family. Over the years, he was approached several times by people who told him, "I have been in Japan, the land of cherry blossoms." His interest was piqued; he researched Japanese sources and discovered accounts from the 1920s. In 2019, I was able to meet Teruo Matsumoto and thank him in person (photo 3.6).

Photo 3.6. Teruo Matsumoto and the author in Wejherowo, Poland

In the same time period, in 2001, I requested Pawel Wojdak's war record from the British Ministry of Defence. The astonishing information arrived in June 2001. There were three massive surprises: it stated that Pawel Wojdak was born in Russia; he was married in Poland; and he had been in the German Army! And further, he joined the 3rd Carpathian Division in Italy in 1944! That he was born in Russia was plausible; it was consistent with him becoming an orphan in Siberia. But by his enlistment date in the German Army, he was not at Tobruk in North Africa, and if he was at Monte Cassino, it had to have been in the German Army, not the Polish or British!

30033370 – PRIVATE Pawel WOJDAK

Born on: 27 July 1912 at Novo-Mikolajewsk, Russia

Parents: Ernest and Marta, nee SZYC [the Polonized version of Schulz]

Marital Status (while serving): Married

Nationality: Polish

Religion: Roman Catholic

Civilian Occupation (prior to Army Service): Blacksmith

Service with the Polish Forces under British Command:

From 7 November 1944 to 24 October 1946

Service with the Polish Resettlement Corps: Enlisted on 25 October 1946 Commissioned

Relegated to: finally discharged Class "W" Reserve on 22 May 1948, relinquished commission on 24 October 1948. Unemployed List (honourably discharged)

Conduct: Good

Former Service and History:

Prior to 1939 lived in Lugowo, district and county of Poznan, Poland – which after the 1939 September campaign in Poland was annexed by the German Third Reich. Consequently, he was conscripted and served in the German Army from 26.01.1944 to 28.09.1944 when taken prisoner of war by the Allied Forces in Italy.

Being of Polish nationality he volunteered and was accepted to serve in the Polish Forces under British command. Enlisted on 07.11.1944 and was posted to 7 Rifle Battalion, 3 Carpathian

Infantry Division, 2 Polish Corps, 8 British Army – served in Italy 1944–1946 when together with the II Polish Corps was transferred to the United Kingdom – date of arrival – not recorded.

Due to gradual demobilization of the Polish Forces under British command, enlisted with the Polish Resettlement Corps (PRC) on 24.10.1946 – served in the UK until finally discharged on completion of his two years contract with the PRC.

<u>Theatre of Operations</u>: Italy 02.01.1945 – 02.05.1945 (action on the River Senio 02.01.45 – 08.04.45); battle for Bologna / Lombardy Plain 09.04.45 – 02.05.45)

<u>Medal Entitlement</u>:

<u>Polish</u>: Army Medal.

<u>British</u>: 1939–45 Star, Italy Star, The War Medal 1939–45 (CS20 enclosed)

Pawel Wojdak was born in Russia, not Poland—little wonder I never located Novo-Mikolajewsk on any map of Poland! I would discover it is in Siberia, 4 000 kilometres east of Poland. My mother said, "I always thought Novo-Mikolajewsk sounded Russian!" She also revealed knowing that my father had been married—a "marriage of convenience," she called it, though I regret not pursuing what exactly that meant. One could marry for convenience for a host of reasons: financial support, legal purposes such as citizenship or exemption from military service, or to legitimize an unborn child.

Moreover, how did Pawel Wojdak's parents come to be in Siberia? Was it a consequence of the First World War or some earlier event? Where and how did his parents die? Harbin is in China: Why was he there and how did that relate to Siberia? I needed a deeper understanding of the history of Poland and of Poles in Siberia. Research in that direction was quickly successful. But for me to understand his participation in the German Army and why he kept that secret took much longer. I had to gain a deeper appreciation of his emotions under duress and to understand memory.

Why were there thousands of Poles in Siberia? The answer lies in two widely separate but linked movements that progressed over decades: Russian expansion into Far Eastern Asia, and the struggle in Europe for the independence of Poland. Curiously, these movements combined to provide the seed of friendship between Poland and Japan that was instrumental in the fate of the Siberian children, including Pawel Wojdak. In the next several chapters, I will look closely at this period of history to uncover the roots of my father's story.

4.

Russian Expansion in Siberia — the Trans-Siberian Railway

Siberia is that part of Russia, east of the Ural Mountains, the 2 500-kilo-metre-long north-south range that runs from the Arctic Ocean to Kazakhstan, and is taken to be the boundary between Europe and Asia. The vastness of Siberia is difficult to comprehend by viewing a very large-scale map (Map 1, prepared from historic data specifically for this document). Siberia is considerably larger in area than all Canada. It is 13.1 million square kilometres, whereas Canada is slightly under 10 million square kilometres. The time zones of Siberia span seven hours compared to Canada's four-and-one-half—once again emphasizing its expanse. Polish exiles to Siberia encountered a vast range of living conditions proportionate to its size. Nowhere in Siberia has a benign climate, but the grassland of Western Siberia is relatively tolerable com-pared to mountains and forest and permafrost and tundra in the east and far north. Tomsk was the largest city in Siberia in the 1800s, but today, the principal cities are Novosibirsk, Omsk, and Chelyabinsk. Important secondary cities include Irkutsk, Khabarovsk, and Vladivostok. Siberia was greatly enlarged in 1858–1860, when Russia forcibly took the area north of the Amur River from China.[7]

Siberia is bounded to the southwest by Kazakhstan, a component republic of Russia. Kazakhstan was the destination of many exiled Polish soldiers in 1940. It is subordinate in size to Siberia, yet it is equal in size to Canada's four western provinces. Kazakhstan has an extreme continental climate, with hot summers, very cold winters, and little precipitation. The terrain is steppe (grassland or prairie), with many salt lakes and the large Aral and Caspian seas. Due to its inhospitable climate, Kazakhstan is sparsely populated, and most people are Muslim, in contrast to Christian Siberia.

In 1891, Czar Nicholas II announced Russia would construct a railway across Siberia to connect with its seaport on the Pacific Ocean. Russia wanted to build its empire and accumulate wealth from colonies, a recipe proven successful for many European nations. Russia wanted its part in world domination. Construction of the Trans-Siberian Railway to full completion took twenty-five years and required 62 000 workers, many of whom were convicts and exiles.[8] Chinese and Koreans were recruited as poorly paid labourers. Two new cities were built because of the railway and figure prominently in Pawel Wojdak's story: Novosibirsk, in Siberia, and Harbin, China.

Russia was a bit late to implement an imperial strategy, and access to the Pacific region was vital to exploit China and advance its Alaska colony in North America. Vladivostok, on the Pacific Ocean, was the destination of the rail line; it was becoming a cosmopolitan and prosperous city by export of Russian grain, import of Alaskan fur, and as an access point for Western business development in Siberia.

Until about 1850, Russia paid little attention to Siberia; it was remote and a convenient place to send prisoners, such as Polish dissidents and other critics of the czar. That view gradually changed, and Siberia came to be seen as a land rich in natural resources that could augment the wealth of

---

7 Wikipedia, s.v. "Amur Annexation," last modified October 6, 2023, https://en.wikipedia.org/wiki/Amur_Annexation.

8 Wikipedia, s.v. "Trans-Siberian Railway, Construction," Wikipedia, last modified October 14, 2023, https://en.wikipedia.org/wiki/Trans-Siberian_Railway#Construction.

Imperial Russia. Western Siberia contains large coal deposits and expansive grasslands suitable for grain crops and grazing animals; eastern Siberia comprises vast forests with fur-bearing animals, rich mineral deposits, and major rivers flowing from mountainous terrane with hydroelectric potential. The Trans-Siberian Railway was the means to unlock that wealth by connecting European Russia with the Pacific Ocean 9 000 kilometres away. Vladivostok, meaning "lord of the east," was established in 1860 to give Russia a Pacific port for trade and further expansion in the region. The impact of the Trans-Siberian Railway was comparable to that of the Canadian Pacific Railway in Canada, which opened western Canada to farming, the founding of new cities, and commerce between eastern Canada and Pacific ports.

The Ob River in Western Siberia was one of the first obstacles in extending the railway east of European Russia. The Ob, the seventh longest river in the world, flows from its source in the mountains of central Asia (Kazakhstan-Mongolia border) to the Arctic Ocean. A railway bridge was required, but Tomsk, the largest city in the area, was considered an unsuitable location because of its swampy ground. A bridge site was selected 250 kilometres south of Tomsk instead, and a new city was established in 1893. Novo-Nikolayevsk was named after Czar Nikolay, the Russian form of Nicholas. The city grew rapidly after the bridge was completed in 1897 and became a major centre; it claims to have reached one million inhabitants faster than any other city in the world. Today, now known as Novosibirsk,[9] it is the third-largest city in all of Russia.

Nikolay is converted to "Mikolaj" in Polish and many other Slavic languages.[10, 11] It is a linguistic quirk to exchange the first consonant. Thus, Novo-Nikolayevsk was referred to as Novo-Mikolajewsk in spelling and pronunciation by Polish people.

---

9 Wikipedia, s.v. "Novosibirsk," last modified, September 3, 2023, https://en.wikipedia.org/wiki/Novosibirsk.

10 "Why Is Mikolaj the Polish Reflex of Nicholas?" Stack Exchange: Linguistics, last modified January 15, 2014, https://linguistics.stackexchange.com/questions/6193/why-is-miko%C5%82aj-the-polish-reflex-of-nicholas.

11 "Poland, Russian Mikolaj I (Emperor Nicholas I of Russia, King of Poland)," Online Coin Club, accessed August 8, 2023, https://onlinecoin.club/Info/Reigns/Poland_Russian/King_Nicholas_I/.

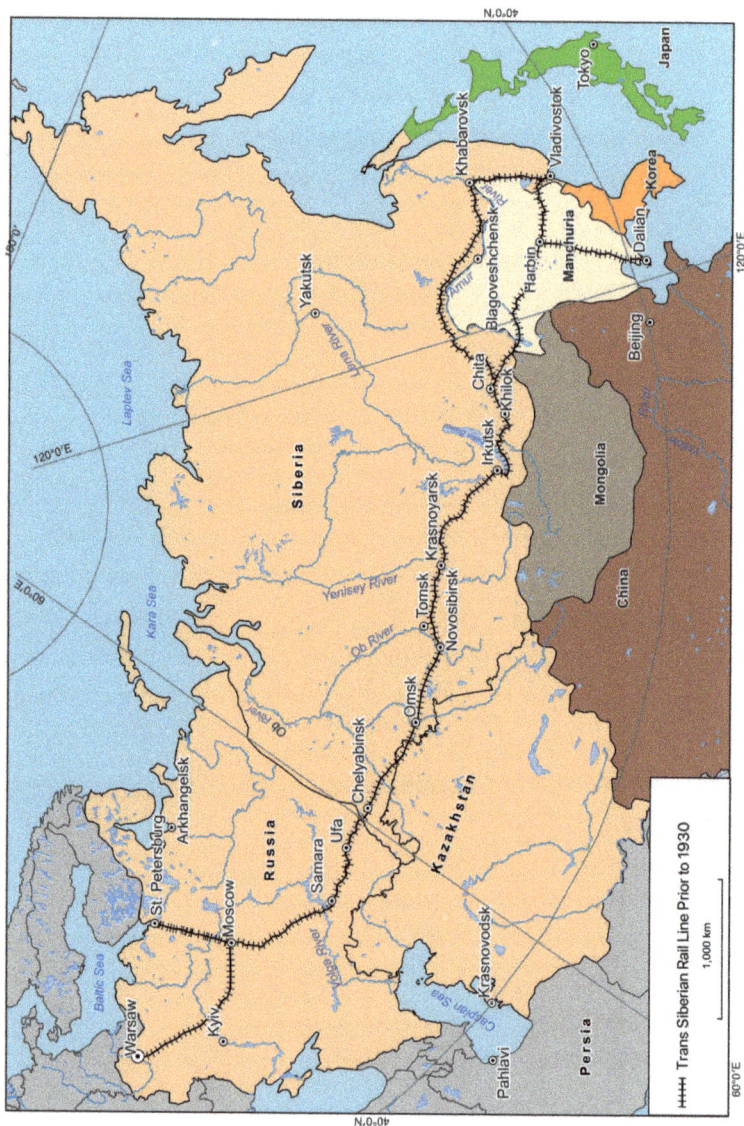

Map 1. *Russia showing Siberia and Kazakhstan; borders of Russia and Manchuria are pre-World War I. There were many rail lines in Europe and eastern Russia, only the pertinent main line is shown. The Trans-Siberian Railway in Siberia and Manchuria consisted of only the lines shown. Map prepared using Natural Earth.*[12]

12 Natural Earth, free vector and raster map data at 1:10m, 1:50m and 1:110m scales, https://www.naturalearthdata.com

This variation in spelling persisted in Polish and British military records and frustrated my efforts to identify the city in tracing Pawel Wojdak's roots. A vivid description of Novo-Nikolayevsk is given by a Polish soldier in *Dzieci Syberyjskie (Siberian Children)*, a thorough documentary book by Theiss.[13] The following, translated from Polish, is entirely appropriate to the early life of Pawel Wojdak:

> At that time, the Russians called Novonikolajewsk "the Polish city" or "Polish town." It deserved this name completely as the Polish language was heard most often on its streets. Not only that, several thousand Polish soldiers were stationed there, and there was also a very rich Polish civilian life. It was possible to recognize this from the great abundance of Polish signs in shops, craft workshops and cafeterias, and from posters announcing performances, dances and meetings or recommending Polish products and companies. It is possible to print such advertisements because there is also a Polish printing house in the city. More importantly, there are various Polish associations, even Polish schools and public educational lectures in Novonikolajewsk. The Polish Army [Siberian Division] is responsible for an awakening of Polish social and cultural activity in Siberia by encouraging the civilian population to openly display their Polishness, to sing Polish songs, to establish Polish societies. By doing so the children and grandchildren of Polish exiles retain their mother tongue, saving them from Russification, and so they realize their far-away Motherland, which they had never seen, still exists. The Army also supported the scouting movement and the Scouts were the first to join the Army when it was created.

The Siberian Division was created by the czar during World War I. The soldier quoted above was taken prisoner by the Red Army at Krasnoyarsk a few years later. He was eventually returned to Poland and became a professor at the Jagiellonian University, in Krakow, where he wrote his memoirs. The

---

13 Wieslaw Theiss, *Dzieci Syberyjskie 1919–2019: Z Syberyii Przez Japonie I Stany Zjednoczone do Polski* [*Siberian Children 1919–2019: From Siberia through Japan and the United States to Poland*], second edition (Krakow: Manggha Museum of Japanese Art and Technology, 2020), 43.

description of the vibrant Polish community in Novo-Nikolayevsk refers to the "children and grandchildren of Polish exiles." Was that the reason Pawel Wojdak's parents were there? Novo-Nikolayevsk was not unusual in having a large Polish community; they existed in all Russian cities and especially in railroad towns in Siberia because Polish engineers and forced labourers, many of whom were also Poles, were required for the railway's construction. Novo-Nikolayevsk was renamed Novosibirsk in 1926, a more familiar placename today.

Railway construction was expensive and technically challenging because of major river crossings and rugged mountains south and east of Lake Baikal, where the route climbs to 1 070-metre elevation. To cut costs, the rail line was poorly built: insufficient ballast for the rail bed; lightweight steel rail; green timber for ties and bridges, which rotted quickly; narrow embankments that eroded easily; steep grades; and sharp curves. Movement of people and supplies was inefficient due to service disruptions that would prove to be an acute problem in wartime.

Russia negotiated (or more accurately, coerced) an agreement with China in 1897 to build a route across the Chinese province of Manchuria that would reduce the length of the rail line by 1 300 kilometres and eliminate part of the difficult terrain. The Manchurian shortcut was named the Trans-Manchurian or Chinese Eastern Railway, but it was effectively the mainline of the Trans-Siberian Railway.[14] A new city was built at Harbin, in Manchuria, to serve as the regional administrative centre. The city was laid out by Polish engineer Adam Szydlowski[15] and buildings in present-day Harbin still portray its Russian heritage.[16]

Manchuria is the name of an historic region of northeast China and part of Inner Mongolia; its boundaries were imprecise. Mongolia lies north of the Great Wall, and historically (pre-1900s), migration of Chinese people

---

14 Wikipedia, s.v. "Chinese Eastern Railway," last modified July 9, 2023, https://en.wikipedia.org/wiki/Chinese_Eastern_Railway.

15 Wikipedia, s.v. "Harbin," last modified October 25, 2023, https://en.wikipedia.org/wiki/Harbin.

16 Tommy O'Callaghan, "8 Mind-Blowing Facts About Harbin, the Chinese City Built by the Russians," *Russia Beyond*, August 19, 2018, https://www.rbth.com/history/328985-harbin-russian.

north of the Wall was restricted, so the region was sparsely populated. Likewise, the migration of Korean people west into adjoining Manchuria was gradual. During the late 1800s and early 1900s, Russia and Japan competed for control of Manchuria. They developed infrastructure and major cities at Dalian (Dalniy) and Harbin. Since World War II, Manchuria has been fully incorporated into China and comprises the provinces of Heilongjiang, including Harbin city; Liaoning, including Dalian city; and Jilin, which adjoins North Korea. Inner Mongolia is an autonomous region of China that includes Manzhouli, in the west of historic Manchuria.

Manchuria appears modest in size in map 1, but it is approximately equal in area to British Columbia. The terrain and climate of Manchuria range proportionate to its size, from fertile lowlands with a warm continental climate in the south to mountains and high plateau in the north with a cool continental to cold arid climate. For Poles who escaped Siberia and lawless Manzhouli, the Polish community in Harbin was a comparative sanctuary.

The Chinese government was weak during the nineteenth century; it was exploited by a series of unequal trading agreements with several European powers whereby they gained access to trade in Chinese luxuries, silk, and porcelain. Britain was first, leasing the port of Canton, which was reduced in 1898 to a ninety-nine-year lease of Hong Kong. Russia's objective at Dalniy was somewhat different: it wanted a port on the Yellow Sea. Vladivostok requires ice-breakers to keep it open, but Dalniy, on the Liaodong Peninsula, is ice-free. China also conceded to Russia the right to build a rail line to access Dalniy. Russia developed a major commercial port and built a railway spur line from Harbin to Dalniy, completing it in 1902. Dalniy was protected by a fortified naval base at nearby Port Arthur on the Liaodong Peninsula.

The Boxer Rebellion in the early twentieth century was a major turning point in this phase of imperialism. Gradually, foreign nations were dislodged from China. Today, Dalniy is known as Dalian (China) and has a population of 7.5 million.

At the dawn of the twentieth century, Russian interests in the Far East competed with Japan, which had similar imperial objectives in Manchuria and Korea. Japan began to exploit the area prior to Russia. Russia displaced

Japan from its lease of the Liaodong Peninsula; this affront led to war between the two nations in 1904. The outcome of the war was disastrous for Russia. Before considering the outcome of the Russo-Japanese War, we should consider the Polish struggle for independence and resultant Polish exiles in Siberia.

5.

Poles in Siberia —Political Exiles

Poland was once a powerful nation in Eastern Europe. At its zenith, in 1619, it included all of present-day Belarus, Lithuania, and Latvia, and most of Ukraine.[17] Poland's fortunes declined as that of rival adjoining nations ascended: the Kingdom of Prussia to the west, the Habsburg monarchy (Austria-Hungary) to the south, and the Empire of Russia to the east. Poland was divided in a series of three Partitions amongst these three nations.[18] After the third partition, in 1795, Poland no longer existed as a sovereign state.

Russia administered the largest area: a puppet state formally named the Congress Kingdom of Poland. It included the cities of Wilno (now Vilnuis), Warsaw, and Lublin. Austrian Poland, or Galicia to the south, included the cities of Lwow (now Lviv) and Krakow. Prussia named its area the Province of Posen; it is where Pawel Wojdak would grow up after escaping

17 Wikipedia, s.v. "History of Poland," last modified September 21, 2023, https://en.wikipedia. org/wiki/History_of_Poland.

18 Wikipedia, s.v. "Partitions of Poland," last modified October 25, 2023, https://en.wikipedia. org/wiki/Partitions_of_Poland.

Siberia. Posen included the city of Poznan and the important steel-making centre, Katowice.

Prussia attempted to Germanize Posen by bringing in 300 000 colonists and eliminating Polish instruction in schools. The Polish population resisted strongly; there was a school strike in 1901–1904, and Germanization had limited success. It is likely the Schulz farm—the farm that took in Pawel Wojdak as a child farmworker—in the Poznan area came into existence during that period.

Partition borders shifted with the ebb and flow of other European rivalries, most notably during Napoleon's conquest. Poles saw Napoleon as a liberator of their nation, and many joined Napoleon's Army, becoming the effective Polish Legion. Napoleon is reputed to have said that 800 Poles would equal 8 000 enemy soldiers. Despite Napoleon's ultimate defeat, the valour and accomplishments of the Legion were legendary in Poland. In addition, the civic and democratic ideals of the French Revolution became a vision for Poles, planting the seeds of revolt in the minds of the Polish upper class. Uprisings in Russian Poland in 1771, 1794, 1830, 1846, 1863, and 1905 were led by the Polish elite and joined by oppressed factory workers and peasants.

In response to Polish unrest, Russian penal law changed in 1847 so that exile and *katorga* (hard labour) became common penalties for Polish insurgents.[19] Exile was a punishment for serious crime and an administrative measure to expel undesirables. Typically, whole families were included so that exile also served to colonize remote areas. The penal colony on Sakhalin Island was used in this manner.[20] Russian author Anton Chekhov visited Sakhalin in 1890 and, angered by what he witnessed, wrote, "There were times I felt that I saw before me the extreme limits of man's degradation."[21]

Hard labour was to extract resources or build infrastructure, such as roads and bridges, and commonly under dangerous conditions. There

19 Wikipedia, s.v. "Katorga," last modified August 23, 2023, https://en.wikipedia.org/wiki/Katorga.

20 Zhanna Popova, "*The Two Tales of Forced Labour: Katorga and Reformed Prison in Imperial Russia (1879–1905)*," *Almanack* 14 (2016): 91–117. https://www.scielo.br/j/alm/a/GySfYqMB6HgDNBQgQqNJXRK/?lang=en&format=pdf.

21 Donald Rayfield, *Anton Chekhov: A Life* (London: Harper Collins, 1997).

was no standardization of practices; some were paid a low wage, and some were shackled. If they were paid, it was to purchase basic amenities. Those sentenced to *katorga* were not necessarily meant to survive. The number of deportees is not easily found. Gentes (2003) determined 36 459 Poles were exiled to Russia after the 1863 uprising, of which about 21,000 were sent to Siberia.[22]

A London newspaper, the *Morning Post*, published a *Reuters Express* article titled "Extermination of Polish Nobles, Landowners, etc. by Russia."[23] It lists 213 individuals who were condemned and transported from Wilno and their location of exile. Their sentences included hard labour, civil death (loss of citizenship), and soldier for life. Several Roman Catholic clergy were included. Such people became known as *Sybiraks*.[24] Commonly, they were not granted exit visas after completing their sentence. Unable to leave, they remained in Siberia as a growing Polish minority. Intermittent protests and disruptions between major Polish uprisings ensured a steady flow of political prisoners to Russia and further east to Siberia.

Russification was attempted in Russian Poland by making Cyrillic Russian script the official language in the 1860s.[25] There were strict restrictions against land reforms and labour unions. Protests in Austrian and Prussian Poland achieved some progress in social conditions, but in Russian Poland, they produced increased repression and restrictions. The Russian-imposed education system was intended to erode Polish language, religion, and culture. Polish patriots established the underground Flying University in Warsaw, so named because lectures were held in different places to avoid

---

22 Andrew A. Gentes, "Siberian Exile and the 1863 Polish Insurrectionists According to Russian Sources," *Jahrbucher fur Geschichte Osteuropas* 51, no. 2 (2003): 197, https://www.jstor.org/stable/41051062.

23 "Extermination of Polish Nobles, Landowners, etc. by Russia," *Morning Post*, September 1, 1863, 2, https://www.newspapers.com/image/396231435/?fcfToken=eyJhbGciOiJIUzI1N iIsInR5cCI6IkpXVCJ9.eyJmcmVlLXZpZXctaWQiOjM5NjIzMTQzNSwiaWF0IjoxN jgxOTM3ODDc2LCJleHAiOjE2ODIwMjQyNzZ9.R-VuiEfMA_BRhKDDsyEJ6kWvRT-1Dm78QNo3LlHsZUWQ. (subscription required.)

24 Wikipedia, s.v. "Sybirak," last modified April 4, 2023, https://en.wikipedia.org/wiki/Sybirak.

25 Wikipedia, "History of Poland."

detection by the Russian authorities.[26] Russia encouraged the Polish elite to assist in administration and to enlist in the Russian Army. Some Poles, no doubt, were loyal to the czar, but history proved repeatedly that Polish noble families gave lip service to Russia and their true allegiance to Poland. Mothers taught their children Polish history and customs in secret at home so that sons and daughters followed their parents, as opponents of Russian rule, to be national patriots and insurgents.

Many *Sybiraks* were from the intellectual elite of Poland and, unable to leave Siberia, became a growing minority that educated their children in their own language. They maintained Polish customs and their devout Catholicism in a nation that was Orthodox or atheist. In addition to Polish churches, there were schools and newspapers in Polish, all to preserve their identity in a foreign land. Some of the intellectual elite emigrated to France, like Frederic Chopin and Marie Curie, for example, and others to England, like author Joseph Conrad. Millions of common people went to America, in particular to the Chicago area, which will figure prominently in the future path of Siberian children.

There is a prominent Canadian connection to Polish insurgents of the nineteenth century. Canadian radio broadcaster Peter Gzowski was a CBC regular from 1970–1997 and became known as "Captain Canada." Peter Gzowski was the great-great-grandson of Casimir Gzowski, a participant in the 1830 Polish uprising, who escaped capture and emigrated to America. Casimir was born in St. Petersburg and the son of a Polish count serving in the Russian Imperial Guard, demonstrating once again Polish nobility feigned loyalty to the czar and fathered patriots. Casimir Gzowski became an engineer and moved from America to Canada, where he was prominent in railroad building in the 1850s, among many other activities.[27]

Jozef Pilsudski was the most effective in a long line of Polish rebels and was also a *Sybirak*.[28] More than anyone else, he was the father of Polish

26 Katarzyna Charzynska, M. Anczewska, and P. Switaj, *A Brief Overview of the History of Education in Poland*, 93, https://files.eric.ed.gov/fulltext/ED567110.pdf.

27 Wikipedia, s.v. "Casimir Gzowski," last modified August 5, 2023, https://en.wikipedia.org/wiki/Casimir_Gzowski.

28 Wikipedia, s.v. "Jozef Pilsudski," last modified October 24, 2023, https://en.wikipedia.org/wiki/Józef_Piłsudski.

independence, winning freedom from Russia. Jozef Pilsudski was born in 1867 into a patriotic and noble but impoverished family. His father and other close relatives participated in the 1863 Polish uprising. In 1887, Jozef and his brother Bronislaw were arrested for a failed attempt to assassinate Czar Alexander in St. Petersburg. Bronislaw was sentenced to fifteen years *katorga* on Sakhalin Island, in Far Eastern Siberia, and Jozef to five years for his minor role in the plot. He had simply provided secure accommodation to his brother and associates and (apparently) did not know their intent. Pilsudski sustained brutal treatment while in Siberia, detrimental to his health for the rest of his life.

Jozef Pilsudski was allowed to return to Poland in 1892 and immediately took up subversive activities again. He joined, and later led, the Polish Socialist Party (PPS) and became the chief editor of an underground newspaper called *Robotnik* (the *Worker*). His printing press was discovered in 1900, and he was jailed in the Warsaw Citadel, an infamous prison. He made a daring escape by pretending to be mentally ill so that he was transferred to a less-secure mental hospital. Shortly thereafter, when Russia's focus on Poland was distracted by war with Japan, Pilsudski was ready for more dramatic actions toward Polish independence in 1918.

6.

Friendship Between Polish and Japanese Peoples

Russia and Japan were in competition for resources, territory, and political influence in Manchuria and Korea. War began in February 1904, when the Japanese Navy made a pre-emptive attack on the Russian fleet at anchor in Golden Horn Bay near Vladivostok.[29] The Russian fleet was confined in port for the remainder of the war. Japanese ground forces captured Port Arthur in January 1905 and won decisive land battles in Manchuria. The war was a humiliating total defeat for Russia. In the ensuing peace treaty in September 1905, Russia agreed to leave Manchuria, including its highly valued port of Dalniy and rights to the Chinese Eastern Railway. Russia also ceded southern Sakhalin Island and recognized Korea as being in Japan's sphere of influence.

Japan defeated Russia despite having a smaller army. Russian soldiers were poorly motivated, and an incomplete gap in the Trans-Siberian Railway near Lake Baikal meant military equipment and reinforcements were unable to reach Far Eastern Siberia in time. Japan captured 75 000

---

29 Wikipedia, s.v. "Russo-Japanese War," last modified October 30, 2023, https://en.wikipedia. org/wiki/Russo-Japanese_War.

members of the Russian Army. Upon interrogation of their prisoners, the Japanese were surprised to hear 16 000 of them declare they were Polish and hated Russians.[30] In this manner, Japan learned the Poles were conscripted soldiers and many were deportees. Japan became aware of the long history of Russian subjugation of Poland and recognized a potential ally.

Bronislaw Pilsudski completed his *katorga* sentence in 1902 and remained on Sakhalin Island after the settlement of the Russo-Japanese War[31] He took up ethnographic study of the indigenous Ainu people, a Japanese ethnic group. He lived with them, learned their language and culture, and married an Ainu woman. Subsequently, he moved to Japan as a recognized ethnologist and, together with writer Futubatei Shimei, founded the Polish-Japanese Society.

Jozef Pilsudski visited Tokyo in 1904 as head of the Polish Socialist Party (PPS) to discuss Japanese assistance to overthrow the czarist autocracy, their mutual enemy.[32] The Russo-Japanese War had begun, and an axiom of foreign relations at the time was "my enemy's enemy is my friend." Pilsudski received some funding but much less than he requested, owing to the disunity of Polish opposition parties. Japan was not convinced Pilsudski would be successful and did not want to alienate a future Polish government. Nonetheless, the sociological friendship begun by Bronislaw consolidated the political effort of his brother: Japan and Poland would become lasting friends. These ties set the stage for Japanese assistance to Polish children in Siberia.

In 1904, friendship between Poland and Japan was unofficial; Poland did not exist yet as a sovereign state. Nationhood was not a requirement for the periodical *Echo of the Far East*, but its inaugural issue, on September 15, 1921, corresponded closely to that event. It was edited by Piotrowski Wienczyslaw for the Polish Rescue Committee.[33] It proudly declared Poland–Japan

---

30 Teruo Matsumoto, lecture in Tsuruga, November 9, 2019.

31 Wikipedia, s.v. "Bronislaw Pilsudski," last modified October 29, 2023, https://en.wikipedia.org/wiki/Bronisław_Piłsudski.

32 Piotr S. Wandycz, *Soviet-Polish Relations 1917–1921* (Cambridge: Harvard University Press, 1969).

33 Piotrowski Wienczyslaw, ed., *Echo z Dalekiego Wschodu* [*Echo of the Far East*] (Tokyo: Anna Bielkiewicz, 1921–1929). http://mbc.cyfrowemazowsze.pl/dlibra/publication/57321?tab=1

friendship, and early issues documented the story of the Siberian children. Its banner states the publication to be the "fortnightly national review of Polish interests in Far Eastern Asia." The opening editorial addressed its purpose to the Japanese nation; it is verbose, but the sincerity and passion of purpose are powerful:

> To give information to the Japanese nation about Poland and the Poles, and to inform Poles about Japan and the Japanese. This idea of mutual acquaintanceship of the two nations was aroused in us by a certain feeling of gratitude for the help bestowed on our nation in caring for Polish children and orphans, as well of the facilities in evacuating them from Siberia via Japan to North America, whither they are dispatched to receive schooling and whence they will eventually be repatriated to Poland.
>
> Up to the present the Japanese knew very little about Poland and the Poles, and even now the majority does not know anything at all about our country. There is nothing strange in this, for Poland in its slavery was divided amongst three powers, namely; Russia, Germany and Austria. Thus it is not strange that the Japanese do not distinguish Poles from Russians. The Poles are, in fact, a nation having traits of different character, different culture and different customs. Poland was once independent and is independent again.
>
> In editing this paper we would like to make it known to the Japanese who the Poles are, so that they will not commit the mistake of taking us for Russians or Germans.
>
> As all the nations in the world are united by one guiding link, to wit—brotherhood of the nations—which, after better acquaintance is tightened by friendship, which leads to one bright future. Therefore, we would like to contribute to this, at first on a small scale by the edition of this periodical. We shall relate to Poland about Japan, about which also very little is as yet known there. Thus, we shall note all worthy remarks from which one may learn and probably derive profit in our country during its reconstruction.

Being confident that the aim which we wish to carry through will find support among the Japanese, the first number of the issue will be distributed free of charge.

Although the "Echo of the Far East" is not a political organ, articles of political content must of necessity appear therein, because the life of nations and countries, their commerce and commercial problems are at every step entangled with politics, so that we cannot possibly omit this question entirely. We shall give extracts of political questions concerning Poland and enlarge thereon from national point of view.

A large section of the periodical will be devoted to the economical world, giving agriculture and social articles and treating on industry and commerce. Nowadays nations and countries give the first thought and careful attention to the world's markets, the exchange of food stuffs and raw materials as also the industrial products of each country, endeavouring thereby to enter into commercial contact and profit thereby.

Poland is the country through which one of the main roads for exchange of products and culture between the East and West leads; so that Poland, when the political situation in Europe has been regulated and is again settled, will become a country where a most vital and rapid current of commerce and industry will pulse. We shall also give information about Arts and Literature.

As our paper has been called to life thanks only to the humane activities of the Japanese towards Polish children in Siberia, which has given the Poles the possibility of knowing the noble qualities of the Japanese character, we shall also enumerate stories from the lives of those children with a highly dramatic strain. According to possibility we shall give illustrations in the Japanese section characteristic of Polish life and in the Polish section of Japanese life.

The periodical will appear bi-monthly, that is, on the 1st and 15th of each month and we beg the Japanese nation and its institutions for heartiest support.

Echo of the Far East is hugely important because it documented the Siberian children during the 1920s by the people directly involved. For children who went to America, it listed their names, ages, family status, and their location in the United States. The actions of the Polish Rescue Committee and the role of the Japanese government were explained and what transpired in Poland. Most articles are in Polish, but some are written in English, perhaps to publicize the desperate condition of Polish children in the United States in order to raise funds.

I attended the Kresy-Siberia conference in Warsaw in September 2018. The group comprised descendants of *Sybiraks,* Poles exiled to Siberia and Kazakhstan in 1940 by Russia. In 1943, out of nearly 2 000 000 deportees there were 114 500 survivors able to leave Russia.[34] Able-bodied men and some women formed the Polish II Corps (within the British Eighth Army), also called the Polish Army, and distinguished themselves in Italy. Other women and children went to camps in East Africa, India, New Zealand, and elsewhere. Because Pawel Wojdak was in the Polish Army and also had been in Siberia, albeit from an earlier generation, I hoped perhaps conference attendees might know about earlier *Sybiraks,* such as my father.

A second objective of my trip to Poland was to learn more about the Siberian children after their return to Poland in 1922. At the University of Warsaw Library, I obtained a membership for a modest fee and accessed their archives for *Echo of the Far East.* After 1922, the periodical was published exclusively in Poland and continued to focus on the Siberian children. After reviewing available issues of 1921–1929, I contracted the staff to prepare scanned copies of selected pages, some in English, others in Polish. These constitute part of my reference material for this work. Many Siberian children, upon returning to Poland, were housed in a special facility in Wejherowo, near Gdansk. The facility and the children's wonderful learning environment are described extensively. Their positive experiences were at odds with what I knew about my father's experience.

---

34 Norman Davies, *Trail of Hope: The Anders Army, An Odyssey Across Three Continents* (Oxford: Osprey Publishing, 2015), 177.

Today, close friendship continues between Poland and Japan[35] demonstrated by activities of the linked organizations Social Welfare Organization Fukudenkai in Tokyo[36] and ASAGAO[37] based in Krakow, Poland. ASAGAO was founded in 2019 by Yumi Yoshida and Ayaka Jimbo, founders of the Japan Poland Student Council and the Japan Poland Youth Association.[38] Krakow was selected as the base because it is the cultural hub of Poland. Yumi Yoshida, in a personal communication, explained the asagao (morning glory) flower was chosen as the name of the organization because it denotes "strong tie," and symbolizes the bond between Poland and Japan. Polish culture has penetrated deep into the fabric of Japan; even the music of Polish composer Frederic Chopin is popular.

In September 2023 my wife and I travelled to Krakow and went to the ASAGAO office to meet Yumi Yoshida and other staff members. We also visited the Manghaa Museum dedicated to cultural relations between Poland and Japan.[39] Our visit to Manghaa coincided with the dedication ceremony of an image of the Siberian children at Fukudenkai in Tokyo. I was fortunate to speak with the Japanese Ambassador to Poland, Mr. Akio Miyajima, about my father (Photo 6.1).

35 Kazihiko Inoue, "Poland Is One of the Most Pro-Japanese Nations. Here's Why," *Japan Forward*, October 18, 2019, https://japan-forward.com/poland-is-one-of-the-most-pro-japanese-nations-heres-why/.

36 Social Welfare Organization Fukudenkai, accessed October 31, 2023, http://www.fukudenkai.or.jp/.

37 ASAGAO, accessed October 31, 2023, https://asagao.pl/ .

38 Japan-Poland Youth Association, accessed October 31, 2023, https://jpya.or.jp/.

39 Manghaa Museum, accessed November 20, 2023, https://manggha.pl/en/about-us.

*Photo 6.1. The author and Japanese Ambassador
(to Poland) Mr. Akio Miyajima at Manghaa Museum
image of Siberian children in background.*

7.

Outcome of the Russo-Japanese War

After Russia lost the war, Japan controlled Manchuria and Russia was compelled to build a much longer all-Russian line for the Trans-Siberian Railway. The route lay north of the Amur River, the tenth-longest river in the world.

The junction of the Trans-Manchurian Railway and the new route of the Trans-Siberian line is in rugged terrain east of the small city of Chita. The boundary between Russia and China follows the Amur River in an 1 800-kilometre northerly arc around Manchuria until it reaches Khabarovsk. At Khabarovsk, the border and the Amur diverge. The river flows north-northeast for 700 kilometres to reach the ocean; its mouth is opposite the north end of Sakhalin Island. The rail line at Khabarovsk turns abruptly south to follow the Russia-China border 750 kilometres to Vladivostok. Passengers and freight were required to disembark from the train and board a ferry to cross the Amur until 1916, when a 2.6-kilometre-long bridge was completed.

Railway construction in the Amur valley caused more Poles to work and settle in Siberia. Not all were forced labourers, as we will learn from some personal accounts. Over several decades, some four million settlers migrated to Siberia, mainly from within Russia and Ukraine, but some were Polish. Land was free—an attractive alternative to working the land of a wealthy landowner or subdividing a tiny farm in Poland. Even before the Russo-Japanese War, Russia began to expunge Chinese people from the Amur area. Thousands of Chinese in Blagoveshchensk, the largest city north of the Amur, were massacred and their property expropriated during pogroms in 1900.[40] Harbin, in Manchuria, continued to host a Polish enclave and became a safe destination for Poles escaping from Siberia. Within a few years, many fragmented Polish families and orphans would come to Harbin.

Significant events were taking place in Russia and Poland, perhaps not a direct consequence of the Russo-Japanese War, but they signalled a growing mood of discontent. In 1905–1906, impoverished peasants in Russia rose against czarist rule, seeking land reform, and this was known as the Agrarian Revolt. Unrest in Poland also led to rebellion because 100 000 people were unemployed.[41] Jozef Pilsudski was encouraged by declining Russian strength, and in the fall of 1904, he formed a paramilitary unit: the Combat Organization of the Polish Socialist Party (*bojówki* or *Bojowa*).[42] The Russian Cossack cavalry attacked a PPS-organized demonstration in Warsaw, and in reprisal during a November demonstration, the Bojowa paramilitary opened fire on Russian police and military. In a single day, called "Bloody Wednesday," in August 1906, the Bojowa assassinated eighty Russian police officers and informants. A total of 336 Russian officials were killed over the entire year 1906. The illegal force had 2 000 members and carried out 2 500 operations between 1904 and 1908. In addition to assassinations, robberies were committed to fund their activities.

---

40 Wikipedia, s.v. "1900 Amur Anti-Chinese Pogroms," last modified October 19, 2023, https://en.wikipedia.org/wiki/1900_Amur_anti-Chinese_pogroms.

41 Wikipedia, s.v. "Revolution in the Kingdom of Poland 1905–1907," last modified August 20, 2023, https://en.wikipedia.org/wiki/
Revolution_in_the_Kingdom_of_Poland_(1905%E2%80%931907).

42 Wikipedia, s.v. "Combat Organization of the Polish Socialist Party," last modified March 17, 2023, https://en.wikipedia.org/wiki/
Combat_Organization_of_the_Polish_Socialist_Party.

By 1905, Pilsudski and the Bojowa induced a series of labour strikes all over the country that involved 1.3 million workers seeking better wages and working conditions. University and high school students protested against a Russian edict banning their education in Polish. These uprisings were met with violence. In Warsaw, on May 1, 1905, thirty-seven in a crowd of thousands were shot and killed. In June, in the city of Lodz, more than 200 were killed and thousands wounded during four days of fighting. The rebellion was subdued by 1907 and was followed by a period of brutal suppression. Martial law was imposed, and promised concessions were revoked or not carried out. School instruction in Polish was disallowed and students barred from entering university. Russian officials strove to eliminate leftist opposition parties and suppress trade unions. Russian military were authorized to conduct executions without trial. Through all this, the Bojowa were considerably reduced yet continued to operate.

The Bojowa's most daring robbery occurred on the night of September 26–27, 1908, when the Russian mail train was held up near Wilno on the main line from Warsaw to St Petersburg.[43] The intent was to steal cash and gold, wealth extracted from Poland destined for the czar. By official Russian count, the train contained 2.7 million rubles, but most of it was in unsigned banknotes and bonds, which were useless to the PPS. Instead of gold bars, the train carried silver, which weighed much more than gold of the same value. The load was too much for the conspirators' horse-drawn cart, and some silver was left behind. Still, the "take" of the Bezdany raid amounted to 200 812 rubles ($100 000 in 1908) in cash and silver,[44] equivalent to at least $3.5 million in current dollars.

The "Great Bezdany Raid" made newspaper headlines throughout the Russian Empire and beyond. Pilsudski was already well-known but became a virtual celebrity internationally and a hero in all of Poland. The magnitude and audacity of the robbery increased Russian determination to capture him. Intense police questioning using the usual brutal methods led to the

43 Peter Hetherington, *Unvanquished, Joseph Pilsudski Resurrected Poland, and the Struggle for Eastern Europe* (Houston: Pingora Press, 2012), 191–215.

44 Wikipedia, s.v. "Bezdany Raid," last modified September 6, 2022, https://en.wikipedia.org/wiki/Bezdany_raid.

arrest of five of the twenty conspirators within weeks of the robbery.[45] Pilsudski evaded capture and escaped to Austrian Poland.

Indirectly and unexpectedly, the Pilsudski train robbery may have had consequences for Pawel Wojdak's father. A young Pole named Wladyslaw Wojdak was arrested on September 27, 1908, for a break-in and minor robbery—the identical date as the train robbery. Was his crime a coincidence of timing? Might the train robbery have caused him to be a suspected subversive, whether valid or not, and be deported to Siberia?

In 1908, Pilsudski recast his paramilitary units into the "Union for Active Struggle" headed by three of his associates, one of whom was Wladyslaw Sikorski, a future general and leader of Poland. Their main purpose was to train officers for a future Polish Army. In 1910, two paramilitary organizations were legally created in Austrian Poland: one in Lvov (now Lviv, Ukraine); and one in Krakow. With the permission of the Austrian officials, Pilsudski founded a series of "sporting clubs" as cover to train a Polish military force. This evolved to become the Riflemen's Association, which, by 1914, comprised 12 000 men. That year, at a lecture in Paris, Pilsudski declared, "Only the sword now carries any weight in the balance for the destiny of a nation," arguing that Polish independence could only be achieved through military struggle against the partitioning powers.[46]

---

45 Hetherington, *Unvanquished*, 213.
46 Wikipedia, "Jozef Pilsudski."

8.

Groundwork for Polish Freedom

Pawel Wojdak was little more than a babe-in-arms in Novo-Nikolayevsk when war erupted in Europe thousands of kilometres away. World War I resulted in new countries from old empires in Europe, triggered revolution and civil war in Russia, and was a disaster for Poles in Siberia. The war also laid the groundwork for Poland to emerge as an independent nation after 123 years of subjugation, a homeland for the handful of Poles who managed to return from Siberia. Jozef Pilsudski foresaw World War I and said in 1914, "At the end of the war conquerors and conquered will be weakened. That will be our opportunity. We must be ready for that end."[47]

The seeds of World War I were sown in the late 1800s when Russia shifted from an alliance with Germany and Austria-Hungary (the Axis powers) to alignment with France and Britain to form the Triple Entente, more commonly called the Allies. Italy dropped out of the Axis alignment in 1914 to become neutral. Poland was not formally aligned with either side because it did not exist; however, it was fully involved because Russian Poland was

---

47 Grace Humphrey, *Pilsudski: Builder of Poland* (New York: Scott and More, 1936), 122.

with the Allies while Galicia (Austro-Hungarian Poland) was aligned with the Axis. Pilsudski's aim was to build a Polish military force, with himself as leader, that was powerful enough to secure Polish independence when the war concluded. His leadership and military skills were such that his troops were loyal to him rather than any non-Polish government. He managed to manoeuvre between Austria, Germany, and even his most hated adversary, Russia, to acquire military supplies and extract pledges of support for Polish independence.

Prior to World War I, Pilsudski resided in Galicia because Austria-Hungary was the only one of the partitioning powers to be somewhat sympathetic to Polish interests, and he was subject to arrest by Russian police. Pilsudski persuaded the Habsburg government to create a small Polish unit rather than be dispersed in the large Austrian Army.[48] Once established, Pilsudski began immediately to overstep his authority and disobey orders, to distance himself from Austrian command. Pilsudski named his force the Polish Legions, a name inspired by the Polish Legions in Napoleon's Army (1797–1803).

Early in the war, the Polish Legions were ineffective, few in number, and poorly equipped. Late in 1914, when Austrian divisions fell back in disorder under Russian attack, the Legions distinguished themselves by forming an effective rearguard despite their deficiency of arms and equipment. Pilsudski bonded closely with his men by being at the front lines under fire by day and visiting the wounded by night. Ordered to withdraw with the Austrian Army to German territory, Pilsudski disobeyed and led half his force dangerously across the face of the advancing Russian Army to the safety of Krakow, where he was hailed a hero by the Polish residents.[49] The Russian advance stalled. The Austrian command promoted Pilsudski to brigadier general, choosing to recognize his military skill and the Legions' bravery rather than his insubordination.[50]

Jozef Pilsudski became increasingly popular with Polish people; he was seen as the personification of Poland's struggle for independence. He

---

48 Hetherington, *Unvanquished,* 251–254.
49 Hetherington, 277.
50 Hetherington, 278–279.

encouraged his soldiers to see themselves as Polish, not Austrian troops. They wore their own distinctive caps, featuring an eagle, the symbol of old Poland.[51] To emphasize their equality, Pilsudski's legionnaires addressed each other as "citizen" in the same manner as in Napoleon's Polish Legions. They also used the Polish two-finger salute instead of the Austrian full-hand salute. And Pilsudski reactivated the battle cry of Napoleon's Polish Legions that became the rallying cry for Polish independence: "In the name of God, for your freedom and ours!" The cry acknowledges the fight by Poles within the army of a foreign nation for the ultimate goal of winning freedom for Poland. It also signifies that God and moral righteousness were on Poland's side. The same cry was used by Polish troops in World War II within the British Army.

Pilsudski's most audacious act—which was surely treason for an Austrian general—was to secretly contact the Allies to explain he was a Polish patriot and his actions in the Austrian Army were directed only against Russia![52] Audacious but perhaps not completely surprising because Pilsudski had a high regard for French and English society, their freedoms, and their government.

While Germany focused on the Western Front in 1915 and 1916, a to-and-fro of offensive and counteroffensive between Russia and Austria was happening in Galicia and Congress (Russian) Poland. The fighting destroyed much Polish territory. Russia adopted a scorched-earth policy, destroying crops in the field, factories, and infrastructure, and deporting vast numbers of Polish people into Russia to prevent their enlistment in the growing Polish Legions or to become forced labourers in Germany. Estimates of the number of displaced people range from 800 000, by R. F. Leslie,[53] to 1 000 000, by Norman Stone.[54]

Germany redeployed troops to the Eastern Front in 1916, when it became clear the Austrian Army was completely beaten, having suffered one million

---

51 Hetherington, 280–281.

52 Hetherington, 283.

53 R. F. Leslie, "The Emergence of an Independent Polish State," in *The History of Poland Since 1863*, ed. R. F. Leslie (Cambridge: Cambridge University Press, 1980), 115.

54 Norman Stone, *The Eastern Front 1914–1917* (Hachette: Hodder & Stoughton, 1975), 183.

casualties and 400 000 captured. Members of the Polish Legions were among them. Pilsudski was discouraged that the war had not produced an uprising for independence in Poland, but that was not a realistic expectation considering that the German Army had quickly regained Polish territory lost by Austria. Pilsudski issued an ultimatum to the Axis powers that they guarantee to establish Poland as an independent country or else he would resign his command. Austria issued a conciliatory response, but Germany refused outright because they considered Pilsudski a threat to their authority in Polish territories.

Pilsudski resigned from the Austrian Army on September 29, 1916.[55] The Polish Legions were demoralized by the loss of their inspirational leader and were assigned the benign role of garrison on Polish lands conquered by Germany. This freed up German soldiers for their ill-advised invasion of Russia.

As German and Russian losses mounted, both sides needed new recruits. There were thirty million ethnic Poles living within the partitioned territories of Poland. Germany and Russia each appealed to Polish nationalism in attempts to induce loyalty to their side and recruitment of soldiers. There were promises of partial self-government, restoration of language rights, Polish currency, and even its own army. Germany's offer had a stronger basis because its troops were in occupation of Poland. But by their actions in Poland, it became transparently obvious their promises were insincere: Poland would still be under the rule of the kaiser. After refusing an oath of allegiance to Germany, Pilsudski was arrested in July 1917 and spent the rest of the war in an internment camp.[56] Pilsudski was stymied in his attempt to lead Poland from within. Fortunately, new Polish heroes emerged from North America.

Polish immigrants could be found in many countries but were most numerous in the United States. There were 2.2 million Polish immigrants in America in 1914, mainly first and second generation, and they spoke out strongly for support of Polish independence, including military

---

55 Hetherington, *Unvanquished,* 298.
56 Hetherington, 314.

intervention. Ignacy Paderewski was a famous composer and pianist resident in America but was born in Russian Poland to a family with a history of rebellion.[57] His prominence as a musician provided him access to President Woodrow Wilson and others in government. He lobbied them relentlessly to support the Polish cause. The Allies had ignored the question of Polish independence, but that changed when the United States declared war on Germany in April 1917.

Poles in America were quick to enlist in a Polish Army in exile; the largest number came from Chicago. The Kosciuszko Army was named after a Polish hero who fought in the American Revolution and later in the Polish Legions of Napoleon. Paderewski's lobbying prompted President Wilson to allow the formation of the 22 700-member force in the United States. Having a foreign army on American soil was an exceptional circumstance.

The Kosciuszko Army trained across the border in Canada[58] and soon deployed to France, where they were commanded by Joseph Haller, a career soldier from Krakow. Haller had commanded the Polish Legions Second Brigade at the time Jozef Pilsudski headed the First Brigade. Haller had a convoluted history during World War I, not unlike Pilsudski, having served in the Austrian Army against Russia and then in the Russian Army against Germany. By a circuitous route, Haller was able to go from Russia to France in 1918 via Murmansk. The Polish Army in France swelled to a force of 100 000 and was important in overwhelming the last of the German offensives. [59]

Thanks to Woodrow Wilson and America's prominent role in concluding World War I, the Allies agreed to the creation of independent states for each large ethnic group in eastern Europe. President Wilson put forward a fourteen-point peace plan; the most relevant to Poland was number 13, at the behest of Paderewski, which stated:

---

57 Hetherington, 320–321.

58 Wikipedia, s.v. "Tadeusz Kosciuszko Camp," last modified June 15, 2022, https://pl.wikipedia.org/wiki/Tadeusz_Kosciuszko_Camp.

59 Wikipedia, s.v. "Jozef Haller," last modified October 29, 2023, https://en.wikipedia.org/wiki/J%C3%B3zef_Haller

An independent Polish state should be erected which should include the territories inhabited by indisputably Polish populations, which should be assured free and secure access to the sea, and whose political and economic independence should be guaranteed by international covenant.[60]

In November 1918, Pilsudski became chief of state for Poland. His enormous moustache made him a recognizable figure everywhere. He had adopted the style during his exile in Siberia when the butt of a Russian gun knocked out several of his front teeth.[61]

Pilsudski appointed Ignacy Paderewski as prime minister and minister of Foreign Affairs. The American-Polish connection was important a few years later when America admitted Pawel Wojdak and 368 other Polish Siberian children. They came to Chicago and then distributed to orphanages from there. In a year or so, they were "repatriated" to Poland. There is a display today in the middle of Warsaw to commemorate and celebrate the role of Woodrow Wilson and the United States in championing the rebirth of Poland.

---

60 Hetherington, *Unvanquished,* 326.
61 Hetherington, 120.

9.

Revolution and Civil War in Russia

The young Wojdak family is presumed to have been fairly well settled in the young city of Novo-Nikolayevsk (or Novo-Mikolajewsk to Poles) in the summer of 1917, when their son Pawel turned five years old. The city was barely twenty years old, had a vibrant Polish community, and was prosperous, thanks to economic growth in Siberia and the city's strategic location on the Trans-Siberian Railway. Living conditions for peasants and factory workers in European Russia were terrible, but Novo-Nikolayevsk was remote from Moscow and even farther from St. Petersburg, the most important city in the country, the seat of government and home to Czar Nicholas II.

The situation in Novo-Nikolayevsk was changing, however. War had begun three years earlier when the Imperial Russian Army invaded East Prussia and Austrian Poland of the Habsburg monarchy. After early success against Austria-Hungary, the war went badly for Russia when its army confronted the German Army. Fighting on the Eastern Front was different from the Western Front, with its stalemate of lengthy trench warfare.[62] As more and more soldiers were killed and Russian peasants and factory workers were conscripted, morale among the troops declined. Food became scarce first in the western cities but soon spread east to distant Siberia.

An epidemic of typhus spread among the people of Novo-Nikolayevsk. The disease broke out in prisoner-of-war camps in Novo-Nikolayevsk in the winter of 1915, and eighty percent of the prisoners died.[63] The disease spread through the civilian and military populations, and up to sixty thousand were estimated to have died in the winter of 1918–1919,[64] half the city's population.[65]

The Polish soldier's description of life in Novo-Nikolayevsk, cited previously in Chapter 4, revealed the important role of the military in the city in protecting the interests of Polish people. In 1914, Polish soldiers in western Russia were grouped into the Pulawy Legion by the czar, and they were mobilized against German forces. Fortunately, the Pulawy Legion was not brought up against Pilsudski's Polish Legion on the Austria-Hungary front, or else one Polish unit could have been fighting the other.[66] In 1915, the Pulawy Legion was reorganized into the Polish Rifle Brigade.

The Russian Revolution was a complex affair that took place in two stages.[67] In February 1917, in Petrograd (now St. Petersburg), the Russian Army began to mutiny due to deprivation and massive losses of men at the Eastern Front. The revolt was instigated by the Russian aristocracy and prominent capitalists, who felt the czar was weak and ineffective. Nicholas II resigned and was replaced by the Russian Provisional Government, which planned to continue the war with Germany.

---

62 Wikipedia, s.v. "Eastern Front (World War I)," last modified October 29, 2023, https:// en.wikipedia.org/wiki/Eastern_Front_(World_War_I).

63 Antony Beevor, *Russia, Revolution and Civil War, 1917–1922* (New York: Viking Press, 2022), 231.

64 Beevor, 414.

65 Theiss, *Dzieci Syberyjskie*, 47.

66 Wikipedia, s.v. "Polish Armed Forces in the East," last modified September 18, 2021, https:// en.wikipedia.org/wiki/Polish_Armed_Forces_in_the_East_(1914%E2%80%931920).

67 Wikipedia, s.v. "Russian Revolution," last modified October 15, 2023, https://en.wikipedia. org/wiki/Russian_Revolution.

The provisional government created the Polish I Corps and it pledged to support the war effort and Russia's alliance with France and Britain in exchange for support of Polish independence. The Poles' intent was to free and unite Poland. Importantly, the Polish I Corps was also to defend Poles in the Russian Empire. The Polish Corps numbered nearly 30,000 men when formed in July 1917.

The revolutionaries of the provisional government did not have the support of most Russian factory workers, peasants, and soldiers to continue the war. As numerous political factions vied for power, the Bolsheviks, a far-left party of ruthless anarchists led by Vladimir Lenin, emerged victorious with an inspired slogan, "Peace, Land, and Bread." "Peace" meant to capitulate to Germany; "Land" signified its redistribution to peasants; and "Bread" promised an end to hunger. In October 1917, the Bolsheviks' Red Guards, the forerunner of the Red Army, overthrew the provisional government.

The new Bolshevik government immediately ceased fighting against Germany and Austro-Hungary and dispatched a team to negotiate a peace treaty. The naive incompetence of the Bolshevik negotiators is described by Anthony Beevor in *Russia, Revolution and Civil War, 1917–1922*, a rare humorous event in his grisly account of the Russian Civil War. The team comprised a sailor, a factory worker, a former terrorist and assassin, and three Jews: a revolutionary intellectual, Leon Trotsky's brother-in-law, and a close friend of Trotsky. En route, they realize they forgot to include a peasant to complete the representation of Russian society. The team stops their car at a street corner and offers a lift to a shaggy old man. When asked about his politics, the old peasant states he is a socialist revolutionary. "A left one or a right one?" he is asked. The peasant apprised his situation carefully to be sure he provided the correct answer. "Left Comrades, of course. The very leftist."[68] With his astute answer, he becomes part of the negotiating team. Upon arrival, the German hosts provide a welcoming dinner. The grey-haired peasant, while enjoying the meal of his life, is asked if he would like red wine or white. He responds, "Which is the stronger? Red or white? It makes no

---

68 Beevor, *Russia, Revolution and Civil War*, 144.

difference to me which I drink. I'm only interested in the strength."[69] The subsequent Treaty of Brest-Litovsk represented complete Russian capitulation to Germany.

The Polish Corps' intent of being neutral toward the new Bolshevik government and continuing to fight against Germany was not acceptable to the Bolsheviks, who ordered Polish forces to disband.[70] The order was refused in January 1918. Clashes between the Red Army and the Polish forces quickly followed. The Red Guard controlled western Russia; the only alternative for the small body of Polish troops was to withdraw to the east. Polish forces and the entire Polish minority scattered across the country; they were enemies of the Bolsheviks. It was particularly bitter for Poles who had risen up against czarist rule for more than a century to find themselves "enemies of the people" and be reluctantly on the side of White Russia in the civil war. All those who opposed the Bolshevik regime and its Red Army were collectively called White Russians and the White Army.

Poles throughout Russia were under threat and felt compelled to form their own military. In July 1918, Poles in Novo-Nikolayevsk formed the Siberian Division. Formally, they were part of the Polish Army in France, known as the Blue Army because of the colour of their uniforms. There were four divisions in France, so the Siberian unit became the Fifth Siberian Division.[71] The Siberian Division comprised 16 000 men, just half the number of the previous Polish I Corps. Major Walerian Czuma commanded the Siberian Division; he was a veteran of the Polish Legion who had been taken prisoner during World War I on the Austrian front. The Siberian Division was based in Ufa, alongside the White Guard of Admiral Alexander Kolchak.

The Polish Siberian Division was tasked with defending the Trans-Siberian Railway, the critical means for moving supplies and troops (photo 9.1). They compensated for a shortage of military supplies with ingenuity,

69 Beevor, 146.

70 Wikipedia, s.v. "Polish I Corps in Russia," last modified September 2, 2021, https://en.wikipedia.org/wiki/Polish_I_Corps_in_Russia.

71 Wikipedia, s.v. "5th Rifle Division (Poland)," last modified July 6, 2023, https://en.wikipedia.org/wiki/5th_Rifle_Division_(Poland)#History.

constructing three armoured trains and gunboats to defend the Ob River bridge at Novo-Nikolayevsk.

Photo 9.1. Polish soldiers of the 5th Siberian Division in transit by train

Armoured trains played an important role for both sides in the civil war. There were approximately 300 of them; about seventy-five were purpose-built in Russian railyards, while the rest were fabricated from industrial flat cars and material at hand, including naval deck guns. All featured thick steel armour. Each train carried a company of infantry, about 135 soldiers, and an associated troop of cavalry to provide added mobility and anti-sabotage reconnaissance. The Zaamurets was the most formidable of the armoured trains (photo 9.2).[72] It was built by Imperial Russia in 1916 for use on the Eastern Front, but it was seized by the Red Army in 1918 and deployed to the Trans-Siberian Railway against White Russian forces and, later, against the Czech Legion.

---

72 Wikipedia, s.v. "Zaamurets," last modified July 19, 2023, https://en.wikipedia.org/wiki/Zaamurets.

Photo 9.2. The Zaamurets armoured train in 1920; it was captured several times by opposing armies and renamed each time.

The Red Army used the many ethnic minorities in Russia to create special regiments, but without any concession to granting them independent states. For that reason, there was not a Polish regiment in the Red Army. The Latvian Riflemen in western Russia were one of the first ethnic regiments, soon followed by the Budenny Cossack cavalry army in the Ukraine. Kazakhstan was the home to the Dungan Calvary regiment (Chinese Muslims of central Asia). Chinese and Korean people were widespread in Far Eastern Siberia and also enlisted in the Red Army. Years later, these groups would provide the vehicle for communist infiltration into Eastern Europe, the Caucasus, Korea, and China.

Shortage of food became critical in the winter of 1920–1921. The government confiscated grain, potatoes, cows, chickens, eggs, and animal hides. Rations were minimal, there was extreme inflation, and people began to starve. The Bolshevik press denigrated Polish people, calling them "noble" and "counter-revolutionary."[73] Poles lost their jobs and were denied food and clothing when these came to be rationed. Poles in Novo-Nikolayevsk and elsewhere began to leave, going in the only possible direction of safety: east,

---

73 Theiss, *Dzieci Syberyjskie 1919–2019*, 47.

away from the Bolsheviks. The exodus included the families of Polish soldiers. Disease continued to be rampant, a consequence of poverty, anarchy, and virtually no health services. Starvation and disease claimed many lives.

Before the revolution and civil war, there were 40 000 to 50 000 Poles in Siberia. As Polish refugees fled toward the Far East, their numbers increased to 150 000 to 200 000.[74] They were intermingled with White Russians and other refugees. Inevitably, they competed with troops for space on trains. The Wojdak family, with their six-year-old son, was somewhere in this flood of humanity in 1918–1919, escaping from a desperate situation. Disease was carried east with the refugees. In 1919, typhus, smallpox, cholera, and Spanish flu reached Harbin and Vladivostok.

Trains carrying refugees were held up while troop trains took priority for locomotives or fuel. Two quotations from historian Antony Beevor's book *Russia, Revolution and Civil War, 1917–1922* capture what it was like:

> In almost all trains, at least one wagon was filled with typhus victims. One train carried nothing but typhus patients, and naked bodies were thrown out into the snow at every halt, "with as little ceremony as the stoker threw out the ashes", as a British officer observed.

> Pity was in short supply everywhere. Women refugees trapped in the icicle-covered cattle wagons gave birth, but had no milk for their babies and they had to watch their small children dying from starvation. Their menfolk, "covered with dirty furs, unshaven, wild-eyed, and desperate", would collapse in self-pity. . . . On the night of 10 January, a temperature of minus 68 degrees centigrade was recorded further east at Chita, where on other nights it was down to minus 40.[75]

Siberia was characterized by anarchy, lawlessness, and regional warlords. Local warlords robbed White Russians; fortunately, Polish refugees possessed little and stood a better chance of keeping their lives. Bands of red partisans sabotaged the train tracks, burned bridges, disrupted coal supplies,

74 Teruo Matsumoto and Wieslaw Theiss, *Siberian Children: Japan's Aid for Polish Children, 1919–1921* (Warsaw: Wydawnictwo Sejmowe, 2018), 178.

75 Beevor, *Russia, Revolution and Civil War,* 413–415.

and, on occasion, attacked trains. Much of the Allied force was required to guard the line and to secure the coal mines necessary to operate trains.

Grigori Semyonov was the most infamous of the warlords (some references spell Semyonov "Semenov").[76] He was born in the Lake Baikal region, his heritage was Russian and Buryat, and he spoke both languages, plus Mongolian. He claimed to be a direct descendant of Mongolian ruler Genghis Khan. Semyonov had been an officer in the Imperial Army. In January 1918, he boldly seized the Bolshevik army garrison in Manzhouli, on the border between Siberia and Manchuria. Manzhouli (Man Zhou Li Shi in Chinese) is where the Trans-Siberian Railway from Chita connects to the Trans-Manchurian line to Harbin and onward to Vladivostok. Semyonov recruited an informal army, characterized better as a gang, of Buryats and Chinese and began to attack the Bolsheviks. Semyonov somehow impressed Allied representatives sufficiently to be given financial aid. At the same time, the Japanese Army guaranteed his protection. Semyonov captured Chita in September 1918 and established a provisional government, calling it the Great Mongol State and his army, the Manchurian Special Detachment. The latter included notorious sadists, who terrorized peasants and executed Bolsheviks.

Nominally, Semyonov supported White Russia, but in fact, he served his own interests foremost and Japan's expansion interests in Manchuria secondly. He had several armoured trains supported by Mongol cavalry and, thereby, controlled the railway line between Chita and Harbin. Semyonov exacted a toll on all train traffic and seized materials that were useful to his army, including munitions intended for White Russian forces. In October 1919, a train carrying 68 000 rifles for the White Army was halted in Chita, and Semyonov demanded 15 000 of them as his share.[77]

The Russian Revolution evolved rapidly. Early "Revolutionaries" were zealous idealists. They were supplanted by the Bolsheviks, who used the Cheka secret police to summarily torture and execute all opponents. This evolved into the communist state known for institutional control of society

76 Wikipedia, s.v. "Grigory Mikhaylovich Semyonov," last modified October 30, 2023, https:// en.wikipedia.org/wiki/Grigory_Mikhaylovich_Semyonov.

77 Beevor, *Russia, Revolution and Civil War*, 370.

using the NKVD (*Narodný komissariat vnutrennih del*, the state security police of the Soviet Union).

Extreme cruelty characterized the civil war—millions died. Both sides tortured and executed prisoners. Bodies of victims were routinely left on display, such as being hung on trees or lamp posts. Known and suspected sympathizers suffered the same fate. The account by Beevor provides sickening detail.[78] Both sides pillaged, plundered, and raped peasants and other innocent civilians in the countryside. Single or widowed women were forced into prostitution. Perhaps to numb the mind from all the horrors, White leaders consumed excessive alcohol and were addicted to opium or cocaine. Antisemitism was rife among White Russians in Ukraine; pogroms killed tens of thousands.

There were endless ways to divide people: by ideology (capitalist, communist, fascist, socialist, or anarchist); by social status (peasant, noble, or bourgeoisie); by race or ethnicity (Chinese, Russian, Buryat, Polish, Korean, Czech, Japanese, or Mongol); or by religion (Orthodox, Jew, Catholic, atheist, or Buddhist). At some point, everyone, or anyone, was cast as an enemy.

---

78 Beevor, 331.

10.

White Russians, Foreign Armies, and Demise of the Polish Legion

Alexander Kolchak was an Imperial Russian admiral who began as a junior officer in the Russian Navy during the Russo-Japanese War of 1904–1905.[79] He was captured at Port Arthur and concluded the war as a Japanese prisoner. He became an admiral during the First World War and saw action in the Baltic against Germany and then in the Black Sea against Turkey. He was relieved of command by the revolutionary government in February 1917. Kolchak had no experience in commanding armies in battles on land. He established an anti-communist government in Omsk and accepted command of all the White armies: those in the South (Ukraine), North (Arkhangelsk), Northwest (Estonia), and the East (Siberia). Kolchak advanced from Omsk across the Urals to Ufa, 1600 kilometres from Moscow.

Historians describe Kolchak as courageous, patriotic, and principled but also moody, stubborn, neurotic, and possessing poor social skills. He

79 Wikipedia, s.v. "Alexander Kolchak," last modified October 29, 2023, https://en.wikipedia. org/wiki/Alexander_Kolchak.

lacked the important political skill of compromise. He refused to consider autonomy for ethnic minorities and would not cooperate with the Socialist Revolutionary Party, the only non-Bolshevik political party with widespread popular support. To restore strict discipline in the armed forces, he considered it necessary to employ capital punishment. Reliance on the old ways of Imperial Russia did not build morale in the army or enlist support from many people. Conscripted peasant soldiers deserted at the first opportunity. Kolchak was called a "Western puppet" by the Bolsheviks.

The withdrawal of the Russian Army from the Eastern Front by the Bolshevik government was a great problem for the Western Allies because Germany could redeploy its forces to focus on the Western Front. Western governments were alarmed by the overthrow of the ruling class in Russia and the abolition of capitalism. Socialism was a worrying movement in Europe, but communism was terrifying. Kolchak asked for military aid from the Allies, promising to stop the spread of communism and reactivate the Russian Army to fight Germany. The Allies accepted readily; troops from Britain, America, France, Italy, and other nations mobilized to Arkhangelsk and to the Caucasus-Black Sea region.

In Siberia, White Russian forces were supplemented by 1 800 British troops, 7 950 American,[80] at least 40 000 Czech,[81] 80 000 Japanese,[82] 4 200 Canadian,[83] 1 850 French (from Vietnam), 2 000 Italian, and 5 000 Chinese. The large number of Japanese reflects a strong imperial motive, to protect their advantage in Manchuria and Korea. The formidable Czech Legion is discussed in the succeeding chapter. Vladivostok became a military camp with troops of so many nations. They were simply called "interventionists" by people in Siberia. The presence of foreign armies was widely resented in Russia, not only by Bolsheviks, but also by peasants. Rebellious peasants

---

80 Wikipedia, s.v. "American Expeditionary Force, Siberia," last modified October 23, 2023, https://en.wikipedia.org/wiki/American_Expeditionary_Force,_Siberia.

81 Wikipedia, s.v. "Czechoslovak Legion," last modified October 12, 2023, https://en.wikipedia.org/wiki/Czechoslovak_Legion.

82 Matsumoto and Theiss, *Siberian Children*, 177.

83 Benjamin Isitt, *From Victoria to Vladivostok: Canada's Siberian Expedition, 1917–1919* (Vancouver: UBC Press, 2010).

were called partisans; they eventually became openly hostile to the inter-ventionists and joined the Red Army.

Maurice Janin was a French general placed in charge of all Allied forces in Siberia, with the notable exception of the Japanese, who had the largest army.[84] The Czech and Polish Legions were under his command, as they were not yet independent nations, along with a French colonial battalion. He was to coordinate with commanders of American, Canadian, Italian, and Romanian troops, and liaise with Alexander Kolchak. Differences between nations on roles and responsibilities led to animosity between the troops[85]—Janin's task was challenging, to say the least. A contingent of the American Red Cross was an important adjunct of the American mission, being the only humanitarian organization in Siberia.[86]

Kolchak drew the ire of the Polish Siberian Division and the Czech Legion by his refusal to recognize their claim to independent homelands, causing both to refuse military support in October 1918.[87] Without their participation, a Red Army offensive in the spring of 1919 easily pushed Kolchak's White Army back east from Ufa. He established a new base 1 200 kilometres farther east in Omsk, but the relentless Red advance continued to gain ground. White conscripts were poorly treated, lacked motivation, and deserted at every opportunity. White Russia's goal to restore an aristo-cratic government was doomed to failure by the length and tyranny of the czar's rule but Kolchak's profound failings accelerated the collapse of the White movement. Refugees and the Polish Siberian Division suffered the most from the rapid Red advance.

Kolchak waited until November, far too long, to retreat from Omsk, and his orderly withdrawal became a rout in December 1919. There was a logjam of trains in Novo-Nikolayevsk that enhanced a dire situation; the city was retaken by the Red Army in December 1919.[88] Poles, Czechs, and Kolchak's army argued about the priority of trains; open fighting erupted

---

84 Beevor, *Russia, Revolution and Civil War*, 292.

85 Beevor, 294, 377.

86 Beevor, 293.

87 Wikipedia, "Alexander Kolchak."

88 Beevor, *Russia, Revolution and Civil War*, 376.

on December 20, 1919, at Tayga east of Novo-Nikolayevsk. A contingent of the Siberian Division marched back along the tracks to confront the advancing Red Army on December 23. More than 100 were killed and many more wounded, but they succeeded in delaying the Red advance.

General Janin consistently favoured the Czechs over the Poles, commanding the Poles to be the rearguard of the retreat. Jan Skorobhaty, Polish liaison officer, protested: "To be the rearguard over a distance of thousands of kilometres may be an honour to the Poles, but it is too heavy a burden to be borne all the time by one and the same Polish division."[89]

There were curt responses from Janin and the Czech commander, both rejecting a change in the disposition of troops.

On January 8–9, 1920, the exhausted Polish Siberian Division was badly beaten at Krasnoyarsk, 800 kilometres east of Novosibirsk, and most of their armoured trains were lost.[90] Five thousand were captured, some while they walked along the tracks. The leading group got away but ran out of fuel and supplies at Uyar, 100 kilometres farther east, and surrendered there. Kazimierz Rumsza, second-in-command of the Polish Legion, refused to surrender. He led 900 officers and men on an ice march through the taiga, slipping through Bolshevik forces, until they reached Irkutsk. From there, they managed to escape to Harbin and finally arrived in Gdansk, Poland, in June 1920. Polish prisoners of war were interned in Krasnoyarsk, where many died in the typhus epidemic that swept through Siberia. Survivors were set to work under difficult to brutal conditions. Some went over to the Red Army; a very small number were eventually repatriated to Poland.

The demise of the Polish Legion meant there was no one to defend the interests of Polish refugees. The Czech Legion, better equipped and with greater numbers, was able to fight its way through Kansk, farther east from Uyar, to reach Irkutsk. Irkutsk was still under the control of interventionist forces, so the Czech Legion was able to escape from there to Vladivostok and, eventually, to Europe.

---

89 Beevor, 412.

90 Wikipedia, "5th Rifle Division (Poland)."

11.

The Czech Legion and Polish Refugees

The Czech Legion, as it was commonly called, was unique and powerful among interventionist forces in the Russian Civil War. More than any other foreign army, it had a major detrimental influence on Polish refugees.

The Czech Legion was composed of ethnic Czechs and Slovaks living in the Russian Empire. Soon after the outbreak of World War I, they petitioned the czar to create a force in the service of the Russian Empire to fight Austria-Hungary. Their intent was to establish an independent country after the war from Austro-Hungarian territory.[91] The czar readily agreed because it was his adversary's territory. The czar made no such promise to the Polish Pulawy Legion. Initially, the Czech Legion was small, but early Russian success against Austro-Hungarian forces led to a large number of prisoners, and by 1916, they were allowed to join. As the war progressed, many more defected to the Czech Legion. They were highly motivated and effective in battle, so the Legion was allowed to swell to 40 000 men.

91 Wikipedia, "Czechoslovak Legion."

The collapse of the Russian Army in 1917 provided a windfall of machine guns, rifles, and ammunition for the Czech Legion, but the presence of the German Army in their homeland prevented their return. The Czech Legion was a potential threat to the Red Army, so the Bolshevik government granted them passage to leave Russia via Vladivostok. On May 14, 1918, with the Czech Legion strung out along the entire rail line, a fight erupted at the Chelyabinsk train station between members of the Czech Legion and Hungarian prisoners of war. Several were killed. Russia had withdrawn from the war, so the Hungarians thought they should be allowed to go home, but the Czechs blocked their passage on the train. Some Czechs were arrested by the city police, but their comrades, 3 000 strong, forced their release at gunpoint and took over the town.

In retaliation, Leon Trotsky (the People's Commissariat for Military and Naval Affairs) ordered the Czech Legion to disarm, that their trains be stopped, and that they should join either the Red Army or labour battalions. Not surprisingly, the Czechs refused. Again, Trotsky upped the ante by charging all Soviets to shoot Czechs wherever they were found. Alternatively, Trotsky said if they laid down their arms, they would be treated as brothers. The Czechs did not trust Trotsky's notion of brotherhood.[92]

Battles ensued along the rail line, train stations, and cities fell under Czech control, beginning with Novo-Nikolayevsk. Irkutsk was the final city to fall under Czech control on July 11, 1918. However, the railway was blocked at Lake Baikal, where the rail line hugs the rugged south shore of the lake. The ferry-icebreaker SS *Baikal* had been fitted with a cannon, and Bolshevik ground forces held strategic points in the mountains above the train line. They prevented arms and other supplies from Vladivostok from reaching Kolchak's White Army and blocked the Czechs from escaping Siberia. The Czechs captured two small steamers at the port near Irkutsk, fitted them with howitzers, and sailed across Lake Baikal. On August 15, 1918, the SS *Baikal* was caught by surprise in the port of Mysovsk (Babushkin) and sunk.[93]

---

92 Beevor, *Russia, Revolution and Civil War*, 202.

93 Wikipedia, s.v. "Battle of Lake Baikal," last modified August 16, 2023, https://en.wikipedia.org/wiki/Battle_of_Lake_Baikal.

The Czech Legion now controlled the entire Trans-Siberian Railway, a 7 000-kilometre span from the Volga to Vladivostok. The Allies were encouraged because the means to support White Russia seemed open. Allied forces in Vladivostok were assigned to support the Czech Legion, to assist their withdrawal from Siberia.[94] The buildup of Allied forces was incompatible with Soviet administration of the city. The first Czech arrivals led an Allied force to overthrow the Bolshevik garrison in Vladivostok. The Czech Legion captured the Zaamurets armoured train from the Red Army, renamed it the "Orlik" ("Young Eagle") in July 1918, and used it to solidify their hold on the rail line to Vladivostok. Progress was slow in moving the Legion due to the poor condition of the railway and a shortage of locomotives. In November 1918, the Armistice ended World War I in Europe, and the Treaty of Versailles, in 1919, created an independent Czechoslovakia. The Czech Legion, with a route home assured, became completely averse to fighting for White Russia.

The Western Allies began to realize their strategy in Siberia was hopeless due to Kolchak's inability to gain support from the people or build a strong army.[95] General Janin turned Kolchak over to the Socialist Revolutionary Party in January 1920; a month later, he was executed by the Bolsheviks in Irkutsk. This left Grigori Semyonov and the Manchurian Special Detachment as the last Allied hope against communism, one they chose not to support.[96]

Resistance to the Red Army evaporated, and it advanced quickly eastward across Siberia during mid-1920. Evacuation of the Czech Legion was well underway; its last members departed Vladivostok in September of that year. The United States reversed its position in February 1920, after Kolchak was executed, by stating it was a mistake to intervene in the internal affairs of Russia and began to withdraw its troops.[97] Japan, with imperialist ambitions

---

94 Wikipedia, s.v. "Allied Intervention in the Russian Civil War," last modified October 30, 2023, https://en.wikipedia.org/wiki/Allied_intervention_in_the_Russian_Civil_War.

95 Beevor, *Russia, Revolution and Civil War*, 326, 328.

96 Beevor, 415–417.

97 *Russian Civil War and American Expeditionary Forces in Siberia, 1918–1920*, Archives Unbound, US National Archives Historical Files M-917.

in Asia, increased its armed force to 80 000. Their purpose was to protect the evacuation of the Czech Legion, protect Japanese citizens living in Vladivostok, and prevent communist expansion into Korea and Manchuria.

Most Allied troops of the Siberian expedition stayed in Vladivostok, venturing inland on rare forays. They were reticent to confront the Red Army and never engaged in battle. Interventionist armies protected the port to assist the Czech withdrawal but did little or nothing to assist refugees. After the destruction of the Polish Siberian Division, refugees were on their own to deal with bitter cold, disease, hunger, hostile partisans, and the Red Army. Their greatest challenge may have been to gain space on trains. The Czech Legion was as desperate as refugees for space on trains but had an advantage: they were armed. Polish refugees were displaced from trains, sometimes forced at gunpoint to disembark.

Warlord Grigori Semyonov made Chita a lawless and dangerous place from September 1918 until November 1920, when the Red Army expelled him and his army from the Lake Baikal region.[98, 99] All refugees from Novo-Nikolayevsk, such as the Wojdak family, and those from elsewhere in Siberia and Russia, passed through Chita at his whim.

Semyonov withdrew to a remote region north of Vladivostok and fled Russia in 1921, targeted by communist assassins. He went to Korea and Japan before going to America in April 1922. There, he was faced with deportation and returned to Asia, sailing from Vancouver to Yokohama. He settled in Dairen (Japanese), also called Dalniy (Russian) or Dalian (Chinese), in the Japanese puppet state of Manchukuo, where he supplied intelligence to the Japanese administrators. Semyonov was finally captured in August 1945 by Russian paratroopers. He was executed by hanging on August 30, 1946, having escaped communist revenge longer than anyone else of the civil war. No doubt, he was tortured during his final year.[100]

The 259th Battalion, 16th Infantry Brigade, Canadian Siberian Expeditionary Force, comprised 4 200 men.[101] Canada's decision to send troops

---

98 Beevor, *Russia, Revolution and Civil War*, 328–334.
99 Wikipedia, "Grigory Mikhaylovich Semyonov."
100 Wikipedia, "Grigory Mikhaylovich Semyonov."
101 Isitt, *From Victoria to Vladivostok*.

was contentious; the nation was war-weary, and among the populace, there was a degree of sympathy for communist ideals. Socialism and trade unions were on the rise in Canada, as elsewhere in the world. Unlike the patriotic and enthusiastic men who volunteered to fight in Europe in 1914 and 1915, two-thirds of the 259th Battalion were conscripts, compelled to serve under the Military Service Act of 1917. They (legitimately) questioned whether the Siberian expedition qualified as "defence of the realm," which was the key phrase in the conscription act. The War in Europe was over, so why were they going to Siberia? On departure day from Victoria, many had to be forced at bayonet point to board the ship; a dozen of the leaders would later face court-martial for mutiny. The Canadian contingent departed from Victoria on December 21, 1918, and returned six months later, in June 1919.

Fifty-five members of the Canadian expedition went to Omsk in late December 1918 to provide leadership and training of White Russian forces, while all the rest of the Canadian force remained garrisoned in Vladivostok. It was a difficult trip because bands of partisans (guerillas) were cutting telegraph lines and sabotaging train tracks and bridges. In Omsk, the Canadians quickly determined the fighting spirit of the Czech Legion had been replaced by desire to go home. At the same time, rail workers and coal miners, who provided fuel for trains, went for months without pay. Obviously, they were not inclined to transport foreign armies in a cause they did not support. Ironically, these train workers had transported one-quarter of Imperial Russia's gold reserve, the largest in the world, to Vladivostok and on to Europe to guarantee loans for the war supplies for czarist Russia. There is no indication the Canadian force was involved with the up to 200 000 Polish refugees, and their impact on hostilities in Siberia was inconsequential.

12.

Rescue of Polish Children from Siberia

In Novo-Nikolayevsk in 1919 the Polski Komitet Wojenny (Polish War Committee) started the campaign to rescue Polish children.[102] The idea was inspired by the knowledge that Poland was free; the country was reborn as an outcome of the World War. The repatriation goal came to Harbin and Vladivostok with Polish refugees. The Polish Rescue Committee was formed, comprising Anna Bielkiewicz,[103] Jozef Jakobkiewicz,[104] and Wienczslaw Piotrowski. I obtained detailed, unpublished biographies in English; these are summarized below.

Anna Bielkiewicz was a remarkable woman. She was attractive and vivacious, but more importantly, she was brave, independent, principled, and determined. She operated far beyond the boundaries of most women of her

102 Theiss, *Dzieci Syberyjskie*, 43.

103 Wikipedia, s.v. "Anna Bielkiewicz," last modified July 28, 2022, https://pl-m-wikipedia-org.translate.goog/wiki/
Anna_Bielkiewicz?_x_tr_sl=pl&_x_tr_tl=en&_x_tr_hl=en&_x_tr_pto=sc.

104 Wikipedia, s.v. "Jozef Jakobkiewicz," last modified July 3, 2022, https://translate.google.ca/
translate?hl=en&sl=pl&u=https://pl.wikipedia.org/wiki/J%25C3%25B3zef_Jak%25C3%2
5B3bkiewicz&prev=search&pto=aue.

time. She was born Anna Malynicz, a noble Polish family with a history of dissidence against Russia. Her grandfather was exiled to Siberia for his participation in the 1863 rebellion, and she was drawn to the Polish liberation movement too (photo 12.1).

Photo 12.1. Anna Bielkiewicz, Tokyo, 1921

In 1904, at the age of twenty-seven, Anna joined a quasi-legal Polish charity to assist political prisoners by bringing food and clothing to their jails, communicating with and caring for their families, defending them in court, and pleading for a reduced sentence if they were found guilty. Many dissidents were arrested during the 1905 uprising, and her efforts saved many from harsher punishment. She was relentless and outspoken, which likely contributed to the failure of her first marriage to an opera singer. In 1906, dejected and sought by the police, she left Poland for France and lived a quiet life for several years.

During the First World War, she went to Vladivostok with her second husband, a Polish railway engineer named Bielkiewicz. At the time, the population of Vladivostok was 170 000, of which one-third was Chinese, but there was also a large Polish community. She became politically active again. She established the Polish Rescue Committee in September 1919, with herself as president, to assist Polish exiles in eastern Siberia and Manchuria.

Jozef Jakobkiewicz was born in 1892 in Perm in the Ural Mountains of Russia, where he developed a love of the outdoors from an early age. He was the son of Poles exiled to Russia after the failed 1863 rebellion. His siblings were all well-educated; Jozef trained in medicine in Moscow and began work in 1915 as a surgeon at a front-line army war hospital. After Russia withdrew from hostilities in 1917, and it became too dangerous for Poles to remain in western Russia, Jozef Jakobkiewicz went by train to Vladivostok.

En route to Vladivostok in 1918, he saw firsthand the plight of refugees while he was working as a railway station doctor in Irkutsk and Slyudyanka in the Buryat province of Siberia. This region was infamous for the internment of Polish people. A prison in Tunka in Buryatia held 145 Catholic priests after the 1863 uprising, and in 1887, Jozef Pilsudski was one of many political prisoners.

Photo 12.2. Dr. Jozef Jakobkiewicz, Warsaw, ca. 1928

Jakobkiewicz became chief sanitary doctor of Vladivostok. He was energetic and popular for eradicating epidemics in the city of cholera, spotted fever, and plague. He also became leader of the Vladivostok Boy Scouts and head of Scouting in the Far East region, a role that put him in direct contact with Polish people and their children as far east as Chita. Patriotic and fiercely committed to the education of children, Jakobkiewicz became vice president of the Polish Rescue Committee (photo 12.2).

Wienczyslaw Piotrowski was the third member of the Polish Rescue Committee. His brother Wladyslaw Piotrowski assisted too, but less is known about him. Wienczslaw Piotrowski was nominally a journalist but, more accurately, a vagabond traveller and adventurer. Born in Chernihiv, Ukraine, in 1871, he participated in the 1904–1905 rebellion, for which he was jailed in Warsaw and exiled to Russia. His sentence was short; in 1906, Piotrowski emigrated to Brazil and farmed there for two years. Subsequently, he lived in France, the Netherlands, and Switzerland and began a personal challenge to walk around the world.

After Piotrowski completed 3 000 kilometres of his walk, war erupted in Europe and he joined a voluntary Polish military unit in France. After receipt of the *Croix de Guerre avec Palme* on the Western Front, he went to Russia via Scandinavia and Murmansk to enlist in the Polish I Corps and fight on the Eastern Front. Following the Russian Revolution and the disarming of the I Corps, Piotrowski travelled through Russia to Harbin, where he became involved in Scouting. He edited and published numerous articles, including "A Polish Scout in Asia." Later, he edited the periodical founded by Anna Bielkiewicz, *Echo of the Far East.*

The plight of Polish refugees in Siberia was daunting, so the Rescue Committee focused on children, to take them to Poland, where they would be the new generation in a free country. Beginning in December 1919, Jakobkiewicz, with the American Red Cross, travelled west through Harbin, at least as far as Chita. He gathered Polish children in need at all train stops. He states in his report:

> We persisted in looking for Polish children who hid in shelters of the Russians and Chinese. There were children who lived in wrecked trains; there were also children who found their

way into military barracks. Whenever we heard that Poles were living nearby, we walked our legs off to find them. In the families that lost their fathers, the mothers, shedding tears, implored us to help at least their children. When we were invited inside by one family, we witnessed an emotional scene. Mother, who entrusted her son to our care, covered the miserable table with a rough tablecloth, softly put Holy Mary's figure on it, and said a prayer. In front of her, she put her son who did not know his homeland nor did he speak his mother tongue fluently, and she gently explained to him: "Your grandpa and your father fought for the independence of the fatherland, and you are their descendant." It sounded as if she wanted to instill the insurgent's soul in her son.[105]

Wienczslaw Piotrowski and his brother Wladyslaw organized a rescue expedition north from Vladivostok to the Amur region, as far as Svobodny. In a petition asking for assistance, Anna Bielkiewicz wrote:

> . . . Having no property to attend to, they are fleeing to the East empty-handed. These refugees have to endure the discomfort of the journey and lack of food, they are decimated by the spreading infectious diseases and by cold. Their pitiful conditions results from the merciless cruelty of the extremists, which we cannot help. Since there are not enough trains, soldiers often throw out the refugees from the trains, even in the middle of a blizzard. One of the witnesses said that when he looked inside one train, he saw several dead bodies, and a boy freezing to death beside his dead mother. He himself saw parents cover children with their clothes, give them what food they had, and they died without knowing what would happen to their children. He saw dead bodies of parents frozen to death among little babies, frozen tears on their blue faces. There are many such children wandering about, and there is no way to inform their parents or brothers and sisters about their fate unless they freeze to death along the way.[106]

---

105 Matsumoto and Theiss, *Siberian Children*, 179–180.
106 Matsumoto and Theiss, 182–183.

In all likelihood, this is the tragic situation that befell my father, Pawel Wojdak, and his parents. These were the train "accidents" he could not describe, memories deeply suppressed in his mind. He spoke of their deaths as two separate events, two different traumas, which is entirely possible during their journey across Siberia. A child does not have a full understanding of time. When I was six years old, I was surprised to learn summer was over and there was a return to school; I had thought the two-month summer vacation lasted much longer. Conversely, for Pawel Wojdak, at a similar age and under horrific circumstances, the death of each of his parents may have been only a month apart but seemed much longer.

Appendix 1 lists all 372 Polish children who were gathered in the first rescue mission: 206 boys and 166 girls and their age. (There will be a second and a third rescue mission.) Their names are important. For too many years, their story and identity were suppressed by Russia after another world war and forgotten in Japan and elsewhere. Each child has a unique personal history, and though we might never be able to know their story, it is real. The children's names also appear in the *Siberian Children* website. Perhaps their descendants can find their origin more easily than I.

The youngest rescued child was just two years old, and the oldest sixteen. Those older than sixteen were deemed to be adults and were not taken in by the rescue mission. They had to fend for themselves in Siberia. The separate listing for boys and girls obscures family ties; one must switch between lists to find brothers and sisters, or cousins perhaps. How different was each child's situation! Some children had one or both parents alive but were living in dire conditions. At least these parents were able to see their children safely onto the train. Some children knew their family history. Some older children were entrusted to care for younger siblings—what a responsibility for a child! Some were young orphans, alone and bewildered in cruel circumstances. Their backgrounds might be different, but they will face an unknown future together—would they survive and go to Poland as the Rescue Committee promised, or would the Rescue Committee fail and they be abandoned somewhere?

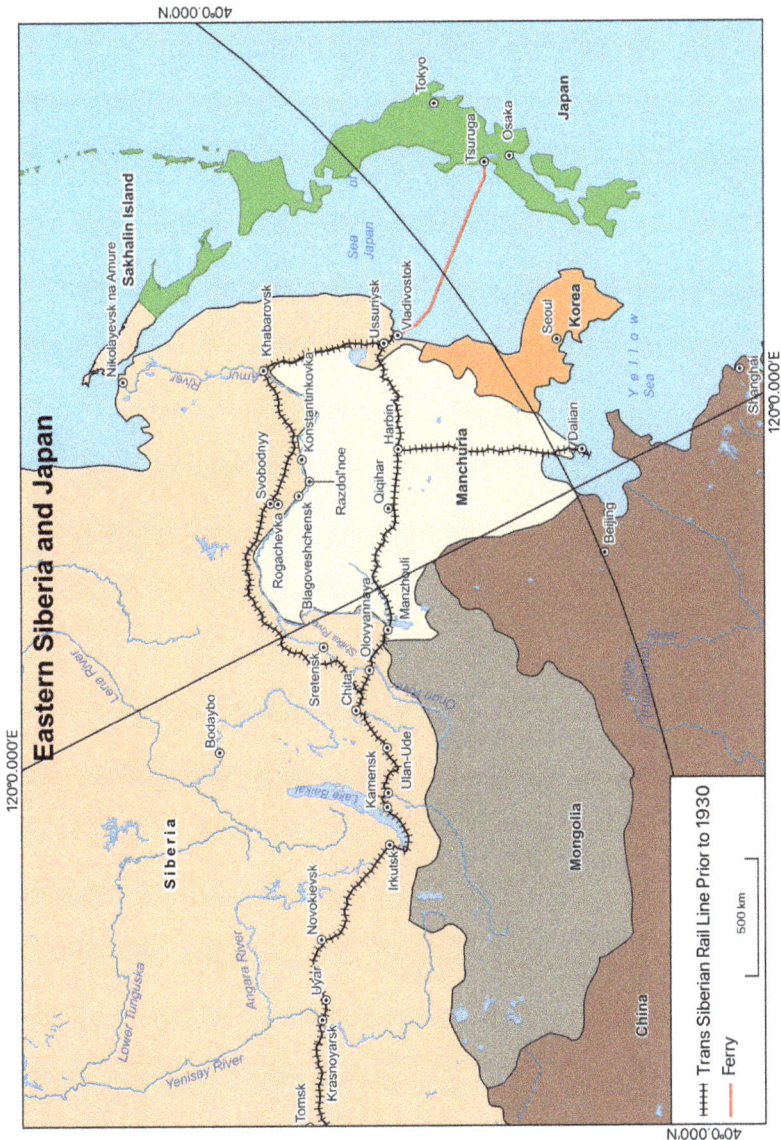

Map 2. Eastern Siberia showing Trans-Siberian and Trans-Manchurian railways and towns where Siberian children were gathered and rescued, and their route to Japan. Location of Nikolayevsk-on-Amur and Bodaybo in the Lena goldfield are also shown. Map prepared using Natural Earth.[107]

107 Natural Earth.

Table 1 lists localities as shown in *Echo of the Far East*—that is, the placenames known to Polish people in 1920 and consequently are spelled with Polish phonetics. Identification of several settlements is challenging because of name changes, modifications in spelling, or more than one location with the same name. Map 2, like Map 1, is prepared from historic data specifically for this document and uses current placenames.

The Rescue Committee took two routes from Vladivostok to find children. One course was directly west on the Trans-Manchurian Railway to Harbin, where there was a substantial Russian and Polish community dating from the construction and administration of the railroad. Jews began to migrate to Harbin in the early 1900s to escape discrimination and pogroms in Russia. In 1913, there were 34 000 Russians, 23 500 Jews, and 5 000 Poles in Harbin.[108] During the Russian Civil War, Harbin became a sanctuary for escaping wealthy White Russians and Polish refugees. The European population swelled to about 120 000. A thorough description of Polish life in Harbin in this period, their background as professionals and refugees from the Russian Civil War, is provided by Mariusz Borysiewicz in his journal article, "Polish Settlement in Siberia (1898–1950): A Brief Historical Survey."[109]

The Rescue Committee found Pawel Wojdak and fifty-eight other Polish children in Harbin. Continuing west, the railway recrosses the Russian border at Manzhouli, where one child was found. Six more were assembled at Olovyannaya (formerly Okieanskaja?), midway between Manzhouli and Chita. Chita is an important centre where twenty-three more children were added. Their rescue journey continued west to Irkutsk, passing through Nikolsk (four children) and Kamiensk (two children). The US Red Cross participated, using the same train to rescue the sick and wounded.

The other route taken by the rescuers was north to Kharbarovsk, where about 1 000 Poles lived.[110] There were 115 children gathered there for rescue. Eight hundred kilometres west of Khabarovsk, there is a cluster of

---

108 Wikipedia, "Harbin."

109 Mariusz Borysiewicz, "Polish Settlement in Siberia (1898–1950): A Brief Historical Survey," *Studia Polonijne* 39 (2018): 125–166, https://doi.org/10.18290/sp.2018.6.

110 Theiss, *Dzieci Syberyjskie*, 45.

communities between Blagoveshchensk, on the Amur River, and Alexeyevsk, located 165 kilometres north where the Trans-Siberian Railway crosses the Zeya River, an important tributary of the Amur. Alexeyevsk, established in 1912 and named in honour of crown prince Alexey, was renamed by the Bolshevik revolutionaries as Svobodny, meaning "Free." The large Polish community in the area can probably be attributed to railway construction.

The Rescue Committee gathered twenty-four children in Blagoveshchensk, twenty-six in Svobodny, and fifteen in the satellite communities of Konstantinovka, Rogachevka, Razdol'noe, and Novokievskii. The four children from Nikolayevsk-on-Amur had a harrowing escape from murderous partisans. They travelled by coastal ferry to Vladivostok. The settlements of Carowka, Kniewiczy, and Sierebranka have not been identified.

Table 1. Locations of Siberian Children, First Rescue Mission

Location (in Polish) Where Found	Current Name (in English)	Number of Children
Aleksiejewsk	Svobodny	26
Blagowieszczensk	Blagoveshchensk	24
Carowka		2
Chabarowsk	Khabarovsk	115
Charbin	Harbin, China	59
Czyta	Chita	23
Kamieniec Podolski	Kamiensk, Buryatia	2
Kniewiczy		1
Konstantyn / Konstanynow / Konstantynopol	Konstantinovka	6
Mandzurja	Manzhouli, China	1
Nikolajewsk an Amurem	Nikolayevsk-on-Amur	4
Nikolsk	Nikolsk, Buryatia	4
Nowokijewsk	Novokievskii	3
Okieanskaja	Olovyannaya ?	6

Razdolnoje*	Razdol'noe*	3
Rogaczewska	Rogachevka	3
Sierebranka		1
Wladywostok	Vladivostok	89
Total		372

*Two places named Razdol'noe, one near Vladivostok,
one near Blagoveshchensk—either one is possible

The children gathered from towns, cities, and railroad stations were assembled in a large villa donated for the cause near Vladivostok in Sedanka. In 2001, one of the children, then in her nineties, said happily, "We got three meals a day and there was water to wash ourselves."[111]

The length of time Pawel Wojdak was in an orphanage in Harbin is unknown. One can imagine he and the other children were bewildered and in a state of emotional shock, no matter how kind and well-meaning the strangers taking them to an unknown destination were.

---

111 Halina Nowika in *Siberian Dreams,* documentary film by Ewa Misiewicz, 2001, video, 52:25, https://www.youtube.com/watch?v=p7zbIogBdbs.

Sidepiece on Svobodny

A deeper look at Svobodny[112] gives insight into the dangerous world in which Poles found themselves during the civil war. There was a calamitous series of events involving the Red Army, remnants of the White Army and independent Korean forces. These are collectively known as the Massacre of Svobodny.[113]

The Far Eastern Republic[114] was created by White Russia. It comprised all the territory from Lake Baikal to the Pacific Ocean along the Amur River, its capital was in Chita. After the death of Alexander Kolchak the Republic was recast by the Bolsheviks as a buffer state between Soviet Russia and territories controlled by Japan; Korea and Manchuria. The puppet state existed from April 1921 until November 1922 when it merged with Soviet Russia. In the transition many White Russians were killed in Svobodny, including many Poles. No one counted the number of deaths.

Koreans opposed to Japanese rule took refuge from the Japanese army in Svobodny, which they called the Free City.[115] The Korean Independence Corps grew to a force of 3500 men in April 1921. Initially they were supported by the Soviets with training and weapons. The Soviets wanted the Korean force to join the Red Army but they refused. The Korean intent was to invade Manchuria and overthrow the Japanese administration. Russia feared this would lead to Japan declaring war on Russia, for which it was not prepared. The Red Army ordered the much smaller Korean force to disarm, and fighting erupted when the Koreans refused. Estimates of Korean casualties range up to several hundred killed and many more taken prisoner. Russia

112 Wikipedia, s.v. "Svobodny," last modified October 20, 2023, https://en.wikipedia.org/wiki/Svobodny,_Amur_Oblast.

113 Wikipedia, s.v. "Massacre of Svobodny," last modified July 28, 2023, https://en.wikipedia.org/wiki/Massacre_of_Svobodny. [page deleted; archived version at https://web.archive.org/web/20230319093319/https://en.wikipedia.org/wiki/Massacre_of_Svobodny].

114 Wikipedia, s.v. "Far Eastern Republic," last modified September 19, 2023, https://en.wikipedia.org/wiki/Far_Eastern_Republic

115 Wikipedia, s.v. "Free City Incident," last modified November 23, 2023, https://en.wikipedia.org/wiki/Free_City_Incident#:~:text=The%20Free%20City%20Incident%20was,the%20Pro%2DRussian%20resistance%20groups.

agreed to Japanese demands to forcibly disband the Korean Independence Corps. Details of the battle and Korean deaths were suppressed by Russia so as not antagonize Koreans serving in the Red Army.

The third stage of the Massacre of Svobodny took place in the summer of 1921. Food shortages were severe, soldiers took what they wanted from civilians by force. Anti-Semitism was strong throughout Russia and Svobodny authorities blamed Jews for the shortages. They instigated a pogrom in which dozens to hundreds of Jews were killed and their homes and businesses destroyed.

Poles were in the middle of these calamities. Fifty-three of the rescued children came from Svobodny, half in the first mission immediately prior to these horrific events in 1920 and half in the second mission in 1922, after the massacres. The memoir of Antonina Liro of Svobodny is related in a future chapter on the second mission. In all likelihood, Antonina's mother and family fled Svobodny during the violence of 1921 to arrive in Harbin and, hence, join the second rescue in 1922.

In 1935, Svobodny was selected as the base for a decade-long construction project to build the Baikal-Amur railroad. The Trans-Siberian line through Svobodny is vulnerable because it runs adjacent to the border with China. The Baikal-Amur line is 700 kilometres north of the Trans-Siberian line and runs parallel to it for 4 300 kilometres. Workers for the project were housed in a "corrective labour" facility in Svobodny, built to hold an astonishing 190 300 convicts, one of the largest in the Gulag system. One may wonder how many guards, machine guns, dogs, and kilometres of barbed wire were required to contain 190 300 inmates in a town named "Free"?

Russian history has a cruel brand of irony.

13.

Siberian Children Speak

Pawel Wojdak was unable to relate what happened in Siberia—as a seven-year-old, he was unaware of what country or region he was in. Any knowledge he may have had of his family origins in Poland or why his parents came to be in Siberia was suppressed or lost from his mind. The "train accidents" in which his parents died were calamities of an unknown nature. We can only draw from accounts of other children to learn why their family was in Siberia and gain insight into what each experienced.

Jan Samardakiewicz's story is told by his grandson, Slawomir Samardakiewicz. Slawomir is a professor in the Faculty of Biology at Adam Mickiewicz University in Poznan, Poland. Jan was a child in the first rescue mission. Shortly before he died in 1985, he told his grandson about his early life. Like Pawel Wojdak, Slawomir's grandfather was reluctant to speak of his childhood, only speaking of individual events. An aversion to describing painful memories is common among people who have experienced deep trauma. The following is drawn from an interview with Slawomir Samardakiewicz:[116]

---

116 Social Welfare Corporation Fukudenkai, "Interview with Slawomir Samardakiewicz," *Siberian Children*, August 2, 2021, https://siberianchildren.pl/en/slawomir-samardakiewicz-en/.

Jan Samardakiewicz was born in 1909 in Malinowka, a town near Tomsk, Siberia. He had a younger brother, Antoni, born in 1911 and sister, Adela, born in 1914. Their parents were Aleksander and Emilia Samardakiewicz. Nothing is known about Aleksander, only that he died when Jan was still young. Emilia was born into the Pawlowicz family in Grauze, now located in Belarus. Perhaps her family was exiled to Siberia because she instilled deep patriotism in her children, a characteristic of Polish insurgents. As a young boy in Malinowka, Jan knew poverty and unimaginable hunger. He had to beg, or steal food to survive. In 1919, when he was 10 he got entangled in a barbed wire fence while trying to steal fruit from an orchard. The orchard owner saved his life but the scars on his stomach remained for life.

A typhus epidemic broke out in Tomsk, forcing the Samardakiewicz family to flee. In 1920 Emilia came to Harbin, Manchuria, as a widow with three children. Poles in Russia saw Manchuria as a place of refuge, especially Harbin with its strong Polish community. Emilia found work as a housekeeper but the pay was insufficient to feed her children so she was compelled to place them in an orphanage. The orphanage for Jan and Antoni was in Mulin, about 300 kilometers from Harbin. When Emilia had the opportunity she passed her sons over to the Rescue Committee, to give them a better life in their homeland. Emilia remained in Manchuria with Adela, her youngest child.

Jan Samardakiewicz's story is comparable to that of Pawel Wojdak. They came from the same district: Tomsk is not far north of Novosibirsk. Typhus and cholera epidemics in Tomsk and Novosibirsk were essentially simultaneous, although living conditions were deteriorating from other causes that could trigger a departure decision. The Samardakiewicz and Wojdak families likely fled their respective cities within the same time period, and there is a remote chance they crossed paths as refugees. What is certain is both children came to be in an orphanage in or near Harbin and subsequently under the care of the Polish Rescue Committee in 1920.

Slawomir Samardakiewicz tells a remarkable story of how he recognized his grandfather as a boy in a photograph in Japan. While attending a conference in Nagoya, he chanced to visit the Meiji-Mura museum and noticed a large picture on the wall. It was a photograph of a passenger ship and a large crowd of children waving handkerchiefs. He saw that the children were Europeans. A label below the picture indicated these were Siberian children. The picture was part of an exhibition about the Japanese Red Cross Society and their first international humanitarian project. In the photo, Slawomir states he "could easily recognize which child was [his] grandfather. His brother Antoni was in the picture next to him, Jan and Antoni always stood together in group photos."

The circumstance of Slawomir Samardakiewicz's chance discovery is amazing. Is it a case of serendipity, or something more mysterious and divine? Slawomir wonders, might those that love us reach out to find us? I experienced a similar feeling when I received documentation of my father's past in Siberia.

The story of Halina Nowicka is drawn from Theiss's *Dzieci Syberyjskie 1919–2019*,[117] together with the documentary film *Siberian Dreams*,[118] in Polish but with English subtitles. The film blends present-day film footage of the Siberian landscape and historic archival images, with the dialogue of the four Siberian children, then in their nineties. They relate their memories of Siberia and Japan and their return to Poland. Halina Nowicka was also on the first rescue mission. Her name appears in Appendix 1 as Halina Szyszkarewska. Her experience gives vivid insight into the train journey from Omsk in Western Siberia, the same district as the Samardakiewicz and Wojdak families began their journey. Once again, the passage is a condensed translation:

> Grandpa was in the 1863 Polish insurrection and was deported to Pskovsk province [adjacent Latvia] and later died of a heart attack. Grandma bore a grudge against all Russians. In the War in 1914 father was mobilized to Omsk. We had a very nice house on the street where all the important people lived. Behind our house was open steppe. Once I got lost while looking for flowers on the steppe but father and the cavalry found me.

117 Theiss, *Dzieci Syberyjskie*, 120–121, 127.
118 Misiewicz, *Siberian Dreams*.

Summers were very hot, all the streams dried up and water had to be delivered in drums. In winter it was -55 degrees and impossible to travel for supplies, everything had to be stored.

There was a military base and a cadet base. In the 1917 Revolution all the cadets were lynched, hung from trees all along the street. Revolutionary patrols demanded to see one's hands. If they were not calloused, you could be shot. One day a warrant officer who had escaped from the Bolsheviks came to our house. He told Mother everyone had been killed including my father. He also told her the last train with refugees was about to leave from Omsk for the Far East. Mother had a sister in Khabarovsk so we were going there. Normally the trip would take 7–10 days but it took us months. It was 1918 and I was nine years old.

At first we were in a regular passenger car with retired officers and mothers with young children and babies. The fuel ran out. Bolsheviks boarded the train and threw everyone off. They lined up all the retired officers who tried to show how important they were by pinning on medals and showing czarist papers. They were machine-gunned—I already knew that sound—and a rifle volley killed who was left. Bodies were left where they fell.

After that we rode in a converted freight car but we waited at the station a long time because there was no locomotive or engineer for refugees. Intervention troops, American, British, Czech were withdrawing all along the Trans-Siberian Railway, their trains went by one after another. Once our car was attached to an American military train because we begged them, other times we sat at a siding for days. Corpses were thrown off the train. One time when we were waiting at a siding we walked to a house though the snow which was up to my neck. The house was empty and we searched for food scraps, we found a few crusts, just enough to fit in the palm of my hand. Mom gathered straw to line the train car. At Khabarovsk we were the only ones to get off the train, everyone else was dead.

In Vladivostok gangs of hungry kids roamed the streets. I was the leader of such a gang. We roamed all over searching for food. Japanese troops gave us a little. The Chinese who owned huge stores gave us a little bread or sugar. Once we saw men with buckets. They had broken into a closed warehouse and found vats of caviar. They filled buckets of caviar for us and I took several buckets home. Another time I stole a sack of dried fish from the harbour and dragged it home. Mother was sick and my two-year-old brother was too, she had to stay with him. I became their "breadwinner."

There was a cholera epidemic. All the Chinese died, not a single survivor. Corpses were left in the street. We weren't scared, we jumped over them. The Japanese put lime on them and disposed of the bodies because they were afraid cholera would spread to Japan. The training I got from these experiences stayed with me all my life. When times were very difficult in 1939 to 1945, I became that little girl again—stealing food, fighting to live. I changed, I became a different person.

There was a rumor that two Polish people began an Aid Committee for the 5000 Polish children in the Far East, to send them back to Poland. Anna Bielkiewicz, a well-known activist, and Dr Jozef Jakobkiewicz, chief sanitary doctor, shuttled back and forth along the 5000 kilometer route of the Trans-Siberian Railway. They risked their lives to collect homeless children from streets and orphanages, and from desperate parents whom Bolsheviks considered enemies, and were unable to provide or protect their children. My aunt came from Khabarovsk with her two kids and told Mom, "Let's send our kids with the Committee. They will go to Poland, we will join them later."

Antonina Liro is featured in *Siberian Dreams* and also furnished an interview in an unpublished paper, "On the Meeting of Descendants of Siberian Children."[119] Antonina states she was born the year before the revolution, therefore in 1916. When Antonina was two or three years old, the family moved to the Amur region of Siberia because there was free land there, but she could not recall where they moved from. Her father was a soldier and, consequently, away for extended periods, and her mother managed the

---

119 Social Welfare Association Fukudenkai, "On the Meeting of Descendants of Siberian Children," (unpublished paper, Warsaw, October 7, 2022), 39–46.

homestead farm on her own. She drove an ox to plow the fields and hauled logs for firewood, leaving Antonina to be minded by her older sister, Anna. Antonina's soother was a piece of cloth soaked in sugar-beet juice. There were ten children, but only six survived. Neighbours were at a distance, and wolves were a constant threat in winter.

The civil war was in progress from Antonina's earliest memories. Food had to be hidden from marauding deserters from various armies: White, Yellow (Korean Independence Corps), and Red. It was only safe to cook and eat at night because the smell could attract hungry men, who were capable of anything. They could walk into the house whenever they wanted. The children were hidden during the day in a hole dug in the floor and disguised by the kitchen table. She says they were like puppies in a den. Young girls could be raped and boys shot. When food ran out, Antonina remembered a special feast: her mother had found a frozen pumpkin. It was cut into pieces, roasted in the oven, and all of it was eaten, including the skin.

The family situation became increasingly desperate. Antonina's mother banded together with some neighbours; they loaded carts and travelled by raft or boat on the Amur and other rivers to Harbin. There, they reunited with her father. The family was housed at a Catholic school. Her older sister, Anna, attended class, but Antonina was still too young for school and followed the priest on his duties. His name was Antoni and he was like a godfather to her. Father Antoni was also affiliated with an orphanage that took in abandoned Chinese girls. Antonina's oldest sister had a job as a typesetter for a Polish magazine.

The Polish Catholic Mission in Harbin was active from the early 1900s.[120] The St. Vincent de Paul Society was established in 1909, a primary school in 1912, a shelter for the homeless and elderly in 1913, and the Henryk Sienkiewicz Secondary School in 1915 (named for a Nobel Prize-winning Polish writer). This surely accords with Antonina's account.

Antonina relates getting her "first doll and a dress" at the Chinese market in Harbin. Soon after, she and her sister, Anna, were put aboard a refugee train to Vladivostok with other children. There was not enough money for

---

120 Borysiewicz, "Polish Settlement in Siberia," 149.

tickets for the others. In Vladivostok, the children were housed temporarily in a bakery; she recalled they slept on bread shelves with their clothes as a pillow. Antonina was separated from her family for the first time in her life; the experience must have traumatized her because she stopped speaking. Until then, she had spoken normally, but she stopped and would not answer when asked a question.

While in Vladivostok, Antonina was parted from her doll. Another girl was crying terribly for her mother and family, and Dr. Jakobkiewicz was trying to console her. "He said to me, 'Give her your doll to calm her down, see how she cries.' I gave it to her even though my heart was breaking because it was my first doll." Later, her sister, Anna, chastised her, "You give everything away! You gave the doll away! You give everything away."

Antonina's revelation that she stopped talking for an extended period is a documented medical condition called traumatic mutism or psychogenic mutism.[121] It can result from physical trauma such as a head injury but is also linked to psychological trauma: separation, disorganized care, or death of a parent. Antonina would not have understood why her mother put her aboard a train in Harbin alone, bound for Vladivostok. For Antonina, as we shall see in a succeeding chapter, there may also have been a confusion of languages: Russian, Polish, Chinese, and their dialects. Antonina's situation is a close parallel to my father's. He was alone in Harbin, perhaps confused by different languages, and put on board a train. Perhaps my father simply stopped speaking and could not, or would not answer when asked his name.

For other children, the train journey was less harrowing, although the family situation was desperate. Henryk Sadowski was eleven years old when his parents turned him over to the Rescue Committee along with his seven-year-old brother, Wladyslaw. Henryk's story is condensed from subtitles in the film *Siberian Dreams:*[122]

> Grandma was sentenced to Siberia so her son [Henryk's father] had to go too. When my father was grown up he wanted a family, but not a Russian wife. So he went to Warsaw to

---

121 "Psychogenic Mutism," *GoodTherapy*, last modified August 18, 2015, https://www.goodtherapy.org/blog/psychpedia/psychogenic-mutism.

122 Misiewicz, *Siberian Dreams*.

propose, was accepted and returned to Siberia with his wife [Henryk's mother].

We lived in Khilok near Lake Baikal. It was not a town, not a village, just a hamlet. In Khilok there were Russians, Chinese, Buryats [the Indigenous people] and some Poles who were the only educated people. I was a sickly child, Mother prayed to the Lady of Czestochowa [religious icon of the Virgin Mary] and took me 15,000 kilometers to Czestochowa [round trip distance]. I guess it worked because I recovered.

The Bolsheviks took Father at gunpoint to drive trains for them and Mother was worried for our lives. Children were murdered, little girls were raped. Mother wanted us to avoid that if she wasn't there. She gave me a box with papers and packages and said, "Father and I can lose our lives, so please remember to give it to Wanda to swallow, then to Wladzio and then yourself" [cyanide pills or other poison]. I promised her I'd do what she wanted. And I would have! [spoken passionately] So help me God!

When the train left, Mother kissed the cross and blessed us, "Henio, you are the older one, take care of Wladzio. Don't let anyone harm him." My father accompanied us to Chita, I watched my mother and sister disappear as the train pulled away from the station.

Khilok is situated in difficult mountain terrain on the Trans-Siberian line. Evidently, Henryk's father, as a locomotive engineer, was able to get his two sons aboard a train safely. Henryk states they were handed over to the Rescue Committee in Chita, but the children's list in *Echo* shows it to be Blagoveshchensk. Perhaps Henryk's father piloted the train beyond the dangers of Chita to the safer location of Blagoveshchensk. Evidently, the Sadowskis decided not to send their youngest child Wanda with the Rescue Committee; parents faced agonizing decisions about what was best for their children.

Two other children related their memories of separation from their parents: Eugeniusz Cytowicz, on leaving from Khabarovsk,

Mum signed us up for the trip a few times and withdrew each time because she didn't want to part with us, until the fourth time she agreed we should go. Four of us left: me and three sisters, my older brother did not want to go and stayed with my mother. On the day of departure, already aboard the freight car, I hugged my mother and did not want to let go of her hand, even though the train had already started. I felt that I would not see my mother again.[123]

And Katarzyna Kuszner, on leaving Kabarovsk,

I remember the moment the boat left the jetty. God, how much I cried! Children were throwing themselves overboard, parents were too. There was so much crying. Even now, I cannot forget it. It was a terrible thing. We sailed on the Amur to Vladivostok. The Amur is a very large river. Oh God, such memories![124]

Older children were compelled to take decisions and undertake responsibilities in caring for younger siblings. They had to be adults before their time. Wladyslawa Lesniewska was one such teenage girl; her location is not stated but was probably Vladivostok:

I found out that the Polish Rescue Committee was taking Polish children to Poland. I decided to sign up for this trip. When my father found out, he objected, "What have you done?! You are their guardian, you would leave the little ones? I am always away from home, who will take care of them?"

Mum was already dead. I was 14 and ran the whole house and looked after my youngest siblings. So I told my father I would go again and ask if I could take my younger sisters and brother with me. They told me yes, but on the condition that I look after the younger ones. They also asked me if I was aware of what it was to take care of such young children, that I would not be able to go anywhere etc. In the evening I told my father everything.

---

123 Theiss, *Dzieci Syberyjskie*, 87.
124 Theiss, 88.

I told him that it would be easier for him to return to Poland on his own.[125]

The most terrifying account I came across is that of Wiktor Andrzejewski, who was sixteen years old and living in Nikolayevsk-on-Amur in 1920. His grandfather was exiled to Siberia for his participation in the 1863 rebellion. The family roots were in Plock, fifty kilometres from Warsaw. Nikolayevsk-on-Amur (abbreviated to Nikolayevsk) was occupied by the Japanese Army in September 1918 because of its strategic location at the mouth of the Amur River. Among a total population of 6 000, there were 450 Japanese civilians and a garrison of 350 Japanese soldiers and 300 White Russians. In January 1920, the town was surrounded by a partisan force of 4 000 under the command of Yakov Tryapitsyn. The following is Victor's dictated account, which was published in instalments in two consecutive issues of *Echo of the Far East* [126]

> I should like to put into writing all that I have lived through during those few terrible months that will forever live in my memory, overshadowing all of my youth and all my life. Sometimes it seems to me that I am only dreaming and that the dear person whom I lost is still alive, but only I must wake up and everything will disappear, the moans of murdered people, the glow of fire and the cries for help and mercy.
>
> I lived for thirteen years in Nikolayevsk-on-Amur and I knew every person and every corner of the town. We lived in the suburb in a house of our own, my father being engaged in the Town Council and after the Revolution of 1917 was engaged as bookkeeper with the Central Union. My mother kept house and myself and my two younger brothers were at school. My father was a very peaceful man and never mixed in politics; he was very fond of his family and home and being a very good-hearted man was always ready to help anyone in need, and was consequently much loved and respected in the town. We were

---

125 Theiss, 88.

126 "Drama of Children in Siberia, Memoirs of a 16 year old Boy," as related to Maria Brant, *Echo of the Far East*, 7 (1922): 13–14, and 8 (1922): 11–12.

very happy under his care but a day came when everything came to an end.

Late in autumn 1919 a small detachment of Partisans under Tryapitsyn approached Nikolayevsk and were robbing the peasants of food, clothing, money and arms. This detachment grew daily in numbers being reinforced by peasants, Chinamen, deserters from Admiral Kolchak's army and workmen from the mines and sawmills. Shortly afterwards Tryapitsyn announced the mobilization of all men between 16 and 55 and all refusing this order were condemned to death. Two large detachments of Kolchak's army in attempting to fight the Partisans were defeated and the majority of soldiers joined the latter. Another small detachment of Russians and Japanese was obliged to retreat into the town, owing to the outweighing numbers of the enemy. The siege of Nikolayevsk began on 18 February 1920. A military corps was formed of the citizens and everyone had to belong to it and on 10 February my father was mustered to it also, it consisting of "Whites" and Japanese. Life in town came to a complete stop, the post and telegraph communication with Khabarovsk was disconnected and everybody lived in expectation of something terrible to happen. The schools were closed as well as pupils were taking active share in operations and defence and a search light was placed in our school.

On February 20 Tryapitsyn commenced bombarding the town. As we lived in the suburbs the constant shooting and flight of shot and shell kept us in a continuous strain and we were obliged to hide in the cellars for days at a time. Fear and extreme nervousness was even imbibed into the Japanese and their military command opened negotiations with the partisans and peace was signed on 28 February, guaranteeing safety to all the inhabitants.

The same day Tryapitsyn entered the town, his partisans carrying red banners with the inscription "Down with capitalism and death to the bourgeois; long life to the workers." A meeting was called at which the people were incited to avenge themselves and the next day all military men were arrested. Thus, at night on 2 March, the immemorial day when my father was arrested came around. I was awakened about eleven o'clock at night by loud knocking, but for some reason or other I did not get up to see what it was about. Had I done so I might have seen my father once more in my life. After a short while the servant came to my room to tell me that my father had been arrested, whereupon I ran to my parents room but I found only my mother and brothers there. I immediately ran into the yard but not seeing my father there I went into the street; however all I could hear there was the sound of receding steps and swearing. Afterwards my mother told me that 12 partisans had led my father away, not even allowing him to say goodbye to anyone and upon mother's asking the reason of his arrest they answered "That's none of your business!" They were swearing and laughing disgustingly all the while.

A voice inside my heart was telling me that I should never see my father again and that he had disappeared forever in the darkness of that night. Our dear cozy home became as silent as a cemetery, full of painful remembrances; the empty place at table and in fact every place in the house reminded us of father. We were in a state of hallucination, we thought we heard his footsteps or even saw him. The strain was ruinous for mother's health and we decided to go and live with relatives, which we were able to only after much difficulty. We tried to see our father but it was useless. Often, I tried to peer into the windows of the militia building where father was imprisoned, to get a glimpse of him and once received a blow with a butt-end from a partisan who shouted, "Clear out, why gaze at those . . ." In the night of 11 to 12 March, many military men from among the imprisoned ones were shot on the ice in the middle of the Amur River, their moans and cries being heard by us on shore.

At the request of the Japanese and Russian population the Japanese Consul sent a severe ultimatum to Tryapitsyn, in reply to which he demanded a complete surrender. The same night the battle began. It was an awful night; mother woke me crying that something horrible was going on around us, as bullets and shot were incessantly flying around. In the centre of the town stood the huge house of the Japanese Yamada together with some other large buildings, which appeared like a huge red-black mass. We hid ourselves among some bushes in our yard, waiting for help that might take us from this inferno, but with the morning the battle only increased. My mother thoroughly exhausted and tired was weeping bitterly and I tried to console her, but my heart was full of anxiety for my father. Where was he, was he still alive? In spite of some terrible foreboding I tried to assure myself that he was still alive and safe. All day and through the next night the fighting continued and only weakened towards the next morning.

The news spread that the Japanese Consulate had been burned and all that had sought protection there had perished. Others had run to the Chinese gun boats but had been refused shelter there and been shot by machine guns. My mother, my brother and I went to seek our father at the militia station, whilst shooting, although seldom, continued and the air was heavy with smoke. Everywhere the bodies of Japanese were lying; I remember them so well, the majority already stripped of their clothing. Ruins of gutted houses resounded with the drunk laughter of robbers. One dead body makes me shiver when I remember it for it showed clearly the brutality of the murderers. The body was in a crouching position, already quite frozen, a bloody cap had been placed on its head and the cross-pole with a bucket of water at each end placed across its shoulders. We proceeded another block but were refused further passage so had to return.

The 13th of March had come, the day when my father and uncles were shot without trial and being guiltless. All the prisoners, including the women and children were shot, or rather murdered, as they were done to death with anything the murderers could lay their hands on, axes, iron bars or were simply thrown through holes in the ice. Tryapitsyn now reigned in town and blood was flowing and people perishing—the angel of death had entered the town. We returned to our empty house, so very different to what it had been formerly. We boys were all the time with our mother as the schools were closed and tried to cheer her and distract her attention from the painful memories, but it was difficult as our thoughts dwelt on the same dear yet bitter memories as hers.

One night, as we were sitting at supper, nine Partisans entered with orders to search the house and one of them smiling asked mother where father was hiding. What could we answer? They were leaving us after the search, having taken all father's clothes and the gold and silver things they found. I felt mad they had taken my watch, a gift from father, and jumped at the partisan snatched it from him and struck him as hard as I could. For this I was arrested and led away in spite of mother's cries, but the leader ordered my release saying "Let the brat go" and pointing at my mother added "It is enough for this . . . that her husband was drowned in the Amur." Two days later the partisans nationalized all our furniture and food, leaving us practically nothing.

In the spring the mobilization of everybody between 16 and 45 was announced, to carry out various kinds of work and I was forced to serve as a deck-boy on a small motorboat. Every morning at six o'clock men and women were taken to the opposite shore to load stones. Thus my mother, aunt and brother were daily taken to some place about 40 versts [a Russian unit of length, about 1.1 kilometres] away, having only bread and a piece of cold meat which they were able to take from home, and used to work there until 11 and 12 at night. I often had to watch my mother being abused but was powerless to protect her.

In the middle of May evacuation began, the preference being given to workmen and partisans, but my mother was afraid to ask for a permit, as many wives who had lost their husbands were thus arrested. But apparently it was our destiny to remain alive. Soon afterwards some Chinese gun boats left Nikolayevsk for the village Mago, about 40 versts away, and towed a number of boatloads of Chinese and Russians with them. Thanks to a Chinaman named Kahan, my mother and brothers were able to get away in one of the boats, but I could not join them as I was not able to leave my launch for a single moment. Thus I remained behind all alone, without my family or even friends who either left or perished. My motor-launch was laid up owing to a motor defect and often at night I could hear the whistles from the boats carrying prisoners to the place of execution. A special detachment was fulfilling this cruel work, and often unseen by them I heard their stories and boasts, so terrible to make one's hair stand on end. The unfortunate victims were taken into the middle of the river, stripped naked, stood in a row in the boat and murdered, their bodies being thrown into the river. The waves rocked them in their last sleep and death was doubtless a blessing for many of the victims, compared with the torture they had passed through.

Hearing and seeing all that was occurring around me, my hatred for the murderers of my father steadily grew, I was nursing and inciting it and looking at the stars I vowed to avenge my father and repay with the same mercilessness and cruelty. I wanted to grow up in this hatred and teach my heart to be devoid of mercy. One sleepless night I lay in the bottom of my boat thinking of our happy childhood and peaceful home life, of my father—so good and quiet—who never did harm to anybody and who taught us to forgive our enemies—and then it was I understood that my intentions were wrong and the vengeance I planned would never please him, but that I must worship his memory in a different, generous way. Thus, although I have no love for my enemies, my hatred does not grow, in fact weakens and may be some day I shall be able to even forgive them.

As I said, I was all alone with nobody but enemies about me. One night I was seized with a terrible longing—the river stretched wide before me with the moon casting a silvery ray across—the idea to escape became strong in me. The day before I had noticed a tiny skiff at the landing stage and in one moment I had pushed it into the water and taking some bread with me I rowed away. A few strong strokes and I was far from the bank and my boat drifted noiselessly down the river on the tide. Luckily I passed the guards unnoticed, for they were asleep around it. Gradually the wind rose and my skiff rocked badly, shipping water and wetting my clothes and sometimes I thought the river would get me.

I felt small and helpless on this mighty river but did not despair and soon noticed an island where I decided to land, eat my bread and also rest a little, as I was very tired. I slept until late in the morning and immediately started on my journey, fighting with all my strength against the up-current. About 3 pm I reached a Chinese village where a gun-boat was loading wood and at the sight of people my energy increased and I rowed with renewed strength in the direction. About six o'clock in the evening I arrived at the Chinese village of Mago, where 4 Chinese gun boats and 15 boats were lying in the middle of the river. In one of those boats my mother and brothers should be, but in which? The sun had set by the time I reached the barges and the shadows were thrown on the river, but suddenly I heard the voice of my youngest brother calling, "Victor, Victor!"—a few more strokes of the oars and I was in my mother's arms. Thus I found my family again and we were once more together. I was surrounded by many asking about their friends and relatives, whether they were still alive and where they were.

The life on the barges was very hard and the people were often drenched by the rain. On May 31st we awoke to see a dense wall of smoke covering Nikolayevsk, which had been set alight by Tryapitsyn. The air was stuffy and the smoke hurt our eyes. Next day, when the smoke had lifted we saw a whole fleet of steamers approaching us, led by a small motor-launch, in which Tryapitsyn and the leaders of his gang were seated. The motor-launch approached the gun boats and asked for permission to pass on and cross over to the settlement Kerb. They were, however, refused passage and in consequence some of the Chinese boats were blown up in front of our eyes, whilst others were set afire and the burning hulls drifted ashore where they burned out completely. Tryapitsyn and his gang landed and vanished into the forests.

At last the belated and long expected Japanese help arrived; June 3rd saw some gun boats and steamers approaching us, flying the Japanese flag, they brought help to the few that remained and deliverance from this inferno. June 5th we were taken back to Nikolayevsk, or rather what was once that town—ruins, houses burned out and blown up and dead bodies by the hundreds, whilst Japanese sanitary workers were burying them as quick as they could, whereas the river threw up bodies by the tens every day. We went with mother to search for father's body but never found it. We saw some horrible sights, bodies with limbs cut off, heads smashed in and terribly mutilated, whilst a woman was drawn from the river with two small children attached to her feet. Apparently the murderers did not wish to separate the mother from her children.

Seeing all these horrifying sights I was seized with despair, fear, madness and wanted to scream aloud and run away from all these horrors. We never ascertained what had happened to father's body. Was he buried in the common grave, or had the waves carried him away, or thrown him up on the opposite bank? We could not render him even the last service and cry over his grave. We were housed in shanties in the market square, as nothing was left of our house.

After a few days Japanese armoured ships and a passenger steamer arrived and we were taken on the transport "Tomas Maru" to Vladivostok. The steamer sailed slowly from the ruined town giving us time to have a last look at what was once the flourishing town of Nikolayevsk-on-the-Amur. I cried a farewell to the place so full of happy memories that were followed by the most tragic and horrible ones, where we had lost what was dearest to us, our father and where for the first time I met with human cruelty and monstrosities.[127]

Wiktor Andrzejewski's description is historically accurate—the tragedy is known as the Nikolayevsk Incident.[128] Tryapitsyn had the rank of front commander in the Red Army when he entered Nikolayevsk under a flag of truce. Once admitted to the town, he began to slaughter supporters of the White movement. Next, he ordered the Japanese garrison to disarm; when they refused, a one-sided battle ensued. The entire Japanese garrison was killed either in the fight or by execution immediately after. All but 122 Japanese civilians were also slaughtered. Next, several thousand of the town's other inhabitants were killed, all those deemed to be dangerous. As a Japanese relief force approached, Tryapitsyn burned Nikolayevsk to the ground and fled.

---

127 Wienczyslaw, ed., *Echo z Dalekiego Wschodu* [*Echo of the Far East*], issues 7, 8 (1922).

128 Wikipedia, s.v. "Nikolayevsk Incident," last modified July 30, 2023, https://en.wikipedia.org/wiki/Nikolayevsk_incident.

Tryapitsyn's atrocities were no different than those carried out by Bolsheviks in Ukraine and elsewhere during the civil war, which gained promotion for many of those perpetrators. But Tryapitsyn was also an outspoken critic of Moscow's policies in the Far East, as demonstrated by the tone of this excerpt from his telegram to Moscow:

> It has become clear to us that you are absolutely incorrectly informed about the situation here, and would like to ask you who informed you about the situation here, as well as to Moscow which passed a resolution on the buffer state [Far Eastern Republic, 1921-1922], the creation of which is absolutely not advisable. . . . And you achieved exactly the opposite results, instead of getting rid of the Japanese, the state gave us an even more bitter war, even more: you ruined the already prepared victory of the Red Army in the East by your stupid buffer.[129]

Further to Tryapitsyn's downfall, Japan lodged a formal protest with Moscow about the massacre of its people in Nikolayevsk and demanded compensation. Russia feared the possible consequence of a war with Japan. The 1905 war had cost Russia dearly; in a return engagement, Russia could easily lose Vladivostok and the entire Amur region. To mollify Japan, the Russian government arrested Tryapitsyn and his entire staff, thirty-two in total, and executed them. Japan was not satisfied; it seized the north half of Sakhalin Island and delayed recognition of the Bolshevik government until 1925.

Leopold Kulesza related his life in Siberia and his experience with the Rescue Committee to his daughter, Anna Domaradzka. Anna grew up in northeastern Poland in the Podlaskie *voivodeship* (province). She was educated in Poland and acquired a master's degree in Polish studies in Warsaw. Anna and her husband came to America in 1981, where he began postgraduate study at Princeton University. When martial law was imposed in Poland in late 1981, the Domaradski family remained in the United States and eventually settled in Los Angeles.

---

129 Wikipedia, s.v. "Yakov Tryapitsyn," last modified September 5, 2023, https://en.wikipedia.org/wiki/Yakov_Tryapitsyn.

I was pleased to meet Anna Domaradzka at a conference in Wejherowo, Poland, in 2019. I was amazed at the depth of her knowledge of her father, complete with photographs from Siberia. The Kulesza family came from Poland by choice to work and live in Siberia and brought their family history with them. That was an amazing contrast with my scant knowledge of Pawel Wojdak. The family prospered until the chaos of the Russian Civil War when, like other Poles, they became enemies and refugees. Anna provided me with a written account:

> The Kulesza family hailed from Podlasie in the northeastern part of Poland. In 1891 Russian Tsar Nicholas II announced the construction of the Trans-Siberian Railway to the occupied territories of Poland and possibilities of employment there for all kind of workers.
>
> At the end of 19th century my grandfather grew up on a farm in a family with many children. Traditionally, only the eldest son of such families would inherit the farm and the remaining siblings would have to support themselves via other means when they reached adulthood. My grandfather Aleksander Kulesza, and his brother Antoni decided to pursue employment on the construction of the Far East branch of tracks of Trans-Siberian railroad. Later my grandmother Marcjanna Jabłońska, also from the Podlasie region joined my grandfather and they were married in Siberia. They had four children who were born between Chita and Harbin during the construction of the railway. My father was born on November 3rd 1908. His government ID card identifies his birthplace as the Buchedu station in Manchuria, then a part of Russia, currently in China. He was baptized in Harbin in a Polish Roman Catholic church at the very beginning of 1909.
>
> My grandfather started to work on the Trans-Siberian construction as a payroll agent. He distributed salaries to employees by traveling all along the railway to far-flung major stations between Chita and Harbin. In the beginning of 1914, Aleksander Kulesza left his job on the railway and moved his whole family to Błagowieszczeńsk on the Amur River in the middle of Siberia. When a new northernly route of the Trans-Siberian rail

reached Błagowieszczeńsk, my grandparents decided to open a dining hall for railroad workers and the surrounding area as well. After a few years of hard work and raising four young children it became increasingly difficult to run this business. As a result, Aleksander Kulesza found more stable employment as a book-keeper/accountant at the local bank. This was a very respected and desirable position that afforded Aleksander Kulesza and his family a good life. Their eldest daughter attended a local Russian high school while the younger kids went to the nearby elementary school. They learned Polish language skills from their parents and in a neighboring Polish Home Association organized by local Polish community.

Life for the Kulesza family was irrevocably changed after 1917 by the Russian Revolution. The historical backdrop of this period was one of constant political upheaval and change in governing powers. The Błagowieszczeńsk region was also fated to experience turmoil of the Russian Revolution and Civil War. Russia under Red Banner rule suffered a period of anarchy, lawlessness, and decay. Human life ceased to have any value to new officials in power during this time and survival, especially for the Poles in Siberia became more and more difficult.

Members of the Polish Home Association of Błagowieszczeńsk decided to write a letter to the de facto leader of Poland at the time, Marshal Piłsudski describing the terrifying reality of life for Poles in Siberia. The letter was signed by around a dozen people including the local Polish priest named Kamiński and was subsequently sent to Poland by a messenger. The River Amur is about three kilometers wide at Błagowieszczeńsk and in the middle of this expansive river the letter's messenger was apprehended by the Bolsheviks. The messenger was imprisoned and everyone who had signed that letter was subjected to a trial and punishment by the New Worker's government. These trials' outcomes were pre-determined and all defendants were convicted and sent to prison for several years. Aleksander Kulesza himself was sentenced to eight years in prison for signing this letter.

My grandmother Marcjanna Kulesza suddenly found herself alone with four children and no means to provide for them during the harsh Siberian winters where food was scarce. Błagowieszczeńsk's bank Aleksander Kulesza worked for was taken over by revolutionaries and all their savings were seized by the Soviets. The Kulesza family lost over 20 years of savings. This money would have been enough for everyone to get back to Poland in addition to affording decent life for all.

During Aleksander Kulesza's imprisonment, at the end of 1920, representatives of Polish Rescue Committee in Vladivostok, the Piotrowski brothers arrived in Błagowieszczeńsk by boat from Harbin via the Amur River. The brothers' mission was to help orphaned Polish children and children from families in tragic situations like those of the Kulesza family scattered through-out Siberia. The brothers promised to help these children by sending them to Poland on a circuitous route via Japan and the United States that bypassed the Eurasian continent caught in the turmoil of the Russian Revolution.

The fear of remaining in Siberia forever, the loss of one's national identity and the uncertainty of one's future became extremely important and more realistic with every passing day. The Polish Rescue Committee gave these families children hope for survival. The Piotrowski brothers were able to gather over 20 children from Błagowieszczeńsk and traveled with them to Vladivostok to join the Polish Rescue Committee.

At the very end of December 1920 my grandparents, both aged 44, decided to send their three eldest children to Poland with the Polish Rescue Committee leaving only the youngest son, aged seven, with them in Błagowieszczeńsk. I have often won-dered if such a decision to leave my uncle behind was related to the uncertainty of the Polish Rescue Committee's ability to succeed in their mission or whether the youngest child was simply too small for such a journey. Among the children leaving Vladivostok there were several seven-year-old children like my uncle, but I can only imagine how difficult it must have been for the parents to send these young children to be on such an arduous journey.

Aleksander Kulesza was able to be granted temporary release from prison during this time and covertly assisted his children's departure to Poland. Aleksander and Marcjanna Kulesza, along with their children, the Piotrowski brothers and roughly 20 other Polish children from Błagowieszczeńsk went by train to Vladivostok via Khabarovsk. Additionally, Aleksander Kulesza's brother Antoni, who was a fireman in Shanghai came up to Vladivostok to support his family in their journey. Unfortunately, this was the family's last contact with Antoni as afterwards he was never heard from again.

The decision to divide the family was very hard on my grandmother as she was seen weeping and wailing when her eldest children boarded the ship heading for the port of Tsuruga in Japan. Afterwards my grandparents and youngest son returned to Błagowieszczeńsk after their eldest children's departure. Aleksander Kulesza had to go back to prison and Marcjanna Kulesza was left alone with her child to fend for herself and survive.

The three of my grandparents' children named Łucja-Czesława age 16, Felicja age 14, and Leopold, who just turned 12 years of age were on a ship that set sail from Vladivostok to Tsuruga, Japan, as the year passed from 1920 to 1921.[130]

Waclaw Danilewicz provides the final account of a Siberian child survivor, twelve years old, during the second rescue. Like Leopold Kulesza, he lived in Blagoveshchensk, and his story is rich in detail. His family evacuated from Russian Poland in advance of hostilities during World War I. Waclaw related his story in *Siberian Dreams* and, in more detail, in "On the Meeting of Descendants of Siberian Children." It is translated and condensed below:

The Danilewicz family consisted of eight children, five daughters and three sons. We lived in Dziergieliszki Latvia where my father was a tenant on the estate of Count Plater. During World War I as the German army approached, my father moved us

---

130 Anna Domaradzka, "Stories of Rescued Children," Oral presentation at Siberian Children conference, Wejherowo Special Needs Education School Complex, Poland, September 25, 2019.

deep into Russia, first to Penza and then to Chelyabinsk in the western foothills of the Urals. We lived there until 1918 and we attended a Polish school. Three of my sisters married members of the Polish Legion who were stationed there. Next we moved to Blagoveshchensk on the Amur River. We continued to attend a Polish school because there was a large Polish community. There was also a large Chinese population; they were pedlars who sold goods at very good prices [despite the pogrom twenty years earlier]. China lay just across the river. During the October Revolution, when sugar ran out, we children crossed the frozen Amur River to the town of Sakhalin where sugar could be purchased and up to one kilogram brought back without issue from the customs officers.

The cultural life of Poles in Blagoveshchensk was focused at the "Polish House" where there was a good Polish language school. Later in Poland I passed the exam to enter the second class of the Classical Gymnasium (secondary school). I had to catch up only in Latin. On 1 August 1922 my parents decided to send their four children to Poland; three sons aged 10, 12 and 14, a 15-year-old daughter, and a 3-year old granddaughter. They said goodbye to us with tears. They had no idea they would never see their children again. My father was shot by the Bolsheviks in 1934 and my mother died in Latvia in 1947.

From Blagoveshchensk we took a boat on the Amur River, then the Sungari River to reach Harbin. It was a dangerous trip because *chunchuzi* roamed the area (these were Chinese bandits, also called hunhuzi by Poles). We were lucky, a boat ahead of us was attacked, five men were killed and the entire cargo was stolen. The rest of our trip was macabre because the boat ahead of us dragged a junk with five coffins on deck.

There was a large Polish community in Harbin, even a Polish junior high school named Henryk Sienkiewicz. Our group of children was joined by others from Khabarovsk, Irkutsk, Chita and other cities. We were taken by freight train to Vladivostok and quarantined until there was a Japanese ship to take us to Japan.[131]

---

131 Social Welfare Association Fukudenkai, "Descendants of Siberian Children," 47–48.

14.

Anna Bielkiewicz — Search for Assistance

By spring 1920, the Polish Children Rescue Committee had assembled 375 children in Vladivostok. The next consideration was how to get them out of Siberia. The Rescue Committee had hoped for further assistance from the American Red Cross, but the withdrawal of American troops on April 1, 1920, caused them to wind up their work with Siberian refugees.[132]

The goal was to get the children to Poland, but not immediately because there were threats of a new war while the country still lay in ruins from the previous war. A safe stopover was needed, away from danger in Vladivostok. The Rescue Committee decided to ask America to accommodate children temporarily. The Polish Legation in Washington and the Poland National Alliance in Chicago agreed in principle, but the issues of funding and transportation remained.

There was no direct maritime service to America and only a small coastal steamer, the *Hosan Maru*, which sailed between Vladivostok and Tsuruga, Japan. It was always packed and unable to carry many passengers.

---

132 Matsumoto and Theiss. *Siberian Children*, 181.

The Rescue Committee decided Anna Bielkiewicz should go to Shanghai to ask for financial help because they knew two important Polish people there: one was connected to the financial business of this rich city; the other to the Catholic Church. The following account is derived from the periodical *Echo of the Far East*.[133]

In Shanghai, Anna Bielkiewicz was told money could not be raised quickly. The French Catholic Church offered to take 100 children for one year, much fewer than the 375 waiting in Vladivostok, and was clearly inadequate. Everyone in Vladivostok and Shanghai advised Bielkiewicz that Japanese people were selfish and would not assist, but there was nowhere else to turn. She went to the northern Japanese island of Hokkaido, the city of Hakodate, to call on the Order of the Trappists, a Roman Catholic contemplative religious order, but her plea was refused outright.

Anna Bielkiewicz returned to Yokohama by ferry and train, greatly discouraged. The situation in Vladivostok was becoming more desperate. The rapid devaluation of Russian currency meant the children could not be fed much longer. She would not accept defeat and, after careful consideration, realized that nothing could be done in Vladivostok without the assistance of the Japanese because they controlled the city. She reasoned that, as the children were the victims of war, she would go to the Japanese Ministry of War—an illogical but bold step for any individual, especially a foreign woman alone in 1920 in an unfamiliar land.

In the war office, Anna Bielkiewicz was fortunate to meet a senior bureaucrat who was fluent in French, a language that she also spoke. After she explained to him the entire situation of Polish children in Siberia, he said, "You want quick help, Madame, and in our ministry the slightest matter must pass through various sessions; it takes a long time. I would recommend you go to the Ministry of Foreign Affairs. Do you know anybody there?"

Of course, Anna Bielkiewicz knew no one in Japan. The bureaucrat was moved by her impassioned appeal and escorted her to the foreign office. He facilitated a meeting with Viscount Mushakoji, first secretary to the

---

133 Wienczyslaw, ed., *Echo z Dalekiego Wschodu* [*Echo of the Far East*] (1924), 25–36.

minister of Foreign Affairs. He listened closely and asked her to submit a written appeal the next day.

The next day, with report in hand, Mushakoji told her that indeed steamers could be arranged to transport the children, but he needed two days to consider if there was a place somewhere the children could stay in Japan before going to America. When Bielkiewicz returned, she was introduced to Mr. Morishima of the Red Cross, who would provide full assistance. Anna Bielkiewicz was given a certificate from the ministry ordering all Japanese government departments to give all possible assistance. It had taken just four days to turn so-called Japanese selfishness into friendship and interagency cooperation. The provision of humanitarian aid to Polish refugees had a substantial cost and support from the Ministry of Foreign Affairs, the army, and the navy.

How did this amazing decision by Japan happen, and so quickly? No doubt, Japan's imperial ambitions in Asia were a factor. Japan also recognized that Russia would continue to be an adversary, as in the war of 1904. The 16 000 prisoners from that war, who turned out to be Polish, emphasized that Poland was a determined enemy of Russia. Furthermore, Jozef Pilsudski, who had been a minor politician in 1904 when he came to Japan for assistance, was now poised to become head of the Polish government. And finally, his brother, Bronislaw Pilsudski, had demonstrated true kinship with Japanese people.

A minor but interesting incident occurred during Anna Bielkiewicz's return to Vladivostok. The train trip from Tokyo requires a transfer at Maibara from the mainline. Suddenly, she discovered she was bound for Kyoto while her luggage, dutifully transferred, was bound for Tsuruga. She got off at the next station and with the Ministry of Foreign Affairs certificate, was given every assistance to board the correct train to get to Tsuruga, reunite with her luggage, and board the steamship to Tsuruga.

In 2019, my wife and I made the same journey from Tokyo to Tsuruga and can attest the transfer in Maibara is a bit tricky. We realized, at the last moment, we were on the wrong platform and dashed to our train barely in time. We had spontaneous assistance many times in Japan from kind people who were quick to recognize any difficulty or confusion. I doubt Anna Bielkiewicz's special certificate was necessary.

In today's world of air travel, it is easy to overlook how arduous a trip Bielkiewicz undertook in 1920. Anna would have gone from Vladivostok to Shanghai by train or ship, then to Nagasaki by ship, followed by a train trip the length Japan, and then a ferry to Hakodate, for the meeting with Trappist monks, only to be rebuffed and return to Tokyo before finally taking the return journey by train to Tsuruga and ship to Vladivostok—altogether, the trip would have taken several weeks.

As a result of Anna Bielkiewicz's determination and Japanese aid, the first fifty-six children departed Vladivostok on a military transport ship on July 20, 1920. The departure of a later group on September 13, 1920, was described by S. Sokolowski (a parent and adult guardian):

> At the front are the two Dzielskis from Khabarovsk [Dreiski on the List of Children], sons of a shoemaker's widow. One is four years old, the other merely a year older. The weaker sex is led by Zoska Kulczycka and a group of little heads: hair light as hemp fibres on a distaff, golden as a wheat-ear, brown and black. The group comprises different types: blue, gray and hazel eyes; oblong, round and oval faces. Here is Wladek Mietek: his eyes a bit slanting, reveal a considerable admixture of Asian blood, the image and likeness of his mother. The mother is Korean, nonetheless she speaks Polish. Further a whirling dervish, little rascal and prankster, 8-year-old Piotrek Sandro, resembling a little Gypsy. He was turned in by the Khabarovsk city management as a Polish child.[134]

The scene provokes a Biblical image of creatures boarding the Ark before the Flood. And the image is valid: these children are the survivors; those left behind will drown in a communist sea. If they do not die literally, they will die figuratively because they will lose their Polish identity. By July 6, 1921, five sailings brought 375 children (205 boys, 170 girls) to the port of Tsuruga in Japan. My father was among them.

---

134 Matsumoto and Theiss, *Siberian Children*, 157.

15.

Tsuruga — Port of Humanity

Tsuruga is an important port on the west coast of Japan used for trade and transportation with mainland Asia. In 1920, there were regular sailings to and from Vladivostok. The first group of rescued Siberian children arrived in Tsuruga, Japan, on the army transport ship *Chikuzenmaru* on July 23, 1920. There would be five sailings in total, the last departing Vladivostok on July 6, 1921, delivering a total of 375 children and thirty-two adult guardians.

Halina Nowicka, as related in *Siberian Dreams*, remembered the sailing from Vladivostok:

> The last view of my mother, she stood alone leaning against a drum—I'm emotional about it now [tears run down her cheek]; I wasn't then. The sea was rough, but I wasn't scared. I held my little brother; he cried terribly and called for Mom.[135]

To streamline the children's arrival, representatives of many agencies teamed up: the Red Cross; the Tsuruga city office and police; army staff for transport and clothing; and Japan Customs. The children were painfully thin and shabbily dressed, some with no shoes. Some were dizzy when

---

135 Misiewicz, *Siberian Dreams.*

walking. Many suffered from typhoid fever, whooping cough, or common colds and required immediate treatment. The children walked to a nearby primary school where they were given a meal, including sweets and fruit, rested, and were fitted with new clothes, underwear, shoes, and socks by the Red Cross. They only stayed a few hours or a day at most before boarding a train to Tokyo.

The first arrivals must have created quite an impression on residents of Tsuruga, who likely had never seen a European before, but they provided a wonderful reception to the children. Henryk Sadowski, of the second rescue mission, remembered: "People cheered, 'Long live Poland and Polish children!'"[136] Their actual cry was likely "Bonzai Porando!" (Long live Poland!).[137]

Siberian children were not the only refugees to pass through Tsuruga. Twenty years later, during World War II, thousands of Polish and Lithuanian Jews escaped Nazi terror by crossing Russia on the Trans-Siberian railroad and taking the ferry to Tsuruga. Chiune Sugihara was vice consul in the Japanese embassy in Kaunas, Lithuania.[138] In July 1940, war in Europe had begun, but had not yet reached Lithuania. Poland was beaten by the combined forces of Germany and Russia, and Jews were fleeing occupied Poland to Lithuania. Jews in Lithuania also feared for their future. A great number of them applied to Sugihara's office for exit visas that would permit them to travel to Japan. Japan required that travellers have a third-country destination visa; they could not remain in Japan. Chiune Sugihara issued ten-day visitor visas to Jews, each valid for an entire family. The Dutch Honorary Consul Jan Zwartendijk issued 2 345 Jews with third-destination passes to Curacao, despite having no authority to do so because the Netherlands had been conquered by Germany two months earlier.[139] Russia occupied Lithuania on August 3, 1940, and closed Zwartendijk's office.

136 Misiewicz.

137 Sylwia Szarejko, *Polskie dzieci w Kraju Kwitnacej Wisni* (Polish children in the land of the rising sun), Siberia Memorial Museum, 2023

138 Wikipedia, s.v. "Chiune Sugihara," last modified October 13, 2023, https://en.wikipedia.org/wiki/Chiune_Sugihara.

139 Wikipedia, s.v. "Jan Zwartendijk," last modified September 4, 2023, https://en.wikipedia.org/wiki/Jan_Zwartendijk.

Sugihara issued visitor visas despite direct instruction from Japan not to do so, a very unusual act of disobedience. Reportedly, he worked on them eighteen to twenty hours per day until September 4, when the consulate was closed. According to witnesses, he was still writing visas while in transit from his hotel and after boarding the train at the Kaunas railway station, throwing visas into the crowd of desperate refugees out of the train's window as the train pulled out. The last visas were blank sheets of paper with only the consulate seal and his signature, which could be later written over into a visa.

As Chiune Sugihara departed, his wife later reported that he said, "Please forgive me. I cannot write anymore. I wish you the best," and then bowed deeply to the people before him. There are conflicting reports as to how many visas were issued: 4 500, 5 000, or 6 000. Sugihara recalled many years later, "No one ever said anything about it. I remember thinking that they probably didn't realize how many I actually issued."[140]

Whatever the actual number, Sugihara and Zwartendijk saved thousands of lives. The actions of Raoul Wallenberg, the Swedish businessman and diplomat whose daring work also saved Hungarian Jews from the Holocaust, are better known to most people than those of Sugihara and Zwartendijk. Polish children from Siberia and Jews from Eastern Europe both passed through Tsuruga; the accolade "Port of Humanity" is well-deserved. The Port of Humanity Museum in Tsuruga commemorates these two actions by the Japanese people.[141]

In 2019, my wife, Teresa, and I went to Japan. Tsuruga was a special destination, and we had made arrangements with Akinori Nishikawa, the director of the Port of Humanity Museum. We travelled on a Shinkansen, the famous high-speed train, and transferred at Maibara to a local train to reach Tsuruga. Akinori Nishikawa escorted us to the Tsuruga city office, where we were introduced to Takanobu Fuchikami, mayor of Tsuruga; and Fujio

---

140 Pamela Rotner Sakamoto, *Japanese Diplomats and Jewish Refugees: A World War II Dilemma* (New York: Praeger, 1998).

141 "Tsuruga Guide, Port of Humanity Museum," Tsuruga Tourism Association, accessed October 10, 2022, https://www.tsuruga.org/en/museum.html. [broken URL; no archived version available]

Katayama, vice mayor. I spoke about Pawel Wojdak, explaining that he could tell me very little of his experience due to trauma but that he retained the ability to sing the Japanese national anthem. I thanked the mayor on my father's behalf for the welcome his city gave him after the misery of Siberia (photo 15.1).

*Photo 15.1. Tsuruga Mayor Takanobu Fuchikami
with the author and his wife, November 2019*

Next, Teresa and I toured the Port of Humanity Museum in the company of Akinori. He explained the exhibits and showed us plans for a marvellous new building for the museum. Members of the media attended City Hall and the museum and asked many questions, facilitated by a translator. The notoriety was unexpected and a little overwhelming. The following day, there was a symposium on Siberian children attended by the representatives of Fukudenkai in Tokyo and the Polish ambassador to Japan, Pawel Milewski. We listened to presentations by Teruo Matsumoto and Wieslaw Theiss, who both came from Poland for the occasion.

Wieslaw Theiss's research of Polish children affected by World War II (mentioned in Chapter 1) extended to a cooperative investigation of Siberian children with Teruo Matsumoto. Theiss traced the lives of the children from their time in Siberia to their lives in Poland. His book, published in 2020, *Dzieci Syberyjskie 1919–2019: Z Syberyii Przez Japonie i Stany Zjednoczone do Polski* (*Siberian Children 1919–2019: From Siberia through Japan and the United States to Poland*) is an important source for this work, which not only adds to Theiss's study by reaching an English-speaking readership, but also provides information about Siberian children in America and relates the continuation of Pawel Wojdak's life and how he struggled with his memories and identity.

16.

Fukudenkai — Then and Now

Fukudenkai operates a group home in Tokyo, offering welfare-type care for children as well as facilities for the elderly. It was established in 1876 by Buddhist sects to care for orphans. In 2010, it had seventy children in care between three and eighteen years old. About half the children in care are intellectually disabled; the others suffered some form of abuse at home, be it mental, physical, or sexual. Orphans are rarely adopted in Japan; once in care, children usually remain there until eighteen years of age.

Japan's role in rescuing the Siberian children was forgotten for as much as eighty years, even at Fukudenkai. In 2010, the Polish ambassador to Japan, Jadwiga Rodowicz-Czechowska, passed Fukudenkai while jogging. Fortunately, she knew the history of the Siberian children and was conversant in Japanese to read the entrance sign. She entered and is said to have asked, "Is this *the* Fukudenkai?" The connection was rediscovered; Japan is rightfully proud of its humanitarian role and has taken a leadership role in connecting with descendants of Siberian children and in strengthening ties with Poland.

When the Siberian children arrived at Fukudenkai in 1920, many were undernourished and afflicted with typhus, cholera, and skin diseases, such as scabies.[142] Those who required medical attention were treated at the adjacent Red Cross hospital. Fumi Matsuzawa was a twenty-three-year-old nurse who contracted typhus from one of the children and died. Other children in the hospital did not know why she was no longer present and kept calling for her, causing other caregivers to break down in tears. The children arrived at Fukudenkai in groups of about sixty, the capacity of the ship from Vladivostok and Tsuruga. They stayed 100 days on average; all 375 children were not present at one time.[143]

Returning to direct accounts by the children, Leopold Kulesza told his daughter Anna Domaradzka:

> One of his first memories of arriving in Tokyo was how the Polish children were brought to a bright but rather small room where they were seated at tables set extremely low to the ground. All the children were provided a meal that needed to be eaten with wooden chopsticks for the first time in their lives. The children had no idea how to use such utensils at first, but thanks to the adaptability of the young, they quickly mastered the skill necessary for using chopsticks.
>
> The Kulesza siblings remained in Tokyo for roughly half a year. It was perhaps the happiest time of their lives, a small fraction of their childhood that was lived among kind, generous and friendly people. My father often spoke about his sojourn in Japan and how he appreciated their culture. He was entranced by the beauty of their springtime and its flowering cherry trees, the gorgeous and neatly kept gardens, and minimalistic but beautiful aesthetics of Japanese greenery seen in their parks. Specifically, because he loved nature so much he fondly remembered this time for the rest of his life.[144]

---

142 Matsumoto and Theiss, *Siberian Children*, 187.

143 Takaaki Ohta and Manabu Tsuchiya, personal communication to author at Fukudenkai, 2019.

144 Domaradzka, "Stories of Rescued Children."

In Japan, the children were looked after very well. Barbers and a dentist donated their services. Japanese children brought toys and other gifts when they came to play (photo 16.1).

（一其）景ノ戲遊童兒蘭波ノ中濟救社字十赤本日

Polish Children at Play (Relief Service of the Japanese Red Cross Society, 1921.)

Photo 16.1. Siberian children at play in Tokyo, 1921 or 1922

They went on field trips to the Zoological Garden and to a children's concert. The children also learned to sing the national anthems of Poland and Japan. Jan Samardakiewicz explained to his grandson that he acquired beginner-level Japanese and that his stay in Japan was "the sunrise of hope," a line borrowed from a Japanese poem.

The presence of Polish children from Siberia was publicized extensively by the Japanese press. As a result, many prominent people came to see the children: members of the Imperial Court, representatives of charity organizations, Buddhist lamas, and others. Their notoriety induced Her Imperial Majesty Empress of Japan to visit on April 6, 1921. This was most exceptional; the Empress was rarely seen in public.[145]

---

145 Matsumoto and Theiss, *Siberian Children*, 187.

On that day, there were 101 Polish children and fifty Japanese orphans present. They stood forty metres away, as is protocol and sang "Kimi Ga Yo," the Japanese anthem, and then the Polish anthem. The Empress signalled for them to come closer, and closer again toward the dais she was seated upon, until they were only ten steps apart—astonishing, and very contrary to Japanese rules of etiquette. Then the Empress asked for the youngest child to be brought right up to her. There was hesitation, so the Empress stepped down from the dais, went among the Polish children, and asked again to see the youngest child. Three-year-old Genowefa Bogdanowicz was brought forward, and the Empress stroked her head, possibly an unprecedented act in the history of Japan. Best wishes were conveyed by the Empress and deep gratitude expressed by Anna Bielkiewicz. Turning once again to the account of Leopold Kulesza, as told by his daughter, gives us more detail:

> The most memorable experience while in Tokyo was when the Empress Sadako of Japan, a very gracious woman, left her royal court for the very first time in her life to visit Polish Siberian Children in the Red Cross center. My father was proud of the fact that he was one of the few kids whom the Empress approached directly. He remembered that she was seen stroking the hair of some of the youngest children as a gesture of kindness.
>
> In Tokyo the Polish Siberian Children went to school, visited Buddhist temples, learned to sing Japanese children's songs, watched Japanese dance shows and performances, and went on numerous cultural trips. This was perhaps the most beautiful period of these children's lives and it left an indelible mark on my father who forever had a high esteem of anything Japanese.
>
> In the family home I grew up in Poland there was a drawer in a wooden kitchen table with maps of the world, Japan and the United States. My father often took them out to show and tell me about these distant countries and their diverse cultures. Particularly for me, these stories from Japan told by my father are the most pleasant and unique memories of my own childhood in Poland. My father sung me wonderful Japanese children's lullabies, told me many stories about this exotic and

faraway country, and taught me a few basic phrases and how to count to ten in Japanese. This provided me lifelong cultural enrichment and became some of the most unforgettable memories of my early childhood, all thanks to the charm of an unknown and unique distant world. I was enchanted by these stories about far-off worlds that seemed to belong to fairy tales and not to the Poland I knew growing up that was so irrevocably damaged by World War II.

Slawomir Samardakiewicz relates the importance of one of his grandfather's mementoes from Japan: a simple postcard with the signature of Takao Atsumi, twenty-four years old. Perhaps he was a caregiver at Fukudenkai, but whoever he was, he was so important to Jan Samardakiewicz that Jan kept the postcard all his life.[146]

Pawel Wojdak spoke of getting medical attention to his back in the hospital. He also remembered the warm rain, remarkable after the cold of Siberia. He did not tell me any Japanese words or the national anthem; these memories only came out when he met the Japanese man at our home in Canada. If I had been more aware as a child to ask him, "What was Japan like? Tell me about it," perhaps I would have drawn out pleasant thoughts. The questions I asked were too harsh: "What happened to your mother and father?"

In 2019, I learned Fukudenkai still functions as an institution named Social Welfare Corporation Fukudenkai. There is a Red Cross hospital close by, perhaps in the same location as it was in 1920. Akinori Nishikawa, manager of Public Relations at the Port of Humanity Museum in Tsuruga, graciously facilitated contact with staff at Fukudenkai, and I arranged a visit. Manabu Tsuchiya and Mizuki Wagatsuma met Teresa and I at our hotel in Tokyo and chauffeured us to Fukudenkai. There, we were graciously received by Takaaki Ohta and Iwao Ito, respectively president and supervisor of the institution. Mari Kagawa translated most ably. After an engaging conversation, we went outside for a group photograph to recreate a memorable image of the Siberian children (photos 16.2 and 16.3). Of course, the steps are rebuilt, but to know I was standing where my father

---

146 Social Welfare Corporation Fukudenkai, "Interview with Slawomir Samardakiewicz."

stood ninety-nine years earlier was very special, as was the thoughtfulness of Takaaki Ohta and the others to prepare framed prints.

Photos 16.2 and 16.3. Siberian children on steps at Fukudenkai in 1920
—re-enacted in 2019 by Iwao Ito, Mizuki Wagatsuma, Manabu Tsuchiya,
Mari Kagawa, the author and his wife, and Takaaki Ohta,
president of Social Welfare Corporation Fukudenkai

The people at Fukudenkai described the Siberian children's stay at the facility, Japan's pride in the humanitarian event, and the current role of the institute. It seemed a poor exchange to relate the few details Pawel Wojdak was able to tell me of his stay nearly 100 years earlier. I was shown photos of large groups of Siberian children, but I could not identify my father out of the close-spaced crowd of faces. Most of the children had only a stubble of hair, as their heads were shaved for lice. I have no photo of my father aged less than thirty-four, as a comparison. We received many thoughtful mementoes of our visit. Teresa and I marvelled at the gracious hospitality of Takaaki Ohta and his staff.

Next, we were invited to lunch on the fifty-first floor of the landmark Mori Tower, with a spectacular view of Tokyo. There was a steady flow of delicious dishes. We were told one contained a very special matsutake mushroom. We laughed when we learned the translation of matsutake—it is the pine mushroom that grows near our home in British Columbia and we came so far to enjoy it!

We enjoyed several days as ordinary tourists in Japan. We went to the Hikone and Nagahama castles and the Kanegasakigu shrine. We admired the Five Lakes of Wakasa, Lake Yogo, and Lake Biwa. We stayed in two ryokans, which are traditional Japanese inns where we wore kimonos, slept on tatami mats, and enjoyed traditional dishes.

On our last day back in Tokyo, we toured the grounds of the Imperial Palace. Amongst many beautiful gardens were marvellous displays of yellow chrysanthemums, the official flower of the Empress and Emperor of Japan (photo 16.4). Realization dawned on me: perhaps Pawel Wojdak favoured this particular flower for my mother because of his early days in Japan.

*Photo 16.4. Cultured chrysanthemums
on the grounds of the Imperial Palace, Tokyo*

17.

The Second Rescue Mission

In the summer of 1922, there was increased urgency for the Rescue Committee to organize a second rescue mission. The Red Army was approaching Vladivostok, and Japanese troops were scheduled to withdraw within weeks. In early July, Anna Bielkiewicz established an evacuation centre in Harbin, safe from the conflict in Siberia, and, from there, travelled by train to Ulan-Ude (Wierchnieukynsk to Poles), Chita, and Sretensk. And she went overland to Blagoveshchensk and Khabarovsk, each more than 700 kilometres from Harbin, using the Sungari, Amur, and Shilka rivers. This route was necessary due to the increased risk of rail service disruption and possible confrontation by the Red Army.

The second rescue mission brought 390 children to Vladivostok. They are listed in Appendix 2 with their age and where they were retrieved, transcribed from *Echo of the Far East*. Table 2 lists the towns and cities where the children were found. It is similar to the first mission, but the proportions are somewhat different. More than forty percent were from Blagoveshchensk (six percent in the first mission) and only ten percent from Vladivostok (twenty-four percent in the first mission). The first mission quickly gathered children at their base in Vladivostok, leaving fewer for the second mission. It is not evident why so many more children were retrieved in

Blagoveshchensk. The family status is not included for children of the second rescue—if a mother or father was alive or if the child was an orphan.

Table 2. Locations of Siberian Children, Second Rescue Mission

Location (in Polish) Where Found	Current Name (in English)	Number of Children
Aleksiejewsk	Svobodny	27
Blagowieszczensk	Blagoveshchensk	169
Chabarowsk	Khabarovsk	68
Charbin	Harbin, China	37
Chajlar	Chailar or Hailar He, China	5
Chilok	Khilok	1
Cycykar	Qiqihar, China	2
Czyta	Chita	14
Imanpo	?	4
Mandzurja	Manzhouli, China	7
Nikolsk-Ussuriyski	Ussuriysk	11
Wierchniendzinsk	Ulan-Ude	4
Wladywostok	Vladivostok	41
Total		390

Children of the second rescue mission went by steamship to Tsuruga, as did the first mission. From there, they went by train to Osaka to stay in a newly built nurses' dormitory associated with the Osaka Citizen's Hospital, which is now part of Osaka City University Medical School. The dormitory was not occupied, and it had large grounds and a garden.

Again, the Siberian children were welcomed with kindness and generosity and received medical attention. One unidentified child was quoted, "When I was sick, the nurse gently caressed my head and kissed me. I had never felt the kindness of such treatment before." They were given new clothes, played, visited the zoo, and other entertainments. The children returned by ship to Poland via the Indian Ocean and Suez Canal.

Antonina Liro, six years old at the time, described her time in Japan in the film *Siberian Dreams*, and also in the booklet, "On the Meeting of Descendants of Siberian Children" (again, it is translated from Polish and condensed):

> I remember Japan very well. They took special care of me there. I was sick, they bathed me and thoroughly washed my head. Then I stood on a table and they smeared me from top to bottom with a gray lotion. My eyes were smeared with a blue pencil because I had conjunctivitis or trachoma or something. I was a picture of misery and despair. Then they wrapped me in a sheet like a mummy. They kissed my nose which was not greased and carried me to bed. I was in the hospital a long time before I was cured of scabies and eczema. The hospital rooms were full of surprises for me. I lay on a mat and my head was on some kind of roll. I rode it like a horse and ruined it. Such savages we were. Nurses and all Japanese people were polite and very kind.
>
> When I recovered we were dressed in kimonos and sandals, in which I could not walk very well. Japanese girls from a vocational school made us kimonos and caps. Socks were intriguing, with a separate big toe. Kimonos were so much fun; cookies, balls and everything were collected in the sleeves, and then they were hard to wear because the sleeves hung to the ground.
>
> In Japan I finally stopped having headaches. At meals we could take whatever we wanted. I wasn't hungry, there was plenty of rice. It was made different ways, with raisins or fish. There were rice cakes with a mint frosting. We ate vegetables we didn't know in Russia.
>
> I must have been there a long time because I went through an introductory writing book.
>
> We learned to write Japanese characters using a sharp flat stick dipped in ink. The Red Cross women were so patient and polite. We climbed all over them and they kept smiling. Japanese people cherish children, a cult of the child as it were. We were free to do as we would, except if we entered their

church in slippers. You had to leave them at the door and go in only with socks. They always took me with them, but religion didn't interest me.

When we left Osaka everyone got a bamboo suitcase with two compartments, one for the journey and the other for later in Poland. We got new (European) clothes for the trip, a check-ered skirt, a blouse and a hat so that we were all alike. On the ship we were in a big room with hammocks. We got seasick, the sight of food made me feel ill so I tried not to eat. The trip took a very long time.[147]

Antonina Liro is Antonina Jerzkowska, listed in Appendix 2, her identity confirmed by her children at the meeting of descendants of Siberian children on September 26, 2023. She was six years old with a ten-year-old sister named Apolonia from Svobodny.

Henryk Sadowski spoke about Japan and his group's departure in *Siberian Dreams*. The English subtitles are summarized below:

Shoemakers measured our feet, the next day we all got shoes. In Tokyo, I really enjoyed looking at the advertising towers with lots of neon signs! We sailed on the *Katori Maru* [departed on August 25, 1922, with 191 children]. We were all given baskets with clothes, a towel, toys, and sweets. First, we sang the Japanese anthem, next the Polish anthem, then "Our Lord Who Saved Poland." *Atsuta Maru* was the other ship [departed on September 6, 1922, with 199 children]. We were shown a map every few days with our location and our route to Poland. The best experience on the ship was talking with the sailors about our future.[148]

Along the same lines, Waclaw Danilewicz recounts when he was a twelve-year-old boy:

I have fond memories of Japan. We were treated with hospital-ity everywhere and there was great sympathy and sentiment for Polish children and Poland. We stayed in a dormitory, wore

---

147 Social Welfare Association Fukudenkai, "Descendants of Siberian Children," 42.
148 Misiewicz, *Siberian Dreams*.

kimonos, slept on mats covered with a mosquito net. Japanese children brought us toys and gifts. We visited a huge zoo. Waterfowl nested in ponds protected by mesh domes. Some of the older children even rode an elephant. We were taught the Japanese anthem and a song about a turtle, I remember the words: "*Mosi, mosi, kamijo, kamisajo, seka ine uduce o mai hodo aimina narai, dosite sana naro inoka.*"

We didn't like Japanese food very much and we had to learn to eat rice with chopsticks. We liked swimming in the ocean where it was easy because of the salinity. We sailed on the Atsuta Maru and stopped in Shanghai, Hong Kong and Singapore. We were warmly welcomed by the Japanese colony, at meals we were seated with the Japanese children. When we stopped in Hong Kong there was a Polish priest, who cried to see Polish children going home.

The Atsuta Maru was a combined cargo and passenger ship, it carried 300 passengers and goods for various ports. We stopped in Colombo and Reda [?] where Maltese boys in small boats begged for money to be thrown to them. One would dive in and get the coin. We children threw tins into the water but they realized our trickery and shook their fists at us. On hot days on the Indian Ocean a tarpaulin on the deck would be filled with seawater for us to play in. We played games on board; running in sacks, racing with egg-in-spoon or being blindfolded and trying to place the eye on a pig drawn on deck. There was always a lot of laughter with that game.[149]

In London we transferred to the German ship, "Baltalantik" but three older boys were missing. There was a search and they were found on the Japanese ship where they hid with the help of the Japanese sailors. Finally the captain ordered them to be handed over on the condition that when they came of age they would be allowed to join the Merchant Navy.[150]

The *Atsuta Maru* and the *Katori Maru* stopped at Kobe, Shanghai, Hong Kong, Singapore, Colombo, Port Said, Tunis, Marseille, Lisbon, and

149 Social Welfare Association Fukudenkai, "Descendants of Siberian Children," 47–48.
150 *Memories of Waclaw Danilewicz*, 3.

London. In London, the Japanese company Nippon Yusen Kaisha, assisted by the Polish Consulate, transferred the children onto a Polish ship for the final leg to Gdansk. After a passage of sixty-three days, the 390 children arrived in Poland at the beginning of November 1922. It was one-and-a-half years after the Peace of Riga confirmed Poland's existence.[151]

---

151 Wikipedia, s.v. "Peace of Riga," last modified October 27, 2023, https://en.wikipedia.org/wiki/Peace_of_Riga.

18.

Siberian Children in Chicago and Milwaukee

Pawel Wojdak was in Japan for 67 days, from July 23 to September 28, 1920. When the Siberian children boarded ships in Tokyo, they sang the national anthems of Poland and Japan.[152] They sang with passion—in appreciation of Japan for their salvation and in excitement to be going home to a new Poland. The importance of this event and of singing the anthem was the reason Pawel Wojdak still knew and sang it four decades later. Ironically, the children only knew about Poland as stories from their parents or their rescuers; almost none had lived there.

The Polish Siberian children arrived in Seattle in eight sailings from Japan between September 1920 and July 1921.[153] Jozef Jakobkiewicz travelled to America on behalf of the Polish Rescue Committee and made arrangements with the National Polish Committee of America, based in Chicago. American authorities permitted entry of the children without the usual documents. Slawomir Samardakiewicz, grandson of Jan Samardakiewicz (see chapters 13 and 16), located the passenger manifest for the boys on the

---

152 Matsumoto and Theiss, *Siberian Children*, 188.
153 Matsumoto and Theiss, 187–188.

SS *Fushimi Maru* from US archives (Photo 29). There should be another page listing twenty-six girls. The *Fushimi Maru* sailed from Yokohama on September 28, 1920, and arrived in Seattle on October 12, 1920, with fifty-six Siberian children; the date indicates its passengers were the first Siberian children to arrive in America. The manifest includes Wladyslaw Wojdak, the name that mysteriously was assigned Pawel Wojdak by the Rescue Committee in Siberia. He is indicated to have been 4 feet tall, with fair complexion, brown hair, and brown eyes. On the ship's manifest, the numerals 3 and 8 are difficult to distinguish. Professor Eiko Uto, historian for Fukudenkai, kindly provided definitive information the departure date was indeed September 28, 1920.

The SS *Suwa Maru* also made regular sailings with Siberian children. Jacek Gronski is a grandson of Leon Lebida, a Siberian child from Nikolayevsk-on-Amur listed in Appendix 1; he discovered the passenger manifest of the *Suwa Maru* arrival in Seattle in early December 1920 (exact date illegible). There were thirty Siberian children; one of them was Leon Lebida. The *Suwa Maru* docked in Seattle again on December 21, 1920. Those children arrived in Chicago on Christmas Day 1920 and were welcomed in a celebration described in *Echo of the Far East* that included a Christmas tree, Santa Claus, gifts, and candy.

The *Fushimi Maru* might have been the last transport of Siberian children, judging by the date in the account of Leopold Kulesza, as related by his daughter:

> On June 18th 1921 my father and two aunts departed Yokohama Japan on the ship Fushimi Maru to Seattle Washington. They arrived in the United States on July 1st and disembarked their ship the next day. Representatives of the local Polonia organization took over fifty Polish Siberian Children into their care, the third such transport from Japan, and moved them into a new building of the Polish Home Association. After a hearty meal they went to a railroad station and continued their journey by train to Chicago. It was at this time when the Kulesza family siblings were separated for the first time. The two elder sisters aged 17 and 15 went to a boarding school in Reading Pennsylvania

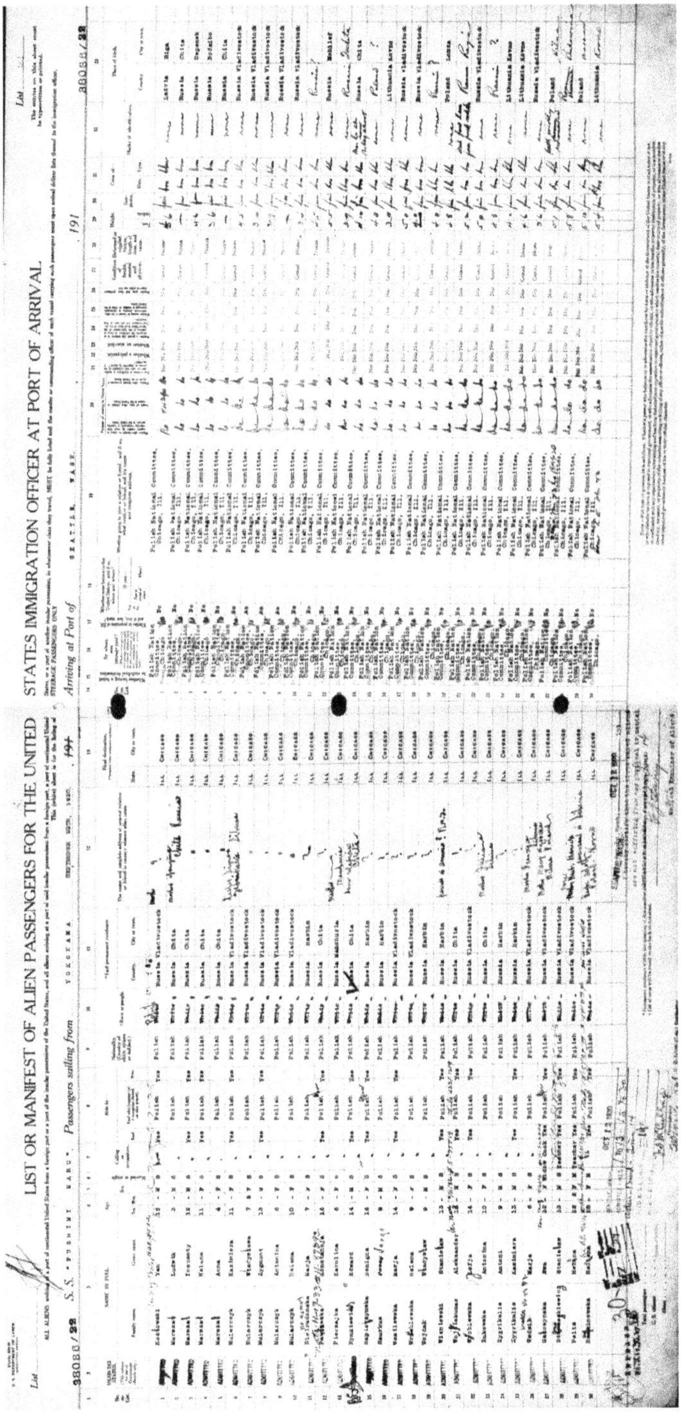
LIST OR MANIFEST OF ALIEN PASSENGERS FOR THE UNITED STATES IMMIGRATION OFFICER AT PORT OF ARRIVAL

Figure 18-1. Fushimi Maru manifest, Seattle October 12, 1920, including Wladyslaw Wojdak and my father, aged 13, went to a school run by the convent in New Britain Connecticut.[154]

In total, there were 369 children and twenty-seven adults transported to America.[155] The number of children is six less than the 375 who arrived in Japan from Vladivostok. The reason for the difference is unknown; some accompanying adults who were parents may have made separate arrangements for themselves and their children to travel to Poland.

Caritas is the Catholic humanitarian organization that Pawel Wojdak recalled as being involved with the Siberian children. Investigation into Caritas activities in USA did not yield a link with the Siberian children. The organization works independently in countries all over the world under the umbrella of Caritas Internationalis in Rome. Globally, their aim is to spread justice and charity, with particular attention to poverty. Their mandate includes social exclusion, attitudes toward foreigners, and migration, linking them to political issues. In the United States, there are two branches of Caritas. Caritas Health Services works within the United States for the well-being of the whole person—body, mind, and spirit. A flagship hospital in Kentucky provides advanced treatment in cancer treatment and pain management. Caritas for Children is a separate group that works to improve the lives of orphans in underdeveloped countries.

A search of the *PolishRoots* website in April 2001 disclosed a curious post: a list of donations for "Polish Orphans in Siberia." The article explained the item came from the archives of the Polish Museum of America and asked for information from the public because their own records did not include the reason for the campaign; somehow, the corporate memory was lost. There was a contribution from the Japanese Consulate in Seattle, which implied a link with Japan and the story of Pawel Wojdak. But at that time, I had not found Teruo Matsumoto to fully understand the connection.

---

154 Domaradzka, "Stories of Rescued Children."

155 Social Welfare Corporation Fukudenkai, "History," *Siberian Children*, accessed September 11, 2023, https://siberianchildren.pl/en/historia-dzieci-syberyjskich/.

The Siberian children were anticipated to be in America for one to two years while the national borders of Poland were resolved, in particular the conclusion of a war between Poland and Russia. Only then would it be safe for the children to go to Poland. Appendix 1, drawn from *Echo of the Far East*, lists where the children were placed and is recast in Table 3: eleven towns and cities scattered from Connecticut to Wisconsin. These were institutions of the Felician Sisters, the Sisters of the Holy Family of Nazareth, and the Bernardine Sisters.[156] Theiss states that Dr. Jakobkiewicz had a high regard for St. Hedwig's in Niles (Chicago), where children seven to twelve years old were taught practical skills, such as carpentry, shoe-making, sewing, cooking, and baking, in addition to schooling and religious practice. In Poland, he would follow a similar program at Wejherowo. Younger children were assigned to other institutions.

Halina Nowicka attended St. Hedwig's. She states:

> In America I was asked if I was Catholic. I answered that I had no time for religion. I was baptized and received Holy Communion. I became very religious. We attended mass three times each day. We had beautiful rooms, good food and nice clothes. The Sisters loved us very much and we were well looked after.[157]

A search of Catholic orphanages in Milwaukee produced a list of facilities, but only one that was focused on Polish children *and* accepted both boys and girls: St. Joseph Orphanage. Many orphanages at that time housed only boys or only girls. St. Joseph was operated by the Felician Sisters from 1909–1959. Subsequently, it evolved to become St. Joseph Academy, comprising a child development function and an elementary school.

Several other facilities were orphanages operated by the Felician Sisters. Education of the Siberian children was a priority. For older teenage boys, who were soon to enter the workforce, it was decided they should learn trades. Forty-six were placed in the Union Craft Institute in Cambridge

---

156 Theiss, *Dzieci Syberyjskie*, 215–216.
157 Theiss, 216.

Springs, Pennsylvania, as reported in *Echo of the Far East*. School fees and expenses were paid by the Polish National Union.

Eleven children—nine boys and two girls—are listed in Appendix 1 to have gone to Milwaukee, but orphanage records prove there were sixteen: nine boys and seven girls. Sister Mary Brendan, director of Mission and Outreach at St. Joseph, confirmed "Wojdak" and several other Siberian children were registered at St. Joseph Orphanage in 1920. Access to the files was delayed for fourteen months until January 2022, due to the COVID-19 pandemic combined with the relocation of St. Joseph archives to a new facility, Madonna University in Livonia, Michigan.

Table 3. Placement of Siberian Children in America

Location	Name of Facility	Boys	Girls
Cambridge Springs, PA	Union Craft Institute (a trade school)	46	
Emsworth, PA	St. Paul Orphanage, Sisters of Charity Orphan Asylum of the Holy Family (Felician Sisters)	56	77
Niles, IL	St. Hedwig's Orphanage (Felician Sisters)	33	32
Polonia, WI	Sacred Heart Church ?	24	
Orchard Lake, MI		2	
Manitowoc, WI	The Felician Home, St. Mary's Village	10	
Milwaukee, WI	St. Joseph Orphanage	9	7
New Britain, CT		11	
Conshohecken, PA		11	
Detroit, MI	Felician Orphanage (later Guardian Angels & Angelus Hall)		18
Reading, PA			30
Placement not known		2	4
Total children		208	166

Orphanage records for St. Joseph Orphanage were kindly provided by Sister Grace Marie Del Priore, library archivist for Felician Sisters at the university. The sixteen children were registered at St. Hedwig's Orphanage in Chicago on October 16, 1920, their personal history recorded and then they were transferred to St Joseph in Milwaukee on October 28, 1920.

Figure 18.2 shows Pawel Wojdak's record at St. Hedwig's and Figure 18.3 his record at St. Joseph. The registrar arbitrarily listed him as Ladislaus, the Latin equivalent of Wladyslaw Wojdak. There is no middle name, birth date or the names of his parents. Even his age was uncertain. Importantly to me, the files confirm my father's account that he was in both Chicago and Milwaukee.

The names of the sixteen children are listed in Table 4 and their orphanage forms at St. Hedwig's are in Appendix 3. The St. Joseph forms are not included because the information is the same as recorded on the St. Hedwig's forms.

The Polish names of the children in Table 4 are maintained in this document. Appendix 3 shows their Americanized first names, for example Jerzy became "George" and Bronislawa became "Regina." These changes may have been acceptable if the children were to remain in America. But it was intended they would go to Poland where they would be known by their Polish birth names. The changes were inappropriate, probably it confused or troubled some children.

Pawel Wojdak was recorded as Wladyslaw by the Rescue Committee in Siberia, and the Americanized form of that name continued to be assigned to him in Chicago and Milwaukee. Interestingly, the forms suggest there was doubt by the comment, "proper name of child unknown." How could his name be "Ladislaus" and, at the same time, "unknown?" This question will be considered in the next chapter. There is no basis for the comment that his mother "probably remained in Novo-Nikolayevsk." The birth year 1913 on the St. Joseph form is probably an estimate derived from his age being "about seven years." While at St. Joseph, Pawel Wojdak saw a tractor and learned the rhyme, "Come, little sister, and sit by me, and I will teach you A-B-C." But he did not retain any other knowledge of the English language.

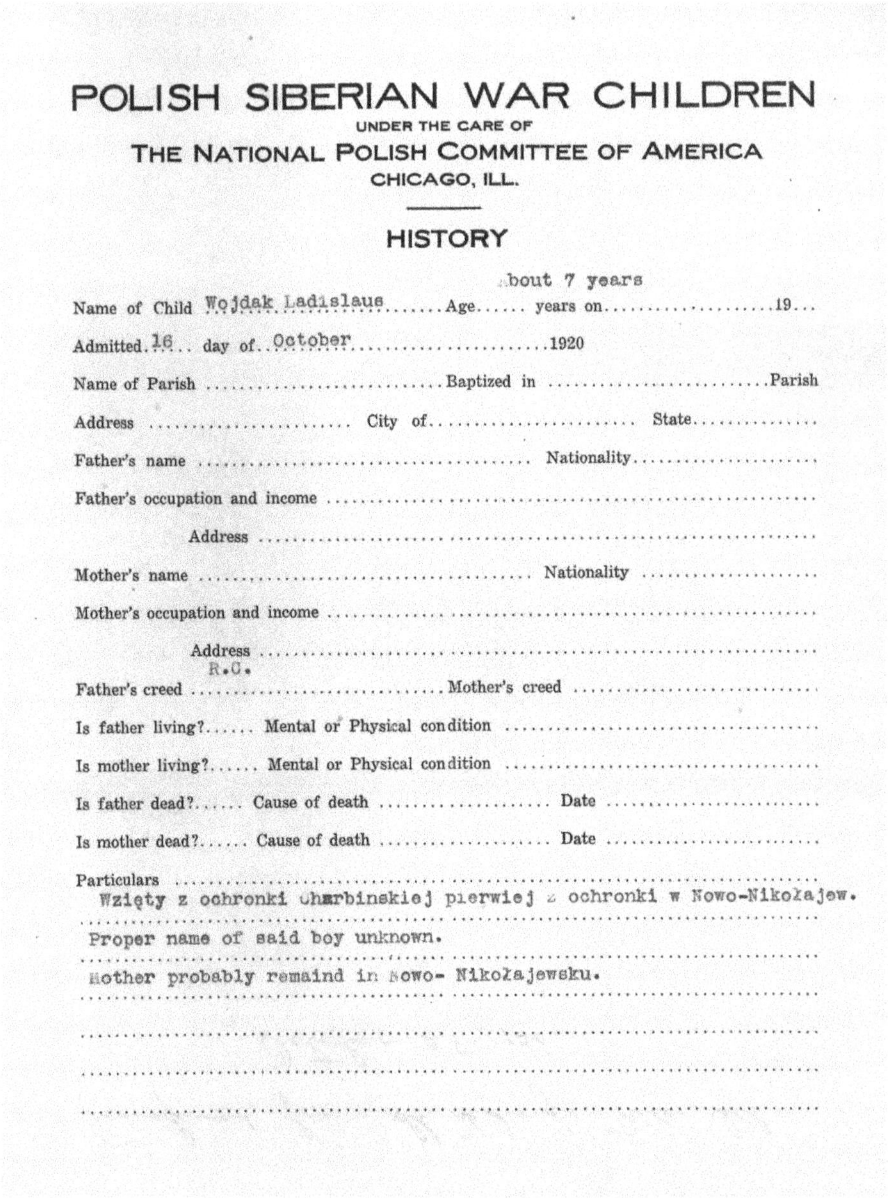

POLISH SIBERIAN WAR CHILDREN
UNDER THE CARE OF
THE NATIONAL POLISH COMMITTEE OF AMERICA
CHICAGO, ILL.

HISTORY

.bout 7 years

Name of Child Wojdak Ladislaus ...... Age...... years on.................... .19...

Admitted. 16 .. day of. October 1920

Name of Parish .... Baptized in .... Parish

Address .... City of....................... State...............

Father's name .... Nationality.....................

Father's occupation and income ....

Address ....

Mother's name .... Nationality ....

Mother's occupation and income ....

Address ....

R.C.

Father's creed .... Mother's creed ....

Is father living?...... Mental or Physical condition ....

Is mother living?...... Mental or Physical condition ....

Is father dead?...... Cause of death .... Date ....

Is mother dead?...... Cause of death .... Date ....

Particulars ....
Wzięty z ochronki Charbinskiej pierwiej z ochronki w Nowo-Nikołajew.
....
Proper name of said boy unknown.
....
Mother probably remaind in Nowo- Nikołajewsku.
....

....

....

....

Figure 18.2. Registration of Pawel Wojdak on October 16, 1920, at
St. Hedwig's Orphanage under the name of Ladislaus Wojdak
(Note: The statement in Polish reads that he was taken from an orphanage
in Charbin [Harbin] and previously from Novo-Nikolayevsk)

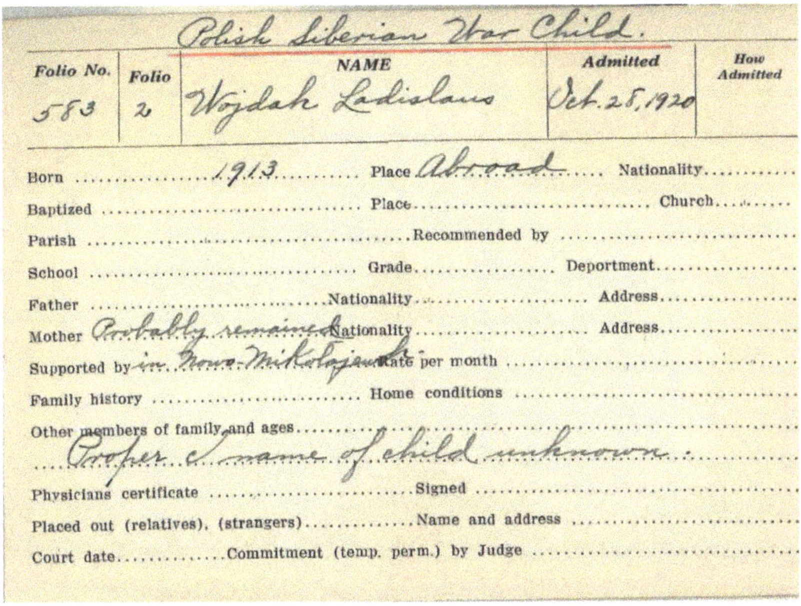

Polish Siberian War Child.

Folio No.	Folio	NAME	Admitted	How Admitted
583	2	Wojdak Ladislaus	Oct. 28, 1920	

Born 1913 Place Abroad Nationality

Baptized Place Church

Parish Recommended by

School Grade Deportment

Father Nationality Address

Mother Probably remained Nationality Address

Supported by in Nowo-Mikolajewsk Rate per month

Family history Home conditions

Other members of family and ages

Proper name of child unknown.

Physicians certificate Signed

Placed out (relatives), (strangers) Name and address

Court date Commitment (temp. perm.) by Judge

Figure 18.3. Registration of Pawel Wojdak at St. Joseph Orphanage under the name of Ladislaus Wojdak

Table 4. Siberian Orphans at St. Joseph Orphanage, Milwaukee

Name	Birthdate	Birthplace or Baptism	Parents
Gryszkus, Jan	1909	Janiszki Chita	Father only
Gryszkus, Jozef	1913	Janiszki Chita	Father only
Gryszkus, Kazimiera	1906	Konwiensk	Father only
Grzegorzewska, Bronislawa	1909	Bujwidzkiej parish	Mother only
Grzegorzewski, Wiktor	1912	Blagoveshchensk	Mother only
Kanezus-Bajlon, August	1910	Chita	Mother only
Kanezus-Bajlon, Flora	1906	Chita	Mother only
Marszal, Anna	1914	Azabu, Tokyo	Mother only
Marszal, Helena	1912	Bodaybo	Mother only
Marszal, Innocenty	1908	Uspiensk	Mother only

Marszal, Ludwik	1917	Chita	Mother only
Sapierzynska, Bronislawa	23/08/1903	Warsaw	Father & Mother
Szurkus, Jerzy	1911	Novo-Nikolayevsk	None
Wedzik, Marja	1914	Vladivostok	Mother only
Wedzik, Wladyslaw	1910	Vladivostok	Mother only
Wojdak, Wladyslaw	1912 or 1913	Novo-Nikolayevsk	None

For children who had lost their parents and were alone, such as Pawel Wojdak, the personal history form from St. Joseph and St. Hedwig's orphanages contains scarcely any information. The most basic genealogical data is absent; core elements of their identity were at risk of being lost. It is disappointing the files did not contain an assessment of child development: their physical and mental health; their aptitude at learning English or other subjects; their leadership and fellowship abilities. Perhaps it would be inappropriate to give out personal information of other children, but there was no mention of such information being available for my father. Did Pawel Wojdak have a close friend among the children? Not only to play with but to share his hopes and confide his fears.

More children were placed at St. Joseph than shown in Appendix 1. This was done to keep siblings together: the Gryszkus brothers with their sister; the Grzegorzewska sister and brother; and so on. The personal histories can be extremely valuable for descendants of Siberian children if they record the names of parents and siblings, their relations, and addresses. Family data of the Marszal siblings—Anna, Helena, Innocenty, and Ludwik (Table 4), and Benjamin (Appendix 2)—reveal the family's history and their connection to an important event in the lead-up to the Russian Revolution.

Birthdates and locations for Innocenty Marszal, and his sister Helena places the Marszal family in Siberia's Lena goldfield at exactly the time of the Lena Massacre.[158] Innocenty was born in 1908, in Uspiensk; Helena in Bodaybo, in 1912 (map 3). The map was created for this document by superimposing a 1912 sketch map by the Lena Gold Mining Partnership onto a

---

158 Wikipedia, s.v. "Lena Massacre," modified July 5, 2023, https://en.wikipedia.org/wiki/Lena_massacre.

Google Earth image. Thousands of men—Poles and Russians—mined the extremely rich gold deposits under brutal conditions (photo 18.1).[159] They were sentenced to hard labour, their families lived in nearby settlements under extremely poor conditions.

In March 1912, 6 000 miners went on strike. Their demands were denied and instead government troops arrested the strike leaders. The miners demanded their release, and 2 500 marched in protest to the government office in Nadezhdinsky. They were met by soldiers, who fired into the crowd, killing 270 and wounding 250 more. The event became known as the Lena Massacre and was well publicized all over Russia. Vladimir Lenin was a young activist who used the massacre to "inflame the masses with a revolutionary fire," causing strikes and protests throughout the country. It was a popular (but false) myth that Lenin changed his name from Ulyanov to immortalize the Lena Massacre.[160]

Map 3. Lena Goldfield (Google Earth image), with settlements of 1912 superimposed including Uspensky (Uspiensk) and Nadezhdinsky, site of the Lena Massacre; Bodaybo is the only settlement that exists today.

159 Wikipedia, s.v. "Lena Gold Mining Partnership," last modified March 15, 2023, https://en.wikipedia.org/wiki/Lena_Gold_Mining_Partnership.

160 Yekaterina Sinelschikova, "Why Did Vladimir Lenin Adopt the Name Lenin?" *Russia Beyond*, October 9, 2020, https://www.rbth.com/history/332831-vladimir-lenin-nickname.

Photo 18.1. Lena Goldfield 1910, hand-mining rich gold deposits in the gravel of the Bodaybo River; the miners are posed in this photograph (reproduced with permission of Alamy stock photography company). [161]

The miners' strike continued until August, when the share price of the Lena Gold Mining Partnership collapsed and the company shut down operations. An estimated 9 000 employees and family members left the area. The company was nationalized following the Russian Revolution. Mining eventually resumed, using dredges, and mechanized mining continues today; workings are visible from satellite, stretching many tens of kilometres along the Bodaybo River and its tributaries. Bodaybo still exists, but Uspiensk, Nadezhdinsky, and all other historic settlements in the Lena goldfield are gone.

The Marszal family are documented to be in Chita in 1917 when Ludwik was born, their youngest child. Chita is 650 kilometres south of the Lena goldfield. Casimir died soon after, and in 1919–1920, widow Antonina surrendered care of Innocenty, Helena, Anna, and Ludwik to the Rescue Committee. A year later, she consigned her son Benjamin to the second mission (Appendix 2), but the fate of the widowed Antonina and her remaining son, Wiktor, is unknown. Six-year-old Anna was baptized in Azabu, Japan, a district of Tokyo, near Fukudenkai. Baptism is very

161 Smith Archive, *Gold Mine in Lena Prior to the Lena Massacre*, Stock Photograph, Almay, 1910, https://www.alamy.com/stock-photo/lena-russia.html?blackwhite=1&sortBy=relevant.

important to devout Catholics—a public profession of faith in Christ and a commitment to a Christian life. Anna's late baptism suggests the Marszal family was unsettled or in difficulty.

Urszula Malewski, a granddaughter of Innocenty Marszal, wrote of her grandfather's life in an unpublished manuscript, "On the Meeting of Descendants of Siberian Children," shared to fellow descendants. It includes an aged photo of her great-grandparents, Innocenty's mother and father. It has fold-lines and crumpled corners; the treasured image had travelled with twelve-year-old Innocenty from Siberia to Japan, to America, and finally to Poland. But Urszula did not know their names. It was a great pleasure to be able to share with Urszula that their names were Casimir and Antonina, as documented in the records of an American orphanage. The files of Anna, Helena, Innocenty, and Ludwik Marszal were forwarded to her also. Urszula did not know anything of her grandfather's brothers, Ludwik, Wiktor, and Benjamin. Sadly, Benjamin did not connect with his siblings in Poland and contact with Ludwik was lost.

Urszula and her son are empowered by the orphanage records to continue and expand their ancestry search and expressed their gratitude to me at learning so much from Siberia and America: "The documents you sent to us are very important and useful to us. We are very happy and thankful that you contacted us. Very grateful!"

Reflecting on the life of the Marszals in the Lena goldfield, water reliably and logically flows downhill, but not so with the course of history. History can take an illogical path. In 1912, in the Lena goldfields, Russians and Poles like Casimir Marszal stood together at the wrong end of a czarist gun—stood together and died together. Six years later, illogically, Poles became "enemies of the people," and their families were torn apart.

Next, consider Bronislawa Grzegorzewska. From the orphanage records, she was born in 1909 in the Bujwidzkiej parish, near Wilno in Russian Poland. Her deceased father, Joseph, had served in the Polish Army, perhaps the 5th Siberian Division, which was almost annihilated during the civil war. The Grzegorzewski family somehow crossed Russia and Siberia between 1909 and 1920 to arrive in Chita. Josephine Grzegorzewska was a widow with five children in Chita, similar to Antonina Marszal with her six children. Chita was controlled by warlord Grigori Semyonov and his private army until 1921. Josephine turned two of her children—Bronislawa (eleven years old) and Wiktor (eight)—over to the Rescue Committee, and they came to St. Joseph in Milwaukee. The records indicate brothers Feliks, Ignatius, and Adam Grzegorzewski remained with their mother. Their outcome is unknown.

Bronislawa Sapierzynska was born and baptized in Warsaw in 1903, but the family came to be living in Ufa, Russia; perhaps they were exiled there. The family became part of the stream of refugees, and seventeen-year-old Bronislawa was in Harbin when taken in by the Rescue Committee. Miraculously, Jan and Francja Sapierzynski survived in Siberia and came to the United States and found Bronislawa. She was released from St. Joseph to her parents on January 25, 1922. What a happy day that must have been!

Flora Kanzus-Bajlon and her younger brother, August, also came from Chita. Their father was dead, and their mother was recorded as "deaf and dumb." Care of the children was shared with a grandfather. The Kanzus-Bajlon family was under stress when they turned Flora and August over to the Rescue Committee.

For young orphans Pawel Wojdak and Jerzy Szurkus, the orphanage files contain little information. Quite possibly, they were sheltered in the same church orphanage in Harbin described by Antonina Liro in Chapter 12.

For other descendants of Siberian children who may read this account and are in search of information, the names of the Felician Sisters orphanages in Detroit, Niles, and Manitowoc are shown in Table 3. Sister Grace also advised that individual records of St. Hedwig's Orphanage reside in the Cardinal Joseph Bernardin Archive.

The orphanage records show there are errors in Appendix 1, which is derived herein from the list published by the Rescue Committee. Kazimierz Gryszkus was actually a girl named Kazimiera and was fourteen years old, not four. Marja Wedzik was six years old, not fourteen, as shown in Appendix 1. Kazimiera Gryszkus is in the records of St. Joseph in Milwaukee, but her personal testimony indicates she was in Detroit.[162] Clearly, some unrecorded

---

162 Theiss, *Dzieci Syberyjskie*, 216–217.

adjustments were made in the placement of children. Kazimiera recalled the following (translated):

> My brothers and I got to an orphanage in Detroit where we were looked after by nuns. We were very comfortable there. The care was great, the food was perfect, we lacked nothing. My brother Jozef was assigned to preschool, my other brother Jan to the first grade of primary school, and I to the second grade. We had a school on-site. Nuns taught at school. Lessons were conducted in English, very little in Polish. The nuns prepared us for First Communion, and after there was a solemn reception during which we received gifts. It was a very beautiful experience that I still remember.[163]

Kazimiera stated in Theiss's 2020 book that she was presented with options about going to Poland:

> In 1922, Mother Superior came to me and said the Polish children with whom I came to America were to be sent back to Poland. She asked me if I wanted to stay in America or return to Poland. She emphasized that there was great poverty in Poland. I replied that I wanted to return to my homeland.

Siberian child Jan Samardakiewicz attended junior high school in Chicago, as related by his grandson Slawomir, and learned about agriculture. His interest and skills in gardening became part of his life. Polish families in America encouraged Jan and his brother, Antoni, to remain, but they were determined to go to Poland.[164]

Pawel Wojdak told me he was presented with a similar question. One day, he and the other children were asked, "Who wants to go home?" They answered in the affirmative, but there was bitterness in his voice when he explained to me, "What child doesn't want to go home?" Probably he was influenced by the other children in agreeing to go to Poland. They had been on such a long journey together and perhaps he thought "home" included love and security within a family. Instead, he had a poor life in Poland,

---

163 Theiss, 226.
164 Social Welfare Corporation Fukudenkai, "Interview with Slawomir Samardakiewicz."

beginning with yet another orphanage. Did he have an ideal image of "home" conveyed to him by his father and mother during their devastating journey across Siberia?

Fifty-seven children chose to stay in America—which ones were not recorded—and two left for Poland earlier; one of them was Bronislawa Sapierzynska. But perhaps her family decided to remain in America. On January 28, 1922, the USS *Princess Matoika* took 310 Polish children "home" to Poland.[165] The ship left from New York and landed in Bremerhaven, the port for Bremen, Germany, after a three-week passage. They were put on a train going to Poznan, Poland, where they were met by Caritas, the Catholic benevolent association. Here, at last, was the connection that my father remembered.

An estimated 2.2 million Poles immigrated to America between 1820 and 1914. It is indeed remarkable that in 1922, eighty-four percent of the Siberian children went in the opposite direction, from wealth and opportunity in America to poverty and deprivation in Poland. The children did not know what lay ahead. Almost none had ever lived in Poland; it was a matter of trust, a leap of faith. That faith came from their parents and from the Rescue Committee; they were Polish patriots a generation or more removed from Poland. This includes Jozef Jakobkiewicz, who was born in eastern Russia, near Siberia. The passion of Polish exiles and their vision for a new and free Poland was deeply rooted in an overwhelming majority of the Siberian children.

The *Matoika* was a transport ship for the US Navy during World War I. She was a German ship that was seized by America in 1917 when war was declared on Germany. In July 1920, the *Matoika* transported the US team to the Olympics in Antwerp. The Olympic team considered her vastly inadequate and published a list of grievances and demands, which came to be known as the "Mutiny of the *Matoika*." But in 1922, the ship was suitable for the Siberian children.

---

165 Wikipedia, s.v. "USS *Princess Matoika*," last modified June 9, 2023, https://en.wikipedia. org/wiki/USS_Princess_Matoika.

19.

Who Was Wladyslaw Wojdak?

Pawel Wojdak's file from St. Joseph intrigued me. How could he be "unknown" and named Ladislaus (or Wlaydyslaw) on the same form? Clearly, there was an uncertainty that was not evident previously. Knowing how difficult it was for him to speak about his childhood, I began to wonder if he could not speak for a period of time when he was an orphan, like Antonina Liro. A child does not carry identity papers. What if his dying father's documentation was transferred to his son and became the only reference when he came to the orphanage in Harbin? If he could not speak his own name, then his father's name might have been assigned to him by the Rescue Committee in Harbin and have remained until he reached America. There, he was at least able to deny his name was Wladyslaw, thereby giving the orphanage doubt.

I hypothesized that my father's father could be Wladyslaw Wojdak and that he was exiled to Siberia. With this rationale, I contracted Your Roots, a genealogical research group in Krakow, Poland, with associates in Russia, to search Roman Catholic birth records in Novosibirsk for Wladyslaw and Pawel Wojdak as well as Russian government records for Wladyslaw Wojdak among those convicted of common and political crimes.

No birth record for Wladyslaw or Pawel Wojdak was found in Novosibirsk parish within the years 1911–1917, but the researcher reported church books are "preserved partially." The following government registers were reviewed: State Archives of Novosibirsk Oblast, State Archives of the Russian Federation, State Archives of Tomsk region (the administrative centre for Novosibirsk), and the Russian State Library in Moscow. I received their report in April 2022.

The report from Your Roots in Poland, by Michal Gierszon and Adrian Jarosz, states that lists of common criminals were published in monthly volumes with an annual or bi-annual index. Complete indexes were available for 1908 and 1909, but for 1905, 1906, and 1907, only half of each annual list was available. No indexes were available for 1910–1913. As with the indexes, many volumes are not available and/or are stored in different locations. Clearly, the records do not allow for a thorough search.

It is rather amazing that two "Wojdak" references were found in the 1908 index of common criminals:

> Wojdak Wladyslaw, son of Franciszek, 139850 in volume 12
> Wojdak Jan, son of Wojciecha, 63111 in volume 5

After some difficulty, the volume with a record of Wladyslaw Wojdak was located:

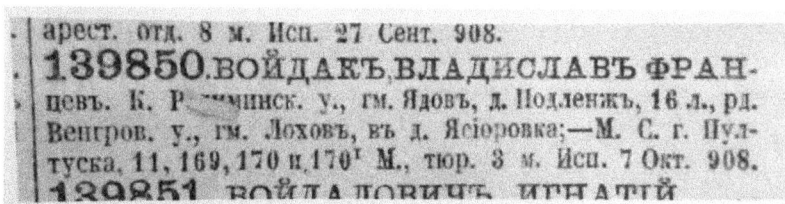

Excerpt from Russian archives pertaining to Wladyslaw Wojdak

The researcher, Adrian Jarosz, supplied the following translation:

> Wladyslaw Wojdak was a peasant of the village Podleze within the administrative district of gmina Jadow. He was born in

the village of Jasiorowka within the administrative district of gmina Lochow. He was 16 years old when he was arrested on 27 September 1908 and sentenced by the Magistrate's Court of Pultusk to 3 months in prison on the 7th of October 1908.

Map 4. Poland showing borders in 1921, post-World War II (1945) and the Curzon line. Also shown are orphanages where Siberian children were housed; Jasiorowka, where Wladyslaw Wojdak may have been born in 1908; and Cieszkow, where Pawel Wojdak lived in 1939. Map prepared from the National Geoportal of Poland.[166]

A Google translation confirms Adrian Jarosz's statement. Gierszon explained the abbreviations in the Statute of Punishment: Article 11

---

166 Geoportal, Poland Head Office of Geodesy and Cartography, accessed July 2023, https://www.gov.pl/web/gugik-en/geoportal

refers to the punishment of minors; Article 169 refers to damages; and Article 170 to theft of an amount not exceeding 300 rubles. The villages of Podleze and Jasiorowka are located 55 kilometres northeast of Warsaw in an area of small farms (see Map 4). The map was prepared specifically for this document to show borders before and after World War II, as well as major cities, orphanages that housed the Siberian children, and settlements relevant to Pawel and Wladyslaw Wojdak.

Podleze is 7.4 kilometres south of Jasiorowka—Wladyslaw Wojdak did not move far from his birthplace. "Gminas" are equivalent to a county. Could Wladyslaw Wojdak possibly be my grandfather? The search for "Wojdak" in the records of political criminals was unsuccessful. However, the archives are similarly incomplete as for common criminals. The only volumes that could be searched were of the Russian Federation for 1904, 1905, and 1914 and those in the Tomsk region for 1905, 1906, 1915, and part of 1916.

Michal Gierszon and Adrian Jarosz commented that common criminals were incarcerated in Poland; there were ample prisons to do so. From the available archives, Wladyslaw Wojdak was not convicted of a political crime, such as involvement in the independence movement, which would have caused him to be exiled to Siberia. They stress there is no evidence that this Wladyslaw Wojdak is linked to Pawel Wojdak.

However, the arrest date of Wladyslaw Wojdak, September 27, 1908, has special significance. It coincides exactly with the Great Train Robbery committed by the Bojowa paramilitary guerilla force headed by Jozef Pilsudski. Perhaps the dates are entirely coincidental. But Russian authorities were enraged by the train robbery and determined to eliminate the Bojowa. A great crackdown and widespread arrests followed the train robbery, as the Russian administration was ready to make an example of anyone who might be connected with the organization. Revenge is a strong (Russian) motive. And conceivably, the Bojowa may have planned robberies simultaneous with the train heist as a display of their strength and determination. Wladyslaw Wojdak might have been a member, as teenagers participated in protests for the right to have school instruction in Polish. Recall from Chapter 7, the organization had 2 000 members and committed 2 500 operations over a few years, so it is a hypothesis that is possible but impossible to prove. All subversive organizations operate as independent cells.

Under martial law at the time, suspicion of a link to the Bojowa might well be enough to render a harsher sentence for a minor crime. An alternative but related hypothesis is Wladyslaw Wojdak became radicalized to the cause of Polish independence while serving his three-month jail term in Poland. Political actions thereafter resulted in an unrecorded arrest and exile. It is all conjecture. If sixteen-year-old Wladyslaw Wojdak was deported to Novo-Nikolayevsk in 1908, the ordeal would mature him quickly. He would gravitate to the large Polish community in the city, and two young people might bond out of loneliness during difficult times. Wladyslaw Wojdak may have become a father in 1912, when he was twenty years old. It is possible, but speculative; there is no firm link between Wladyslaw Wojdak of Podleze and Jasiorowka to a hypothetical Wladyslaw Wojdak in Novo-Nikolayevsk.

When I presented my Canadian passport at Polish Customs in Warsaw in 2018, the agent studied it for a moment before stating, "Hmm, typical Polish name." Never have I been told my name is typical. I was surprised to feel a soft warmth of welcome. Indeed, Wojdak is a typical Polish name, but not overly common. Census data for 2023 indicates there are 1 418 people named Wojdak in Poland, in a population of 41 million. This equates to one Wojdak in approximately 30 000 people. Another example: the online list of 29 000 members of the 3rd Carpathian Rifle Division in World War II contains just one Wojdak and that is Pawel Wojdak.[167] Wladyslaw is one of the most common boy's names among the lists of Siberian children. Combining a very common first name and a not-very-common last name, how many people named Wladyslaw Wojdak might there have been in 1912?

I propose to visit Podleze and Jasiorowka to inquire about Wojdak and Wladyslaw Wojdak in particular. Of course, this in itself will not prove anything—unless there is some family memory of a Wojdak being exiled to Novosibirsk. A slim chance, but recalling the thought of Slawomir Samardakiewicz, "Might those that love us reach out to find us?"

---

167 "Pawel Wojdak, List of 3rd Carpathian Rifle Division," *Kresy Siberia Virtual Museum*, accessed November 2, 2023, https://kresy-siberia.org/list-3rd-carpathian-rifle-division/?pagenum=160.

In September 2023, my wife and I travelled to Poland for the Kresy-Siberia conference in Bialystok, and to attend a gathering of descendants of Siberian children in Warsaw. Both events had been delayed several years due to the pandemic. There was more than a week between the two events, enabling us to explore the places where Pawel Wojdak lived and where his hypothesized father, Wladyslaw Wojdak, lived.

Our enquiries began in the town offices of Lochow and adjacent Jadow, which administer, respectively, Jasiorowka and Podleze. Despite language challenges, people did their best to help, possibly because many Poles have a family mystery of a lost or displaced relative. Staff at the town offices told us the name Wojdak was unknown to them.

The village of Jasiorowka, where a Wladyslaw Wojdak was born, consists of a single street about one kilometre long lined with houses, most of recent construction but interspersed with abandoned square-timbered houses perhaps 100 or more years old. Farm fields behind the houses were once worked individually. There is no school, church, or shops.

Photo 19.1. Square-timbered house in Jasiorowka, possibly 100 or more years old

One inquiry led to a meeting with local historian Karol Suchocki. Karol found the birth record of Wladyslaw Wojdak, son of Franciszek Wojdak and Marianna Ziolkowska, born August 15, 1891, in Jasiorowka.[168] It is handwritten in nineteenth-century Russian, but we obtained a translation. Franciszek was thirty years old, a labourer in Jasiorowka, and Marianna was twenty years old. Baptism was in the parish of Kamionna, a village six kilometres southeast of Jasiorowka.

Karol Suchocki used a Polish genealogical database to determine people named Wojdak are concentrated in Masovian voivodship (province) both now and historically. It is centred on Warsaw. Most voivodships in Poland contain no Wojdaks. Suchocki found that people named Wladyslaw Wojdak are only recorded in Masovian voivodship in the latter nineteenth century, thereby having an appropriate age to be my grandfather. And there were five men named Wladyslaw Wojdak. Two can be eliminated because death certificates indicate they died in Poland; they did not die in Siberia. The three remaining possibilities are:

- Wladyslaw Wojdak in 1882, son of Adam and Marianna, born in Starawies,
- Zygmunt Wladyslaw Wojdak in 1888, son of Adam and Aleksandra, born in Prazmo,
- Wladyslaw Wojdak in 1891, son of Franciszek and Marianna, born in Jasiorowka.

None of the three are known to have a connection to Siberia. Prazmo is located south of Warsaw, but Starawies is just twenty kilometres southeast of Jasiorowka, which suggests these families were related.

The nearest cemetery to Jasiorowka is five kilometres to the east in the parish of Majdan and Ostrowek. There, we chanced to find a Wojdak family mausoleum containing the remains of Konstanty Wojdak (died in 1940 at sixty years), Czeslaw Wojdak (died in 1996 at seventy-five years) and Janina Wojdak (died in 2019 at ninety-one years). Karol Suchocki found

---

168 Wladyslaw Wojdak birth record, https://metryki.genealodzy.pl/index.php?op=pg&ar=21 &zs=0180d&se=&sy=1891&kt=1&plik=144-145.jpg&x=0&y=350&z oom=2.600297176820208.

the marriage and death certificates of Konstanty Wojdak. He was married in Kamionna parish in 1913 to Franciszka Puchta. This is the same parish where the birth of Wladyslaw Wojdak was recorded in 1891.

Karol Suchocki states the deaths of Czeslaw and Janina Wojdak are too recent for their data to be publicly accessible. No records were found that link Konstanty to Wladyslaw Wojdak, who was born eleven years later and only five kilometres away. Jasiorowka, Kamionna, and Maidan-Ostrowek cemeteries form a compact triangle. There must be a descendant of the Wojdak family who maintains the grave so well, as shown in the photo. Karol will continue the search, on my behalf. In the search for traces of my father's family, each door that is opened leads to another door.

Photo 19.2. Wojdak family mausoleum containing remains of Konstanty, Czeslaw and Janina Wojdak

Podleze is uninhabited and overgrown. All that remains is an abandoned farm and a nearby house at the end of a dirt road through fields and forest. Historian Suchocki identified Podleze as one parcel of extensive land holdings of the Zamoyski family in the nineteenth century that was worked by peasants like Wladyslaw Wojdak. The Zamoyski family was influential in Polish politics for several centuries and was deeply involved in the Polish independence movement.[169] Count Wladyslaw Zamoyski was exiled to Russia after the November Uprising (1830–31), and Count Andrezj Zamoyski was exiled after the January Uprising (1863–64).

A later local connection to the independence movement, Medard Downarowicz was born in Lochow in 1878. He was a close associate of Joseph Pilsudski and co-founder of the PPS (Polish Socialist Party) Combat Organization, the Bojowa.[170] He did not participate in the Bezdany train robbery in 1908 because he was arrested and sentenced in 1906 to six years hard labour in Siberia. Lochow lies on the main train line between Warsaw, Wilno, and St Petersburg. We can speculate the Downarowicz estate in Lochow[171] was a safe hide-out for some of the forty-member robbery team on the 500-kilometre trip to Bezdany.

There was a vast social gulf between the Polish nobility like Pilsudski and Downarowicz, despite their being impoverished, and peasants like Wladyslaw Wojdak. The evidence to link Wladyslaw Wojdak to the independence movement and the train robbery that would warrant exile to Siberia remains circumstantial. Perhaps Wladyslaw Wojdak simply served his three-month jail sentence, remained in Poland, and is buried somewhere else than Jasiorowka. And was unrelated to my father Pawel Wojdak. In addition, the Wojdak family may have been in Siberia for a generation or more, in which case there is no hope of tracing a family connection to Poland.

---

169 Wikipedia, s.v. "Zamoyski Family," last modified October 12, 2023, https://en.wikipedia. org/wiki/Zamoyski_family.

170 Wikipedia, s.v. "Medard Downarowicz," last modified October 24, 2023 https:// pl.wikipedia.org/wiki/Medard_Downarowicz.

171 Piotr Libicki and Marcin Libicki, *Dwory i pałac wiejskie na Mazowszu* (Country Manors and Palaces in Masovia, Palace in Lochow) (Rebis Publishing House, 2013).

20.

Securing Polish Freedom, 1919–1921

A full month prior to when Armistice Day officially ended World War I, Polish people began taking action in excited anticipation that their country would soon be reborn, free. German soldiers still occupied all three former partitions, but they were demoralized by the certainty of defeat. Poles ignored them and the German administration. Polish political factions clamoured for different directions to be taken by a government that was yet to be elected. Some favoured welcoming communism, the goal of Lenin's new Bolshevik government, but most wanted Poland to be independent. A county near Krakow took the lead by unilaterally declaring its independence two weeks before the Armistice, with the provision it would join the Polish Republic as soon as it formed.[172]

In 1920, Poland was a concept, not yet an established country with a government and secure borders. The Siberian children in America and Japan, and Polish refugees remaining in Siberia were in no position to come to Poland.

---

172 Hetherington, *Unvanquished*, 328–329.

Poland needed a leader capable of uniting all Poles. Roman Dmowski and Jozef Pilsudski were the two alternatives. They had been political rivals for decades, and their ideologies were diametrically opposed. Dmowski saw Germany as Poland's greatest enemy and had favoured accommodation with Russia to advance Polish independence. During the war, this fell in line with Allied thinking, as the Allies wished to believe communism was a temporary aberration and an Imperial Russian government would be restored. Pilsudski recognized Russia to be Poland's prime enemy. Dmowski was an elitist and strongly antisemitic, while Pilsudski was egalitarian and a socialist. He endorsed inclusion of ethnic minorities in a Slavic federation that would be a bulwark against Russian aggression. A delegation of socialists met with Pilsudski, including former colleagues from his underground days, and addressed him as "comrade." Pilsudski immediately corrected them while simultaneously declaring his political direction by stating,

> "Gentlemen, I am no longer your comrade. In the beginning we followed the same direction, and took the tramway painted red, but I left at the station – Poland's Independence; you are continuing the journey as far as the station – socialism. My good wishes accompany you but be so kind as to call me Sir."[173]

Pilsudski's credentials were impeccable in Poland, whereas Dmowski was endorsed by the Allies. Pilsudski was selfless and charismatic, thereby engendering loyalty among his followers. He was a martyred freedom fighter, imprisoned by both Russia and Germany. He established and commanded a heroic Polish military early in the war. Pilsudski strived to make the Legions distinct from the Austrian Army, and he eventually resigned his command, yet the Allies distrusted him on that account. Dmowski, on the other hand, spent part of the war years safely in Paris as a lobbyist for Poland, but that did not endear him to Poles suffering at home. Jozef Haller's well-equipped army, sometimes referred to as the Blue Army, was loyal to Dmowski.

Jozef Pilsudski accepted the position of commander in chief of the almost non-existent armed forces on Armistice Day, November 11, 1918, and,

173 Hetherington, 344.

two days later, was sworn in as provisional head of state by the Regency Council. Ignacy Paderewski, the influential Polish-American, brokered an accord between Pilsudski and Dmowski.[174] The former controlled the country; the latter brought Allied support and Haller's Army, which was urgently needed to defend Poland.[175]

A guiding principle of the Paris peace treaty after World War I was that ethnic groups should comprise their own country; the principle of self-determination was championed by the United States. Thirty-two countries participated in negotiations, but there were effectively four leaders, each with their own priorities: Britain, France, the United States, and Italy. Defeated nations Germany and Austria-Hungary were not invited to the table, nor was Russia, where civil war was raging and the Western Allies were actively supporting the losing side. The new Bolshevik government had repudiated the war debts to the Allies incurred by the czarist regime. Poland and the plight of Polish refugees in Siberia was, at best, a minor issue in treaty discussions. President Woodrow Wilson was a proponent of Poland, no doubt because of the sizable Polish community in America and the famous and passionately outspoken Ignacy Paderewski. Wilson's role continues to be acknowledged in Poland today.

Poland was one of a multitude of new countries created in the redefining of Europe. Polish partitions previously governed by czarist Russia, Germany, and Austria-Hungary were to be amalgamated, but setting its boundaries was difficult. Eastern Poland, referred to as Kresy, was a patchwork of Polish, Lithuanian, Latvian, Ukrainian, and Belarusian people. In the west and north, there was a mix of Polish and German people. To the south, there was clearer separation of Czech, Slovak and Romanian peoples. Figure 20.1 displays the ethnic and language heterogeneity of Poland in 1931. And Jews were present throughout these ethnic communities, forming a distinct subset of people.

---

174 Wikipedia, s.v. "Ignacy Paderewski," last modified October 29, 2023, https://en.wikipedia.org/wiki/Ignacy_Jan_Paderewski.

175 Hetherington, *Unvanquished*, 352–355.

Figure 20.1. Ethnicities of Poland from 1931 census; white line is the Polish border and shows the complex distribution of ethnicities in the Kresy (Eastern Borderlands) region

The Curzon Line was a proposed boundary between Poland and the Soviet Union, put forward by Britain, as shown on map 4.[176] In theory, the line separated the area where Polish people were the majority. However, the proposed division excluded the predominantly Polish cities of Wilno, Kaunas, Lvov and Tarnopol, as well as Polish rural areas. These were surrounded by large areas where more than a third of the people were

---

176 Wikipedia, s.v. "The Curzon Line," last modified October 20, 2023, https://en.wikipedia. org/wiki/Curzon_Line.

Polish.[177, 178] Two variants of the Curzon Line were discussed at the peace conference: one favoured Ukraine by including Lvov, but neither favoured Poland because both excluded Wilno.

Jozef Pilsudski was born in a village close to Wilno, and he considered Wilno to be integral to Poland; he did not agree with either variation of the Curzon Line. Two days after the Armistice ended hostilities in western Europe, Russia annulled its peace treaty with Germany (Treaty of Brest-Litovsk) and positioned its army to the western frontier, signaling its intent to recover its lost territories. In early 1919, the Red Army was still preoccupied with its internal civil war, and Pilsudski took advantage of this by seizing most of what is now Lithuania, Belarus, and western Ukraine. Ukraine was a new country, but without an army and, therefore, under threat from the east by the Russian Army. Ukraine formed an alliance with Poland; their combined forces occupied Kiev in May 1920. The Soviet Army avoided confrontation and withdrew.

The Soviet Army counterattacked soon after, first on the southern Ukrainian front and then in the north. Polish forces were steadily pushed back to the outskirts of Warsaw. Defeat seemed certain, but in the Battle of Warsaw (August 1920), Pilsudski led the Polish Army in a daring outflanking manoeuvre and routed the Soviet Army, which had over-extended its supply lines. The Polish victory was decisive. They pursued the retreating Red Army and broke a Russian defensive line in a battle at the Niemen River in September. Total Russian casualties, killed and captured, in the two battles amounted to 191 000. It was "an unqualified Polish victory and signalled the end of the Bolshevik vision of a communist Poland for at least a generation."[179] In his biography, Peter Hetherington also states, "Pilsudski's actions at the August 1920 Battle of Warsaw changed the strategic situation so completely, abruptly, and unexpectedly that it is difficult to think of

---

177 Hetherington, *Unvanquished*, 238.

178 Wikipedia, s.v. "Kresy," last modified October 30, 2023, https://en.wikipedia.org/wiki/Kresy.

179 Hetherington, *Unvanquished*, 465.

another comparable operation in the annals of military history."[180] British and French observers, including a young Charles de Gaulle, were astonished.

Pilsudski's "Miracle on the Vistula" was not achieved by Napoleon or by Germany in either of the two world wars. The ensuing treaty (Peace of Riga, March 1921) placed Poland's eastern border 200 kilometres east of the Curzon Line. Pilsudski's goal of retaining the predominantly Polish cities of Wilno and Lvov was achieved.

Formal talks between Russia and Poland for the return of Poles from Siberia began in June 1918. Russia wanted to return Polish refugees who were indoctrinated in communism; Poland refused to admit communists who were aligned with Russia.[181] By December 1918, Russia was openly using the return of refugees as a bargaining chip in setting the eastern boundary of Poland. Russia sent communist agents to Warsaw, disguised as Red Cross staff, to conduct negotiations. The agents were discovered and killed—a crime never solved but made less relevant when the Polish-Soviet War erupted in 1919. Due to the war, Polish refugees became hostages. During the protracted period of negotiation and war over Poland's boundaries, the fate of the Siberian children was in limbo. They needed time in Japan to recover their health and for the leaders to make arrangements for ongoing travel. The long period of instability in Poland meant the first group of children went to America before going to Poland.

Vladimir Lenin and Jozef Pilsudski had opposing visions for the future of Eastern Europe. Lenin saw himself as the leader of an expansion of communism; Poland would be the first in a series of communist revolutions. He intended Russia should rule all Slavic peoples, an aim no different from the czars. Pilsudski wanted a voluntary federation of Poles, Lithuanians, Latvians, Ukrainians, and Estonians as a bulwark against communism and an alignment with Western European culture and values. Constrained between Germany and Russia, he felt Poland had to be a strong nation if it was to exist in the long-term. Pilsudski was sure that Germany and Russia would seek to reclaim territory lost in World War I—which history would

---

180 Hetherington, 459.
181 Wandycz, *Soviet-Polish Relations.*

prove to be true. Pilsudski recognized the duplicity of Lenin when he stated, "Let us imagine for a moment that I have concluded peace with [Russia]. I must then demobilize the army . . . And I will become powerless at the border. Lenin will be able to do what he wants, because he will not hesitate to break even his most solemn word."[182]

Poland gained substantial territory in the Kresy region during the Polish-Soviet War, but the new countries of Ukraine and Byelorussia (Belarus) were officially recognized as constituents of the Soviet Union. This was a blow to Pilsudski's goal of a federation to counter Russia. Perhaps one hundred years later, in 2023, Ukraine will overcome Russian aggression and a variation of Pilsudski's dream will emerge in an alignment with NATO.

Following the Treaty of Riga, Polish refugees, adults and orphaned Siberian children were able to travel across Russia to Poland. In January 1923, Anna Bielkiewicz arranged a special train with 117 children to leave Vladivostok—the third rescue mission.

Settlement of the German-Polish border was also a difficult process that involved violence but did not require a war to settle. There were protests and demonstrations before two plebiscites produced a settlement in 1922. However, ill feelings by German people persisted and would affect Pawel Wojdak and many more Poles in a few short years.

The Paris peace treaty had provided for Poland to have access to the Baltic Sea, important for the economic viability of the new nation. Danzig, a largely German-inhabited city, was given special status that guaranteed its use as a port by Poland. In Poland, it is called Gdansk, and we will see it became important to some of the resettled Siberian children.

From the perspective of the future, it should be noted that census data in 1931 shows Jews comprised twenty to fifty percent of the Kresy region.[183] Distinguishing people by ethnicity and religion adds to a blurring of boundaries, emphasizing the diversity of the region and that Poles and Jews lived side-by-side peaceably. Polish society was not characterized by the frequent Jewish pogroms in Russia. The future extermination of Jews by German

---

182 Hetherington. *Unvanquished,* 406.
183 Wikipedia, "Kresy."

genocide and the massive displacement of Poles by Russia render the 1931 statistics irrelevant today, but they give historical perspective.

21.

Polish "Homecoming" and Wejherowo

To summarize what is known or can be inferred about Pawel Wojdak's journey: He left Novo-Nikolayevsk on a train with his parents in 1919, probably in the fall, certainly by early winter. They were fleeing a typhoid epidemic and the advancing Bolshevik Army and competing for rail passage with increasingly desperate Czech soldiers and other refugees. His mother first, then his father died from some combination of exposure, disease, or possibly violence. When he came to an orphanage in Harbin, during the winter of 1919–1920, he was alone, perhaps dropped off by surviving refugees. He was retrieved from the orphanage sometime during the winter, perhaps as early as December 1919, when Jozef Jakobkiewicz came there on his first rescue trip. He was in Sedanka near Vladivostok for up to six months and probably on the first sailing to Japan on July 20, 1920. Pawel Wojdak was not in Japan very long; he left in late September after a stay of no more than two months, less than the 100-day average for Siberian children. He arrived in America in mid-October and was in Milwaukee for fifteen months until late January 1922. For that length of time, it is disappointing the St. Joseph file contains so little information as to his social adjustment and development.

The 310 children of the first mission arrived at their new residences in Poland in mid-February 1922. They were entrusted to Caritas, which divided them into groups for orphanages in the Poznan region located in Mielzyn, Broniszewicz, Dolsk, and Bojanowo.[184] The *Echo of the Far East* indicates there was also an orphanage in Cerewicka. The Mielzyn facility was operated by Dominican Sisters and housed at least fifty girls. Forty-three children at Bojanowo were transferred to better facilities in Pniewy.[185] Theiss also relates that some children were placed on farms near the various orphanages. Pawel Wojdak was one who went to live and work on a farm.

The 290 children of the second rescue joined the children who came from America nine months later, in early November 1922. Another 117 children of the third rescue mission arrived in January or February 1923, giving a total of 817 rescued from Siberia. It is estimated less than thirty percent of the children were reunited with parents or relatives.[186] Therefore, at least seventy percent, about 570, were placed in care in Poland.

Poland struggled with a host of issues as a new and poor country in 1919. There had not been an independent government nor civil service in over 100 years. Three partitions with different legal systems had to be amalgamated. The land had been crisscrossed by advancing and retreating foreign armies. Railroads, bridges, homes, and factories were destroyed, and whatever was portable had been looted. The population was greatly reduced. Poles had served in German, Austrian, and Russian armies. Some 450 000 had been killed and 900 000 wounded.[187] An unknown number of civilians also died, and at least 800 000 people had been forced into Russia, never to return.

There was excitement and optimism in the Polish people, but receiving the Siberian children was an additional challenge. The children were dismayed by their poor reception and to discover their poor living conditions. Most children did not blame Poland; they acknowledged theirs was a rebuilding nation and were optimistic of a bright future. The recollections of several children follow.

---

184 Wieslaw Theiss, personal letter to author, 2019.
185 Theiss, personal letter to author, 2019.
186 Matsumoto and Theiss, *Siberian Children*, 203.
187 Hetherington, *Unvanquished*, 337.

Henryk Sadowski arrived on the SS *Katori Maru* and, after some time in an orphanage, was reclaimed by his parents, who had made their way from Khilok in Siberia. In *Siberian Dreams*, he relates:

> No one was there to greet us except four people organized by Dr Jakobkiewicz. We lined up in a double row to walk to Gdansk where we got a half sandwich and coffee, taken to the train station and divided into several groups for various destinations. After the train trip we had to walk a long way until we arrived in front of a huge iron gate, inside we were told to sleep on rotten sawdust with no food or anything. It was the Bojanowo facility. We stayed a long time. There was nothing for us, we couldn't ask for anything, our Japanese baskets were taken away so we had no towels and we couldn't wash. We were taken from Bojanowo to Pniewy. We got used to a deprived life. One day during class there was a knock on the door, it was my parents! We hugged with such emotion that nobody could separate us. Mom and Dad were crying, I was crying, my sister too, and all the children in the class cried to see my joy.[188]

Halina Nowicka described her experience at another orphanage in *Siberian Dreams*:

> Poland was not ready to accept 800 children, it was unable to feed and house us. Poland was completely destroyed, devastated by Russian, Bolshevik, Austrian and German armies. It was simply awful, no food, nothing. I was in Mielzyn near Witkowo—a terrible place. There was a nice house nearby where Dominican nuns lived, we were in [uninsulated] huts. In winter it was too cold to sleep, children huddled around the stove. No bread except a small piece on Sunday, other days we got potatoes that were meant for pigs and a watery soup with some flour in it.[189]

---

188 Misiewicz, *Siberian Dreams*.
189 Misiewicz.

Caritas was insufficiently funded to care for the Siberian children in Poland, and nuns may have been loving but were not trained as teachers.[190] Some children were placed with craftsmen for training; others were placed on farms. Pawel Wojdak was one of the latter. Anna Bielkiewicz and Dr. Jozef Jakobkiewicz learned of the situation and took the issue up with the Department of Labour and Social Welfare. A better facility was arranged in Wejherowo near Gdansk, a building that had been a German Army hospital during World War I. The department transferred 400 children from orphanages to the new facility. Bielkiewicz and Jakobkiewicz became directly involved in their well-being and education, Jakobkiewicz as head of the school and Bielkiewicz in charge of the dormitories. One of the children said, "We were rescued a second time." In 1924, there were 331 children in kindergarten and primary school at Wejherowo, which implies about seventy were in secondary school. By arithmetic, some 170 children were placed on the land or with tradesmen.

Halina Nowicka described her transition to Wejherowo in *Siberian Dreams*:

> At Wejherowo I was diagnosed with trachoma and scabies and I had lice. I was bathed and received medical treatment. We had to be self-sufficient, there was no staff. Older girls were in charge of ten younger ones and assigned tasks. 'Girls who wants to scrub the stairs?' I was first to volunteer. It was same with the laundry. They sorted out who could read and write etc. Later I enrolled in Grade 6 in a regular school. Girls who were on duty in the kitchen brought meals to the dining room, we lived like sophisticated people. Dr Jakobkiewicz used to come to the dining room in the evening and asked who wanted to arrange a concert? We sat on the floor, lights turned off and he began to play, he told us about Chopin and Beethoven.[191]

Young Antonina Liro recounted her return to Poland as a "nightmare. We stayed in tents at first, in the morning there was ice under my bed."

---

190 Theiss, *Dzieci Syberyjskie*, 250.
191 Misiewicz, *Siberian Dreams*.

She goes on to describe Wejherowo (translated from "On the Meeting of Descendants of Siberian Children" and summarized):

> There were no adults, older girls cared for ten younger ones. Doctors from Gdansk came on the first night to assess our condition. We were always hungry but I wasn't sick. Some girls suffered from tuberculosis. They didn't want cod liver oil but the duty person was supposed to pour a spoonful into the soup. [In the early twentieth century cod liver oil was used as a treatment for tuberculosis.] When I was on duty, I put in four or five spoonfuls because I knew it was good for our health. Some girls didn't want to eat that soup. On Fridays for dinner there was herring straight from the barrel, and potatoes.

> There was a lake near Wejherowo where we used to go to swim. On the way there were farm fields and meadows where there were peas. Once I took a turnip and I was a hero, all the girls wanted a bite! Another time there was rhubarb on a cart. We didn't know what it was, but we took some and ate it.

> I was in the nursery at first and then kindergarten. I had to learn Polish because I spoke poorly. We studied outside. There was a beautiful avenue under the trees where we sat on benches. The birds distracted us but it was wonderful. I got in big trouble at school. We were meant to learn Polish but I translated into Russian to answer the question and then translated back into Polish.

> During school breaks Jakobkiewicz took us camping. We had a camp stove and stayed under the trees. No tents, we cut fir boughs, covered them with a waterproof sheet and that is where we slept. Soup was cooked on the stove. It was a great life. We collected mushrooms and made mushroom soup with noodles. We ate blueberries until our faces were black. People thought we were such poor children.

> In the morning there was a wake-up call, you had to get dressed and comb your hair. Although we had nothing to comb because we were shaved to the bare skin so as not to have lice. Then there was roll call around the quadrangle, according to classes. We hoisted the flag and sang the Japanese anthem. Next it

was breakfast, then school and then work, whatever you were assigned. Some had duty in the kitchen, others in the canteen or the laundry or the sewing room. I did nice needlework for slippers. Things that we made were sold in shops in the city, they sold well.

The school received a zloty a day for each child, for everything. It wasn't enough to feed and clothe us. When I was seven years old and in first grade, I wore a uniform. There was a green denim pleated skirt, a blouse, a yellow scarf and a large hat tied at the neck. I was proud to finally have the uniform. I was at Wejherowo for two years and I got to Grade 2.[192]

Kazimiera Gryszkus shared her account in a letter to Theiss (translated):

In the dormitory Anna Bielkiewicz assigned me with cleaning the rooms. I did so as a student, without any remuneration. Later the dormitory was taken over by the Kresowiaks. Mr. Zablocki assigned me to purchasing food that was kept in a storeroom. I took over that job from Zofia Tatarynowicz who was promoted to bookkeeper. I accounted to her for the money I used to purchase food. I had a salary of 55 zlotys a month.

Waclaw Danilewicz describes his arrival in Poland. After sailing from Japan on the *Atsuta Maru* to London, he came to Gdansk on the Baltalantik, from there to Warsaw. His description of life and education at Wejherowo is nearly idyllic. Training in sailing, swimming, and seamanship shows that Jakobkiewicz recognized the importance of Poland's new access to the Baltic Sea (translated from "On the Meeting of Descendants of Siberian Children"):

In Warsaw we were placed in barracks of the emigration type in very primitive conditions. We could not have imagined that we could be so disappointed in the homeland we missed so much. We wandered around various cities and hospitals. Finally Dr Jakobkiewicz collected the scattered children. He had found a suitable place for us in Wejherowo, a former psychiatric

---

192 Social Welfare Association Fukudenkai, "Descendants of Siberian Children," 43.

institution built by the Germans that also housed the deaf and mentally handicapped.

Our buildings were beautifully situated in a park with farm facilities and a garden. Wejherowo itself is located on the Reda River and was very nice, quiet and clean. The head of the department was Mrs. Maria Buglewska who came with us from Blagoveshchensk where she was Polish language teacher. She was very energetic and devoted to education of young people, we respected and trusted her. In Siberia she had lost her parents and lived very poorly, my parents had us take milk and other food to school for her every day.

At Wejherowo the children, about 300, were divided into groups according to age. Those under six were placed in Treblowka, an orphanage. For the older children Dr Jakobkiewicz based education on the scouting model. He organized Scout teams almost immediately. The day began with a wake-up call, gymnastics, singing a religious song and The Lord's Prayer. After these we ate breakfast and then to various schools such as preparatory (grades 1–4), craft and agricultural school or a teachers' seminar and apprenticeships in various trades. After school and homework and a short rest there was supper, evening roll call, evening prayers and singing of "God Save Poland" or "Bogurodzica" [Polish hymn, "Mother of God"] and then bed. We spent our holidays working on a farm with a large orchard and orangery next to the school. There were hiking trips in the countryside. We got badges for physical fitness, first aid and other things that were sewn onto our uniform sleeve. Your rank as a scout depended on how many badges you acquired so you wanted to progress. We attended services in the chapel every Sunday and holidays. A women's choir sang in Latin during mass.

In 1925 Dr. Jakobkiewicz organized a sea camp in Hel [town at the end of a thirty kilometre-long sand spit]. We were taught to distance swim, fitness and ocean rescue. We were taught sailing; we had our own yacht and sailboat. We were instructed by General Mariusz Zaruski. Physical education on land was taught by Major Bobrowski. Rhythmic exercises were led by the wife of the poet and novelist, Artur Gorski. In 1925 we performed a rhythmic show for the President of Poland, Stanislaw Wojciechowski in Gdynia.

Our Maritime Corps had a large lifeboat with oars and a sail with a crew of 14 scouts. We went on a cruise in the Gulf of Gdansk despite a squall. At first we rowed but the wind and waves were too strong and we raised the sails. We were struggling to maintain course and then we saw a ship coming toward us. It didn't see us, we might have been rammed. We broke the kerosene lamp, soaked rags in kerosene and lit it. Fortunately the ship saw our signal and changed course.

When I was 15 five of us were assigned to return a missing lifeboat. We set off for Hel [24 kilometres off shore from Gdansk] but a strong wind came up that began to take us toward open seas. We took to the oars but what we made by rowing we lost in drifting. We began to lose strength and decided to go back to Gdansk. It was night when we got to shore near the port. We were so tired we just lay on the beach, covered ourselves with the sail and hugged each other to stay warm because we were dressed only in scout uniforms. In the morning a German policeman asked us what we were doing. We showed him the certificate for our destination in Hel and he allowed us to continue.

On another occasion we went with Dr Jakobkiewicz in the large rowboat and decided to swim. A very large wave knocked (Alfons) Bogucki, the scout next to me, into the water. The sea was so strong we could not reach him, and it was carrying him away. Dr Jakobkiewicz shouted for some fishermen to help and we managed to get him to shore before he drowned. [Bogucki is listed on the second mission, rescued from Ulan-Ude.]

The sea camp developed courage and physical fitness. One of our members, Swiechowski and his friend Bochomold, became famous sailors. They sailed a yacht called the Dal to Canada. The boat is to be put on display in a museum.

Wejherowo had some deficiencies. There was never enough food and many children contracted tuberculosis. The entire Wojcik and Zielinski families died, also Albin Godlewski and

Jadykin [one of two boys]. The eldest of the Wojcik brothers stayed in America and graduated from a technical school in 1931.[193]

The list of children on the first mission shows five Wojcik children: three boys and two girls. There were five Zielinska girls and two Jadykin boys on the first mission. Albin Godlewski was on the second mission—a sad outcome to die within a few years in Poland, having survived so much. Psychological rehabilitation was necessary for some children. At meals, some took extra food to hide. They had to learn trust, altruism, and social skills.

During the partition of Poland, the country did not have port access to the Baltic Sea. The port of Gdansk and later development of Gdynia was enormously important for commercial activity and military security. The crossing of the Atlantic Ocean by three Poles in an 8.5-metre sailboat in 1933–1934 mentioned by Danilewicz was a famous event in Poland when the story was published in 1936. Andrzej Bohomolec, Jan Witkowski, and Jerzy Swiechowski navigated by the stars and a sextant. Their destination was the World's Fair in Chicago. The story was forgotten during the World War II, and after the war, Russia banned the book—as well as the sport of sailing because it was not considered an appropriate proletarian activity.[194] Bohomolec, leader of the sea voyage, lived an adventurous life eventually becoming a cattle rancher in Alberta. Surprisingly, the name Swiechowski mentioned by Danilewicz is not on the list of Siberian children.

In the mid-1920s, a combined vocational school and residence for Siberian children was built in Warsaw at the intersection of Niska and Okopowa streets. The five-storey building housed eighty students. Sixty percent of the building was funded by the Ministry of Labour and Social Welfare and forty percent by the Rescue Committee.[195] Waclaw Danilewicz attended the new facility and describes it below:

---

193 Social Welfare Association Fukudenkai, 49–51.

194 Hallie Cotnam, "Polish Seafaring Yarn Gets Canadian Reboot," *CBC*, February 24, 2020, https://www.cbc.ca/news/canada/ottawa/sailing-adventure-polish-hero-autobiography-translation-history-1.5449662.

195 Jadwiga Danilowska, *Echo of the Far East* 12 (1929): 25–27.

The Wejherowo school was closed once the school and residence were completed in Warsaw. The Marine Battalion of the Polish army took over the Wejherowo facility, they were part of the September campaign against Germany in 1939. The Niska dormitory had three floors, living conditions were different there. Near the dormitory there was a tannery which emitted terrible fumes. The street was ugly, full of Jewish shops with the Daughters of Corinth [prostitutes?] who accosted us boys. Unfortunately the Niska building was built on peat and there was fear it might collapse, so it was torn down. The Siberian children, boys and girls were scattered to various boarding schools and so lost contact with each other. My youngest brother Witold and I were placed in a neoclassical school that was some distance away, we had to walk an hour because no one had money for a tram.[196]

The Siberian children at Wejherowo learned much more than to read and write. They were taught self-reliance, responsibility, and how to manage one's affairs. The morning flag-raising ceremony and other activities were designed to instill patriotism. *Echo of the Far East*, published until 1929, described how they learned all aspects of Polish arts, history, and culture. Many Siberian children became young Poles equipped to make their own way in life: educated, self-confident, patriotic, and imbued with Polish culture. They were ready to contribute to the new Poland, fulfilling the dreams of their parents and the Polish Rescue Committee.

Wejherowo students did not forget Japan. Japanese cultural evenings were held in full costume to honour the nation that rescued them from Siberia and gave them a chance at life in Poland.

---

196 Social Welfare Association Fukudenkai, "Descendants of Siberian Children," 51.

22.

Wejherowo in 2019

The inspiring accounts of the Siberian children at Wejherowo published in *Echo of the Far East* gave an impression that *all* the Siberian children were housed there. It was at odds with what I knew about Pawel Wojdak. Might he have been there and not spoken about it for some reason? To learn more about Wejherowo, I attended a meeting there of Siberian children's descendants in 2019.

The Wejherowo conference was marvellous; a dozen or more second and third generation descendants attended. Most were from Poland and did not speak English, but there was one from America and myself from Canada. Presentations, meals, and accommodation were all held in the same facilities, remodelled of course, that housed the Siberian children. Currently, Wejherowo serves as a school for special needs children, analogous to the function of Fukudenkai in Tokyo (photo 22.1). Malgorzata Wozniak, head of the school, welcomed us individually. Discussion with attendees and listening to presentations on the Siberian children was an emotional experience.

Photo 22.1. Wejherowo in 2019, now a school for special needs children; it had accommodated Siberian children in 1924.

Photo 22.2. Special needs student at Wejherowo School performing a samurai dance; cherry blossoms in the background symbolize Polish memories of Japan.

In attendance, there were Polish and Japanese university students and several Polish national politicians. Their participation showed both the importance of the event and that close ties between the two nations continues. At the conclusion of the presentations, students at the school performed several interpretative cultural dances. One boy conducted a samurai dance to honour guests from Japan and to demonstrate the continuing bond between Poland and Japan (photo 22.2). I met Teruo Matsumoto and Wieslaw Theiss from Poland, key researchers of the Siberian children, and Akinori Nishikawa from the Port of Humanity Tsuruga Museum. I enjoyed a discussion of the Siberian children with them over dinner, including the experiences of Pawel Wojdak (photo 22.3).

Photo 22.3. Discussing Siberian children with Akinori Nishikawa
(Port of Humanity Tsuruga Museum), Teruo Matsumoto (journalist),
and Wieslaw Theiss (professor emeritus)

As a result of the conference my increased understanding of the Siberian children comprised several elements:

- They were housed in orphanages while in America—this prompted a search of orphanages in Milwaukee and locating St. Joseph Orphanage.
- The names of orphanages in Poland where children were housed, and thereby their locations.
- Some children were placed on farms and did not attend Wejherowo, confirming Pawel Wojdak's experience.

Pawel Wojdak did not gain the level of education, nor the camaraderie and awareness of Polish culture as those children who attended Wejherowo. These were building blocks of Polish patriotism. One small comment at Wejherowo held special significance. Jozef Jakobkiewicz had such a special relationship with the children as a teacher and mentor that many called him "Father." That explained Pawel Wojdak's puzzling answer to my childhood question, "Who brought you to Japan?" and his reply, "My father." Now I understood: Jozef Jakobkiewicz was a father figure to the Siberian children—another boyhood mystery was solved.

Conversations during the conference with Anna Domaradzka, daughter of Leopold Kulesza from the first rescue mission and Lukasz Grabowski, great-grandson of Jan Jankowski (second rescue mission), were bonding and fruitful. The connection with Anna led to her sharing the story of her father. Lukasz Grabowski explained he only learned of his great-grandfather's experience in Siberia and Japan when he announced doing an internship in Japan. The story was nearly lost in just three generations. This is reminiscent to Slawomir Samardakiewicz's grandfather confiding his experience in Japan so late in his life. Jan Jankowski, Jan Samardakiewicz, and Pawel Wojdak all had a great aversion to bringing painful memories to the surface.

An interview with Lukasz Grabowski is available on the Siberian Children website.[197] Lukasz related to me a sad story about his great-grandfather. He was in the Polish Army in World War II and was captured. The

---

197 Social Welfare Corporation Fukudenkai, "Lukasz Grabowski," October 25, 2020, https://siberianchildren.pl/en/interview-lukasz-grabowski-en/

prisoners were told if anyone escaped, in reprisal, one of them would be shot. One did escape and Lukasz great-grandfather, then thirty-one years old, was randomly selected for execution. Such is the randomness of life and death—his boyhood good fortune to escape Blagoveshchensk, Siberia, only to meet an arbitrary death in Poland. Does it matter whether the bullet came from a Russian or German gun?

The Wejherowo conference confirmed to me that Pawel Wojdak did not attend the care facility there. Like all the Siberian children, he was in an orphanage for a period of time, but instead of Wejherowo, he was placed on a farm. Limited capacity of Wejherowo and tight funding probably precluded Jozef Jakobkiewicz and Anna Bielkiewicz from seeking out children who were on farms. No record has been found of these children on to which farms they were placed. Pawel Wojdak was ten years old in 1922, the year he came to Poland; perhaps he was twelve when he went to live on a farm.

For several years, the Siberian children were in groups: in Japan, on long sea voyages, in America, and in care homes in Poland. But steadily their lives diverged as they grew up and made their own way as individuals. Some adjusted readily to changing conditions, especially older children who had been grounded by a strong family before leaving Siberia and were supported by their siblings. This was the situation for the Danilewicz, Gryszkus, and Kulesza children. Young children from fragmented families and without siblings were at risk of being overwhelmed, their minds provoked toward dark and difficult places. This was the situation for Antonina Liro and Pawel Wojdak.

23.

Poland Between World Wars

Poland existed as a truly independent nation for only twenty years from 1919–1939, a period sandwiched between two world wars. Pawel Wojdak grew from a boy to a twenty-seven-year-old man during that time when his life was influenced by war again. There is no information about his orphanage; he did not even to tell me its name. The farm where he lived belonged to a German-Polish couple named Ernest and Marta Schulz. My father slept in the barn and had shoes only in winter, suggesting it was a small and poor farm. He did not mention any other children on the Schulz farm. If the Schulz family had children, perhaps they were killed or displaced during World War I, which may be the reason Ernest and Marta needed help on their farm. My father's terse description of life there was devoid of affection; he certainly was not adopted, even "fostered" seems generous. He was taken in as a labourer for farmwork.

Pawel Wojdak accompanied the Schulz on trips to Breslau, probably to sell farm produce, perhaps to visit friends or relations. Breslau was in Germany at that time, but after settlement of World War II, the border was moved over 100 kilometres west so that Breslau, now called Wroclaw, lies in Poland. Over a long history, the city has at times been in Bohemia, Hungary, the Habsburg monarchy of Austria, Prussia/Germany, and Poland. Logically, the Schulz farm lay near the German border in the 1920s for there to be regular trips to Breslau. Extending this logic another step: perhaps Pawel Wojdak was at the Bojanowo orphanage because it lay only a few kilometres from the German border, much closer than the other orphanages as shown on map 3. His childhood account of a German friend at school who shared his food augments the hypothesis he lived in an ethnically mixed area near the border. My father told me that Polish and German people were friendly toward each other prior to World War II and that animosity was induced by propaganda.

Pawel Wojdak shared with me no more about his early adult years in Poland than he had about his youth in Siberia and Japan. He became a blacksmith, a common trade at the time, one who forges and shapes metal to make tools, agricultural implements and gates, and, in wartime, armour and weapons. He told me nothing about when he left the Schulz farm or what blacksmith work he performed. So many questions were left unasked! Pawel Wojdak was not religious; he never attended a church or discussed faith. Once when pressed about his feelings, he said the Church was for the rich and did not genuinely care about the poor. He saw himself as an outsider who did not belong—did these feelings derive from his early life in Church-administered orphanages? Most Polish people are devout Catholics, so Pawel Wojdak's alienation from the Church was unusual.

Once again, I turn to the experiences of other Siberian children to enhance the account of their life in Poland, their challenges with war and the shifting political climate, and their careers. First, Jan Samardakiewicz had a more positive relationship with the Church than Pawel Wojdak, as related by Slawomir Samardakiewicz. It is a continuation of his interview on the Siberian Children website, and is summarized:

> Jan and Antoni Samardakiewicz were in the Broniszewicz orphanage. Little is known about their lives there, except that their legal guardian was Father Walenty Dymek, also a director of Caritas and a future archbishop. Jan was placed on a farm in Szelag Poznan where he practiced gardening. Later, he married

and had six children. He hoped to establish his own gardening business, but his savings were essentially lost when the Polish zloty was re-dominated in 1950 in a ratio of 100:3. Instead, Jan eventually was employed by the Poznan city park service as a gardener.

Poznan hosts a famous annual fair, the largest in Poland and one of the largest in Europe. Slawomir relates that in the 1960s visiting Japanese and Chinese delegations were surprised by his grandfather's ability to speak to them in their language. Slawomir concludes, "I must add here that my grandfather spoke beautiful Polish all his life. There was no influence from the accent of other languages that he learned in his childhood, such as Russian. Despite the strong pressure from Russian authorities which aimed at denationalization of Poles in Siberia, he was not Russified. It is because his family had a patriotism for Poland."[198]

Halina Nowicka described her life:

> When Wejherowo closed I left with nothing more than a towel and a blanket. I was obsessed with learning and finished school in 1932. Jobs were hard to find but I got a position on the census. After that I worked in the Statistics office until 1939. There were many left-wing people there and I started to become a communist. In 1940 I was in Lwow, life was very difficult. One morning I got up at 2 am to stand in line in the freezing cold. I was about to get bread when a man tried to push me out of line. I bit his hand very hard. It was as though the years 1922 to 1939 had not happened. Music, culture—there was none. But Siberian children were tough.[199]

Antonina Liro described the considerable difficulties in her life. Recall that she was the six-year-old girl who became temporarily mute after being separated from her family, a condition called traumatic mutism. She was reunited with her family in Poland, but after years apart, they are virtual strangers. Her account gives insight into the psychological issues of one

---

198 Social Welfare Corporation Fukudenkai, "Interview with Slawomir Samardakiewicz."
199 Theiss, *Dzieci Syberyjskie*, 358, 364–366.

Siberian child (again, summarized translation of her account in "On the Meeting of Descendants of Siberian Children"):

> My father and mother came from Russia. My father found Nela and Anna [Antonina's sisters] but for a time couldn't find me. I was happy not to be found. When my parents came to Wejherowo, I didn't remember father at all, I could have passed him on the street. When they said, "This is your mother," I shrugged and turned away. I only recognized Anna. Apparently my sister Halina died of diphtheria in Manchuria while the train was delayed on the way to Vladivostok. Mother took her and was walking to find a doctor but she died on the way and was buried near the railroad tracks. My brother Franus got a splinter in his leg and a big ulcer developed. Father operated with a razor but it wasn't disinfected and Franus died.
>
> Father arranged for Polish passports so they were able to come to Poland, but it was hard for people who came from Russia. We were in a warehouse, everyone slept on bunks separated by a curtain. Life was terrible, there were always quarrels. My father didn't work for three years because he couldn't speak Polish. And I didn't understand him because he didn't speak Russian.
>
> It took me a long time to learn Polish, I couldn't understand anyone and no one could understand me. It was scary living like that in a big city. I ran away back to Wejherowo but I couldn't stay there because my parents had taken me out. We lived on benefits and food for the poor. I spent the whole winter in my school uniform, a skirt and knee-high stockings. My legs were blue when it was 26 degrees below freezing.
>
> After a few months we were moved to another building where we had a place for ourselves and proper beds. Later father got us an apartment, it was also just one room and a kitchen and there was no bathroom. My sisters were not nice to me, they called me a foundling, a stray. Anna said I was eating their food. So if Anna didn't give permission I didn't touch the food. I went out and walked the streets. It's strange, people say that blood ties but that isn't true, it all depends on the atmosphere at home.

Life got better when my father found a job and my sisters began earning money too. My teacher's brother was a legionnaire buried in the military cemetery. We lived close to the cemetery and my teacher paid me to water flowers at his grave. I earned enough to buy new clothes, even new shoes. Soon after I moved out of the house, I couldn't stand it.

There was a dormitory at the corner of Niska Street, I didn't know some of the Wejherowo children were living there. I attended a trade school and was walking there one day when my friends from Wejherowo recognized me. They called my name, ran out and dragged me inside. They said, "Where are you hiding? We were looking for you!"

During the War I worked in a tractor factory near Warsaw. I operated a metal lathe. The German labour office put me on a list to work in Germany so I had to hide. There was a German policeman waiting in front of my apartment. I found out one of the Siberian children worked in the labour office and he helped me evade the authorities so I wasn't sent away.

In difficult times I thought about Japan, I remembered they were so kind to us.[200]

Antonina Liro's account is puzzling but a discussion with her son and daughter gave some explanation. Our discussion took place at a gathering of descendants of Siberian children on September 26, 2023, in Warsaw. They related that their mother suffered from a speech impediment, accounting for her difficulty in communication, and that Antonina's father spoke only Ukrainian.

Antonina's account is also troubling and gives insight into the psychological issues of some Siberian children. It is plausible that she did not recognize her father in Wejherowo; he had been away from home extensively. But surely, she would know her mother. And her mother is not mentioned at all in her account of life in Warsaw. Did Antonina carry a deep animosity, causing her to "turn away from her mother and shrug," signifying "*I know who you are but you hurt me; I don't trust you, I won't love you.*" Antonina's

---

200 Social Welfare Association Fukudenkai, "Descendants of Siberian Children," 45.

relationship with her sister Anna was also difficult, with many questions there too.

Antonina roamed the city streets inadequately dressed and unable to communicate easily with people due to her poor command of Polish. She epitomized the psychologically damaged "wandering child" characterized by Wieslaw Theiss, as discussed in English by Aneta Boldyrew.[201] Wieslaw Theiss focused on Polish children after World War II, an entire generation of children who were forcibly separated from their parents to be educated, or more properly stated, indoctrinated in German or Russian culture so as to exterminate Polish culture and the intellectual elite.[202]

The life-outcome of the dispersed Danilewicz family after Wejherowo is told in the document, "On the Meeting of Descendants of Siberian Children."[203] There is a sharp contrast between the lives of the three Danilewicz siblings who came to Poland compared with their three married sisters who remained in communist Russia. The siblings in Poland were determined students who contributed substantially to their nation in their professional lives, despite disruptions by war and the arrival of communism. Their accomplishments and contributions not only to Poland but to humanity are notable and a credit to the Rescue Committee.

Waclaw Danilewicz graduated as a veterinarian in 1937. His research discovered how to eliminate tuberculosis from cattle. He learned the disease could be transmitted to people through cows' milk. His work was interrupted by military service during the war, and later, his veterinary clinic was expropriated to the benefit of a *Volksdeutsch*, who "was a Pole before the war." (The term "*Volksdeutsch*" is explained in the next chapter.) During the war, he assisted farmers and secretly supplied the Home Army with medical supplies. After the war, his research eradicated the cattle disease brucellosis, and he introduced artificial insemination to greatly reduce the effects of

---

201 Aneta Boldyrew, "Education and Socialization of Polish Children During World War II: Sources, Methods and the Areas of Activity of the Historians of Education," *Piotrkowski Zeszyty Historyczne* 14 (2013): 171.

202 Wieslaw Theiss, *Zniewolone Dziecinstwo: Socjalizacja w Skrajnych Warunkach Spoleczno-Politycznych* [*Enslaved Childhood: Socialization in Extreme Socio-Political Conditions*] (Warsaw: Zak Academic Publishing House, 1996).

203 Social Welfare Association Fukudenkai, "Descendants of Siberian Children," 53–56.

bovine trichomoniasis, a venereal disease of cattle that causes cows to abort their fetus.

Witold (Wincenty) Danilewicz graduated as a doctor in 1938 but was mobilized to the Polish Army in 1939. He was interned in Hungary and worked in the Budapest Hospital, where he and his wife helped many Jews escape to Canada. After the war, he worked in a refugee camp in Bavaria. Subsequently, Witold and Waclaw moved to a picturesque area near Gdansk, which they cherished from their time in Wejherowo. Witold became head of infectious diseases at the area hospital. He was an excellent diagnostician; people came from far and wide because of his expertise. To their amusement, Witold and Waclaw were sometimes confused; Witold was once called to assist in the birth of a heifer and Waclaw to attend to a sick woman.

Wilhelm, eldest of the Danilewicz brothers, graduated from agricultural school. He and his family lived in eastern Poland. After World War II, he applied to Soviet authorities to return to their pre-war home. To his great surprise, the official was a former co-resident of the Siberian Children Institute in Wejherowo, so his application was approved. He became head of cadastral mapping in Wroclaw.

Kunegunda Danilewicz, sister of the three boys, was seventeen years old when she came to Wejherowo. She became a pharmacist, but during the war, she was taken to Germany as a forced labourer. She died at forty-seven years of age; whether from disease or wartime maltreatment is unknown.

The three Danilewicz sisters left in Russia had troubled lives. Otylia, widowed in Siberia during the civil war, relocated from Blagoveshchensk to Leningrad in 1926. She and her daughter survived the siege of that city, since renamed as St. Petersburg. Otylia and her two sisters from Chelyabinsk returned alone to Latvia, their home before World War I. Their husbands had all been murdered by the NKVD. After a separation of thirty-four years, Waclaw Danilewicz was permitted to visit his sisters in Latvia, but their mother died without seeing any of her children after they left Siberia.

The lives of all Poles were devastated by World War II. The generation of the Siberian children were all young adults, beginning their careers and starting families, when war began again. The lives of Leopold Kulesza and his two sisters were greatly affected.[204] Leopold Kulesza enrolled at a horticultural school when he came to Poland in 1922 and, three years later, began work at the Urban Gardens in Katowice, a city in Silesia, close to Germany. Life became difficult for Poles in Silesia in the buildup to World War II; Katowice was predominantly German, but the surrounding area was mainly Polish. German agitation for reunification of all German-speaking people resulted in discrimination against Poles. Leopold Kulesza lost his job. He returned to his family home in Podlasie, in northeast Poland. He was drafted into the Polish Army in August 1939 and then became a German prisoner of war but escaped and returned home.

Leopold Kulesza joined the Polish Home Army in January 1942 and was given the operative name Echyl. He was a courier, carrying military documents and communications between Polish Home Army commanders until the end of the war. In 1947, he was pardoned for his involvement with the Polish Home Army in an amnesty by the communist Polish government. He worked at a railroad repair plant, unable to resume his career in horticulture. He and his wife had two children.

Lucja-Czeslawa Kulesza was seventeen years old when she arrived in Poland in 1922. She and her sister, Felicja, two years younger, entered teachers' college in Wejherowo. Lucja-Czeslawa was a primary school teacher until the outbreak of the war. In 1934, she married Witold Malukiewicz, an employee of Polish State Railways, and they lived in Torun. In December 1939, Witold was arrested by the Gestapo and taken to Berlin for interrogation; he was released but arrested again in 1941 and sent to the Mauthausen concentration camp, where he died a year later. Years after the war, Lucja-Czeslaw searched for any record of her husband but could find nothing.

After her husband's arrest, Lucja-Czeslawa went into hiding and taught school children in secret—a historic tradition of Polish women. In 1942, she was arrested by the Gestapo, badly beaten, and forced to work as a servant for a German family. Hard work and ill treatment made her very ill. After the war, in poor health, she returned to live with her family in northeast Poland.

---

204 Domaradzka, "Stories of Rescued Children."

In 1950, she became mayor of the city of Lapy, near Bialystok, and was active in charitable circles. She remarried and worked part-time in rural schools.

Less is known of Felicja. She married and lived in the Warsaw area. A positive note for the two sisters: they were able to keep in touch with Jozef Jakobkiewicz all their lives. Their contact was disrupted during the war but resumed afterward when he worked at a hospital. He had a sincere interest in the lives of his pupils.

Aleksander and Marcjanna Kulesza—parents of Leopold, Lucja, and Felicja—returned to Poland in the mid-1920s. Recall that Aleksander Kulesza was imprisoned for signing a letter to the new Polish government imploring help for beleaguered Poles in Siberia. He was sent from prison in Blagoveshchensk to the infamous Moscow Lubyanka prison. After the Polish-Soviet War with Russia, Aleksander was one of the 208 Poles who returned to their homeland via an exchange of prisoners of war. He and his wife returned to Poland in 1925 or 1926 with their youngest son, Stanislaw. He bent his knee to finally kiss Polish ground in elation. They made their way to Podlasie, where parents and children were finally reunited. After a few years of hard work, Aleksander and his two sons, Leopold and Stanislaw, bought a house and a plot of land in Lapy. Aleksander lived there until he died in 1968.

The Rescue Committee brought Polish children together in Siberia for a common purpose: to save their lives, get them to Poland, and preserve their culture from assimilation. The children came from diverse backgrounds and had travelled different paths. Many were descendants of political exiles, first or second generation. Others were children of Poles, seeking a better life in a frontier country with good farmland and well-paying jobs. Some children were old enough to understand what was happening; others were young and confused. Some had full knowledge of their parents, plus the comfort of several siblings, though that carried the weight of responsibility for the oldest child. Some barely knew their parents and were alone. But the Rescue Committee could not control events that affected the Siberian children in Poland.

24.

Deteriorating Polish-German Relations

When Pawel Wojdak came to Poland, he had met peoples from several nations. He would fear and distrust Russians, perhaps be ambivalent toward Chinese, be trusting and appreciative of Japanese, and like Americans because many were Polish immigrants not so different from himself and other Siberian children. He had no experience with German people; he would have no bias. Probably, he was in the Bojanowo orphanage, very close to the border between Poland and Germany, where there was overlap of German and Polish people with a complex history. Poznan and Silesia comprised the German-administered partition of Poland prior to World War I. After the war, the border between the two countries was determined by plebiscite and negotiation. The mixed population would have a range of feelings about the outcome, from satisfaction to resentment. Pawel Wojdak would have been ambivalent.

In rural areas, the border between Poland and Germany passed between villages, between farms, and between neighbours. When Pawel came to the Schulz farm, he no doubt lived in better conditions than the deprivation of the orphanage described by Henryk Sadowski; a farm grows crops and raises livestock. If the Schulzes were not loving, they were at least congenial. As Pawel grew up, he developed a positive relationship with Germans, learned their language, and was comfortable travelling to Breslau in Germany. But the resentment toward Poland felt by some Germans was enflamed by a new political element called Nazism in the 1930s. This change happened first in the cities of Silesia and Poznan, where people of German descent outnumbered those of Polish descent, as shown by Leopold Kulesza losing his job in Katowice. A change in attitude developed more slowly in rural areas, where Poles predominated, and perhaps because farming communities are more stable than city peoples, and farmers often need to cooperate with tasks.

Photo 24.1. German recruitment poster for Polish farmworkers. The caption reads, "Let's go for farmwork in Germany! Report immediately to your mayor."

In the 1930s, Poles were recruited for farmwork in Germany.[205] They were induced by a Germany that was shown in a recruitment poster to be rosy and prosperous (see photo 24.1). Germany needed foreign farmworkers

---

205 Wikipedia, s.v. "Forced Labour under German Rule during World War II," last modified October 29, 2023, https://en.wikipedia.org/wiki/ Forced_labour_under_German_rule_during_World_War_II.

because its citizens were drawn to manufacturing industries and to the military. As explained by my mother years after my father died, Pawel Wojdak voluntarily went to work in Germany. It is likely that his residence and labour in Germany came to be involuntary—forced. As Nazi racist policies took hold, Poles were classed as subhuman, *Untermensch*.

During the war, ethnic Germans in Poland, about two percent of the population, were recruited for the Wehrmacht, but ethnic Poles were not recruited until Germany began losing the war. According to the British record, Pawel Wojdak was conscripted in January 1944. Until then Poles were used as slave labour; they were not worthy or trusted to be in the Wehrmacht.

My mother seemed unsurprised when I showed her the British record indicating my father had been in the German Army. When I was at the Wejherowo conference in 2019, I learned from one of the Polish politicians about a recent agreement to share wartime information. Accordingly, I requested Pawel Wojdak's military record from the German Federal Archives. The report arrived fifteen months later, in late 2020; it is brief and translated from German below:

> There are usually no personal files for members of the Army and Air Force. Therefore the information you are looking for must be found elsewhere.
>
> Woidak, Paul, born July 27th 1912 in Novo-Nikolaiwak (registered here in this spelling), can be found in the Wehrmacht dog tag lists and transfer reports:
>
> The requested person is registered for the first time on 7 March 1944 in the Grenadier Replacement Battalion 360 unit (Oels location)
>
> He had identification (dog tag) – 2913 – Stamm.Komp.Gren. Ers.Batl.360 (Federal archive signature: B 563/655612 page 299)
>
> The following information from the directories:
>
> Parent company Grenadier replacement – reported according to federal archive signature: Battalion 360 List from: B 563/65612 page 322.

March 8, 1944 – transfer to the Hunter Replacement Battalion 49

The last entry was made on February 22, 1944 as a member of 4th Company, Reserve Grenadier Battalion 375. There is an entry through Hunter Replacement Battalion 49

(Federal archive signature: B 563/80063 page 121).

Next of kin – wife, Sophie W. born Solarc, address Freyhan, Militsch

The dates are confusing because they are nonsequential, but the letter from German Archives concludes by explaining the exact dates of transfers could be recorded up to three months before or after the actual date. For deployment and operational information for Wehrmacht units, they advise making a separate inquiry to other agencies or searches of public sources.

Pawel Wojdak's name and birthplace are modified to suit German phonetics, and his first name is shown as Paul (not Pawel). Interestingly, he had acquired a birthdate of July 27, 1912. Because his birthdate was unknown at St. Joseph Orphanage, the date in the German records can only have been assigned at some point in Poland. There is no chance his actual birthdate could be determined. Eventually, every government bureaucracy or military requires a birthdate; it is part of a person's identity.

Learning Pawel Wojdak was married was not a complete surprise to me. The maiden name of his spouse, Sophie (Zofia in Polish), is unusual as written because "Solarc" is not Polish or German. However, Solarz is a common Polish name, and to produce the same sound in German, it would be written as Solarc, a transliteration. The box of photographs that my mother and I chatted about, one Sunday afternoon in my boyhood, contained an unlabelled image of a young woman that she would skip over. Sensing it was important, I asked about it, and she said, "An old girlfriend of your father." Probably, it is a photo of Zofia Solarz.

The home address of Pawel and Zofia Wojdak was in Freyhan, a village in the *gmina* (district or county) of Militsch in Lower Silesia, different from the British record. Neither the British nor German records indicate there were any children. Lower Silesia was German territory prior to World War

II, but Freyhan was only one kilometre from the Polish border. After World War II, Lower Silesia was ceded to Poland, and the village and district were renamed Cieszkow and Milicz, respectively. It is a farming area sixty kilometres north of Wroclaw, formerly Breslau, the city Pawel Wojdak knew as a boy. The town of Oels is now Olesnica and is located between Wroclaw and Cieszkow.[206] Notably, there was a prison and a forced labour camp in Olesnica during World War II. Olesnica has an extensive Polish history.

The former Bojanowo orphanage is fifty kilometres west of Cieszkow and only five kilometres from where the German border lay in 1922. If Bojanowo was the orphanage where Pawel Wojdak was interned, as seems plausible, his life from 1922, when he came to Poland, until 1944, when he was conscripted into the German Army, was constrained to lie in a fifty-kilometre strip along the Polish-German border.

In September 2023, my wife and I travelled 320 kilometres across Poland from Lochow, where we searched for traces of my grandfather, to Cieskow, where I know my father lived as a young man, and Bojanowo, where he may have been placed as an orphan in 1922. At the Bojanowo town office, we were graciously given a book on the history of the community and given directions to a building where a Polish school was established in August 1921. The book explains that Bojanowo was strongly Germanized in 1918 because Poznan province had been ruled by Germany for 125 years. Transition to a Polish administration was difficult; armed conflict erupted between factions that did not end until February 1919 and Bojanowo was officially incorporated into an independent Poland on January 17, 1920. The population of Bojanowo decreased in the early 1920s due to emigration of German people; an influx of Polish people followed. Logically, this would include newly arrived Siberian children. The establishment of Polish schools was considered very important, after years of language and cultural suppression. The school, in a building dating from 1839, had an enrolment in 1922–23 of 154 students, although the building did not have electricity until 1927.[207]

---

206 Wikipedia, s.v. "Olesnica," last modified February 9, 2023, https://en.wikipedia.org/wiki/Ole%C5%9Bnica.

207 Stanislaw Jedras, "Miastro i Gmina Bojanowo," *Leszno*, 2005, 103.

*Photo 24.2. Bojanowo school attended by Siberian children
from 1922, perhaps including Pawel Wojdak*

The historical account does not mention a Bojanowo orphanage but a Catholic church is located nearby. Presumably, the Siberian children were housed in the vicinity. Wieslaw Theiss described the difficult living conditions encountered by the Siberian children in an address to the Descendants in Warsaw on September 26, 2023. Theiss states, "the situation was particularly dramatic at the facility in Bojanowo, simply referred to as prison by the children."[208] On December 23, 1922, forty-three children were transferred by the Grey Ursuline nuns from Bojanowo to Pniewy (refer to Map 4), where they lived under far better conditions.

I cannot know with any certainty if my father was at Bojanowo, but I am more certain he was not at Pniewy. My reasoning is that there is a record of Ernst and Marta Schulz, my father's foster parents, in Milicz, a town south

---

208 Wieslaw Theiss, "Siberian Children – Two Meetings," speaking notes of an address in Warsaw, September 26, 2023.

of Cieszkow, in Germany. Historian Karol Suchocki employed an online database to find:

| 1894 | 2 | Ernst Gottlieb August | Schulz | Ernst, Dorothea Liersch | Margarethe Ella Elise | Finger | Fritz, Marie Kuckol | Milicz-Militsch (garn.) (ewang.) |

Marriage record of Ernst and Margarethe Schulz from geneteka.pl.
Ernst and Dorothea were parents of Ernst; Fritz and Marie Finger were
parents of Margarethe. They were married in the evangelical garrison church
in Militsch, 13 km south of Cieszkow.

Ernst and Marta were married in 1894. At that time, the whole area was German, the provinces of Silesia and Posen (Poznan to Poles). Probably after 1918 there was an exodus of German people from the new Polish territory of Poznan, as occurred in Bojanowo. However, farmers, tied to their land, would be less likely to move. I assume the Schulz farm lay in Poland because I cannot imagine a Polish child being placed on a farm on the German side of the border. The Schulz marriage in 1894 implies they were aged between fifty and sixty in the 1920s and, if childless as a result of World War I, they might apply for a foster child.

My father said the Schulz were a German-Polish couple. But both their names are German, not Polish. This could contribute to Pawel Wojdak gradually losing his Polish culture and becoming partially Germanized.

Some one million foreign volunteers and conscripts of at least seventeen nations served in the German Army during World War II.[209] Estimates of the number of Poles who served in the Wehrmacht range from 250 000 to 500 000.[210] Some 50 000 Poles formerly enlisted by the Germany Army served later in the Polish Armed Forces in the West. They either defected or were freed from prisoner-of-war camps.

"*Volksdeutsch*" was a term coined by Adolf Hitler to mean the German people or race, regardless of citizenship.[211] His rationale for aggression was

---

209 Wikipedia, s.v. "Wehrmacht Foreign Volunteers and Conscripts," last modified October 17, 2023, https://en.wikipedia.org/wiki/Wehrmacht_foreign_volunteers_and_conscripts.

210 Wikipedia, s.v. "Poles in the Wehrmacht," last modified July 20, 2023, https://en.wikipedia.org/wiki/Poles_in_the_Wehrmacht.

211 Wikipedia, s.v. "Volksdeutsche," last modified October 31, 2023, https://en.wikipedia.org/wiki/Volksdeutsche.

all German people, the whole German race, should be in one nation. This was the pretext for Nazi seizure of the Sudetenland in 1938, a Germanic area in Czechoslovakia. That action was not opposed by other European powers, an appeasement that emboldened more aggression.

An estimated ten million *Volksdeutsche* resided in Poland, Lithuania, Ukraine, and Russia. The Nazi goal was to give them German citizenship and to elevate them to power over native populations. For Poland, the roots of this policy lie in earlier history. During the partition of western Poland in the 1800s, Prussia encouraged colonization by German people in Poznan (called Posen by Germans). After World War I, when Poland was reborn as an independent country, the German people in Poznan became Polish citizens. The Nazis alleged there was discrimination of German minorities. This was Nazi propaganda to build a "fifth column" in Poland and elsewhere in Eastern Europe. Leopold Kulesza experienced the consequence of alleged discrimination when he lost his horticulture position in Katowice.

After the invasion and occupation of Poland in 1939, *Volksdeutsche* in western Poland, called *Warthegau* by Nazi Germany,[212] were compelled to register on the *Deutsch Volksliste* (German People's List). There were four categories:

- persons of German descent committed to the Reich before 1939
- persons of German descent who had remained passive
- persons of German descent who were partly "Polonized" by marrying a Polish partner or through working relationships
- persons of German descent who were "Polonized" but supported "Germanization"

The provinces of Poznan and Silesia of western Poland contained 510,000 *Volksdeutsche*, whose names were on the *Deutsch Volksliste*. Poles in Poznan and Silesia were listed as German citizens in 1939 and subject to conscription into the armed services. During the war, *Volksdeutsche* were treated by other Poles with contempt, and after the war, the term was synonymous with "traitor." *Volksdeutsche* benefited from the expropriation of

---

212 Wikipedia, s.v. "Warthegau," last modified September 28, 2023, https://en.wikipedia.org/wiki/Reichsgau_Wartheland.

Polish property and businesses, as demonstrated by Waclaw Danilewicz's loss of his veterinarian practice.

Pawel Wojdak was associated with Germans in Poland and, in Germany, most likely had become Germanized before the war, but did that make him *Volksdeutsch*? Exploring for an answer to the question, we can consider an analogous situation today. Some Canadians are drawn to America for employment, such as nurses, or for seasonal residence, both requiring a "green card." They come to own property and other assets, hold bank accounts, and obtain medical services. They become friends with Americans and can be said to be "Americanized," but they consider themselves to remain fully Canadian. Poles who worked in Germany in the 1930s, like Pawel Wojdak, likely felt they were still fully Polish.

Yet there is a fine line. The foreign resident, be it a Canadian in 2023 or a Pole in 1933, might say they do not agree with or participate in politics, but can it be avoided? In 1970, I considered going to graduate school in the United States, but I was deterred from doing so. There were several reasons, but one of them was the war in Vietnam and the knowledge that American students were being drafted into the armed services. I could not be drafted under US law at that time, but politicians can change laws, as happened in Nazi Germany. Voluntary guest workers, or *gastarbeiter* in Germany, constituted a small proportion during the war as far greater numbers of forced labourers were brought to Germany from conquered nations.

From pre-war to early war years, Pawel Wojdak would have witnessed a steady increase in aggressive German militarism, violence against Jews, and the mistreatment of fellow Poles and other Eastern European Slavic people. There was an abrupt escalation from guest workers to forced labourers when the first countries were overrun. Polish forced workers were forced to display a large *P* on their clothes and were badly treated. Some five million Poles were forced into slave labour in Germany to keep war industries going. It is likely that Pawel and Zofia Wojdak were among them. Pawel was conscripted, but what became of Zofia? Pawel Wojdak would have felt his friendship with Germans was betrayed and confused. Probably, he was ashamed or guilty of having been wrong about Germans.

An incident from my boyhood gives insight into how Pawel Wojdak was affected. I was about fourteen years old when two of my schoolmates joined cadets. Jim joined the Sea Cadets and Frank, a close friend that my parents knew, joined the Air Cadets. My mother was shocked, but my father was devastated. My mother felt the purpose of cadets was to attune young people to militarism and that was too reminiscent of the Nazi Youth in pre-war Germany. My father concurred but took it to a deeper level: he saw cadets as the beginning of shaping the minds of young boys to begin their indoctrination.

Basic facts of the British and German army records are in agreement for Pawel Wojdak. His pre-war domestic history is more detailed in the German record; his military history is more detailed in the British record. He was conscripted into the German Army on January 26, 1944, and deployed to Italy on March 7, 1944, but there is no deployment location of either Grenadier Battalion 360 or Hunter Battalion 49.

Grenadier, Volksgrenadier,[213] or Panzergrenadier[214] were Wehrmacht Army divisions that combined infantry and armoured personnel carriers and tanks. They were structured for defensive battles necessitated by setbacks on the Eastern, Western, and Italian fronts. To cope with a shortage of manpower, Grenadier battalions were organized around small groups of veteran soldiers supplemented with hasty conscripts. By the date of Pawel Wojdak's German Army service, he was a late conscript.

At the end of 1943, the tides of war had turned against Germany on the Eastern Front: the Russians were winning important battles, and the German Army was in stubborn retreat. On the Western Front, the Allied invasion of France was anticipated but still months away from happening. In the south, Germany had withdrawn from North Africa and a combined force of British, Canadian, and American forces took Sicily in 1943. This was followed by the Allied invasion of the toe of Italy in late 1943, but their drive northward was stalled by a series of strong German defensive lines. This is

---

213 Wikipedia, s.v. "Volksgrenadier," last modified May 31, 2023, https://en.wikipedia.org/wiki/Volksgrenadier.

214 Wikipedia, s.v. "Panzergrenadier," last modified August 30, 2023, https://en.wikipedia.org/wiki/Panzergrenadier.

where Pawel Wojdak was deployed and where he learned of a Polish Army in the opposing forces to which he would defect—the final step in ending his relationship with Germany.

Poland had been invaded and conquered by a combination of German and Russian armies in 1939. Where and how did the Polish Army in Italy come to exist?

25.

Polish II Corps

After Poland was defeated by the combined forces of Germany and Russia, the Polish government-in-exile was established in France and a new army of 80 000 men was formed. After France was defeated, the government-in-exile and armed forces relocated to Britain; the latter are referred to as the Polish Armed Forces in the West and comprised ground, sea, and air forces. [215]

The Polish Armed Forces in the East, the Polish II Corps, was formed by a more convoluted process. There are two outstanding accounts of how it reformed and its actions in World War II. Wladyslaw Anders was a colonel in a cavalry unit in 1939; he rebuilt and became commanding general of the Polish II Corps. His firsthand account of war action and behind-the-scenes politics is given in the book *An Army in Exile: The Story of the Second Polish Corps* published in 1949.[216] Norman Davies is a British historian and Oxford University professor emeritus who focused much of his career on Polish

215 Wikipedia, s.v. "Polish Armed Forces in the West," last modified August 29, 2023, https:// en.wikipedia.org/wiki/Polish_Armed_Forces_in_the_West

216 Wladyslaw Anders, *An Army in Exile: The Story of the Second Polish Corps* (London: MacMillan & Co. Ltd., 1949).

history. His treatise *Trail of Hope: The Anders Army, An Odyssey Across Three Continents* is not a dry tome; it is filled with personal stories and photographs.[217] These two works are the basis of the following synopsis.

Some 150 000 Polish soldiers were captured by Russia at the outset of World War II. In 1940, they were deported and scattered throughout Russia; their families were rounded up and sent with them. In the Kresy region of eastern Poland, all professionals, government officials, and landowners received the same treatment, bringing the total deportations to 1.5 million people. This carefully planned program constituted a cultural genocide to eradicate the Polish people, their institutions, and their traditions from the Kresy region. Under direct order from Joseph Stalin, 22 000 military officers, all those above the rank of sergeant, were executed in the Katyn Forest, a location now in Belarus. Stalin's intent was to eliminate the possibility of a revived Polish Army.

Colonel Wladyslaw Anders was the single Polish officer who survived Katyn by being imprisoned at the infamous Lubyanka Prison in Moscow. He was a remarkable person: brave, iron-willed, and a natural leader. Anders was questioned under torture but survived and retained his sanity, which was not the case for many other inmates of Lubyanka. Polish exiles were in forced labour camps from Arkhangelsk and Murmansk in the western Arctic, to Irkutsk and Krasnoyarsk in the Far East, and to Kazakhstan in the south.

Polish deportations were interrupted when Germany betrayed its alliance with Russia in 1941. It invaded and advanced deep into Russia, whose army was vastly under-equipped. In exchange for a massive supply of war materials, the Western Allies requested Stalin to pardon and release the imprisoned Polish soldiers and their families. Why Stalin agreed is a mystery. Norman Davies suggests Stalin feared the repercussions of German discovery of the secret Katyn graves: the negative publicity could stop an alliance with the West. Vast numbers of exiled Poles had died already in Russia from deprivation and disease. The survivors were given no assistance from the Russian government; they had to make their own way to assembly points in

---

217 Davies, *Trail of Hope.*

southern Kazakhstan. Some rafted down rivers; many did not make it. They died en route or were absorbed into a polyglot of ethnicities in desolate regions of Russia.

Hundreds of thousands of Polish deportees were still alive in Russia in late 1941. General Anders was unable to evacuate them all. He gave priority to three groups; men and women of military age, their dependents, and thirdly, to orphans[218]. The rescue of orphans from Kazakhstan in 1942 is analogous to the rescue of Siberian children twenty years earlier from Siberia. A total of 114 500 men women and children were transported across the Caspian Sea in the spring of 1942, less than ten percent of the 1.5 million Polish soldiers and civilians who were deported. They were evacuated on Russian ships from Krasnovodsk, in Kazakhstan, across the Caspian Sea to Pahlavi in British-controlled Persia, now Iran (refer to Map 1).

Davies states there were 78 000 military personnel, including army cadets and the Women's Auxiliary. They went eventually to British Palestine for training, where they recovered their health and fitness. They evolved to become the Polish II Corps. The balance of 36 500 women and children included 10 000 orphans went to refugee camps in India, British Africa, New Zealand and Mexico. One teenage girl, the only survivor of her family, remained in Persia. She married and settled there. Her story is told in a recent documentary film called *Madame*.[219]

The newly arrived Polish soldiers joined with the 3rd Carpathian Rifle Division in Egypt to form the Polish II Corps of the British Eighth Army. Informally, they were the Polish Army. They were transferred to Italy in February 1944, almost coincidentally with Pawel Wojdak's conscription into the German Army and deployment to Italy.

---

218 Norman Davies, *The Odyssey of the Anders Army, 1941-1946*, Polish Cultural Institute in London, 2020, https://www.youtube.com/watch?v=bXM38FI2VpQ

219 Narges Kharghani, *Madame: One of the Last Polish Refugees in Iran*, documentary film, 2017, video, 70:00, (trailer).

26.

Pawel Wojdak Joins the Polish II Corps

Pawel Wojdak was in Italy by March 1944 but in the German Army. The Battle for Monte Cassino began in mid-January 1944 and lasted four months, until mid-May. From the description he told on numerous occasions, he participated in the Battle of Monte Cassino, but by his service dates, it can only have been on the German side. He spoke vividly about Monte Cassino, that one side used Red Cross ambulances to carry munitions to front-line troops, so the other side responded by shelling Red Cross vehicles. As a result, dead and badly wounded soldiers remained where they fell. In hindsight, he did not say which side began using Red Cross vehicles for ammunition and which side responded by attacking them. It was difficult for me to accept that my father was on the German side, in light of his account in my boyhood.

Monte Cassino was the major fortification of the Gustav Line, a German defensive alignment across the Italian peninsula.[220] The terrain is mountainous, rugged, and rocky, very difficult for mechanized equipment such

---

220 Wikipedia, s.v. "Battle of Monte Cassino," last modified October 31, 2023, https:// en.wikipedia.org/wiki/Battle_of_Monte_Cassino.

as tanks. Vegetation is sparse due to thin soil and provides little cover for ground troops. The 29th and 90th Panzergrenadier divisions are among those that participated at Monte Cassino and presumably included the 49th or 375 battalions in which Pawel Wojdak served. It took four major assaults by British, American, French, Indian, New Zealand, and Canadian troops to turn the tide; the scale of the confrontation was massive—a terrifying experience. The cliff-top monastery at Monte Cassino, established about 529 AD by Saint Benedict, overlooks the Liri Valley and controlled access to Rome. American bombing after the first failed assault destroyed the abbey because it was incorrectly thought to be a critical German observation post. The ruins were then utilized by the Germans (photo 26.1).

Photo 26.1. The Abbey of Monte Cassino after the battle in 1944

It was the Polish Army who finally captured Monte Cassino on May 16–18, 1944, as part of a 20-mile-wide Allied assault. The victory was their greatest military achievement of the war. The Polish war cemetery at Monte

Cassino holds the graves of 1 072 who died during those three days in May. Photo 26.2 is reproduced from Davies with permission. A great many more Allied and Wehrmacht soldiers died there during the full four months of the battle. The German Army formed a series of defensive lines in Northern Italy after the Gustav Line was broken by the Allies at Monte Cassino. The US 5th Army chose to celebrate the liberation of Rome instead of pursuing the retreating Germans. This gave the German Army time to build the Gothic Line, using 15 000 slave labourers.[221]

Photo 26.2. The rebuilt Abbey of Monte Cassino © Janusz Rosikon/Rosikon Press
'Trail of Hope' by Norman Davies, Osprey Publishing.
The Polish military cemetery is in the foreground; the dedication plaque reads,
"We Polish soldiers / For our freedom and yours / Have given our souls to God /
Our bodies to the soil of Italy / And our hearts to Poland."

Fighting on the Gothic Line took place from August 1944 to March 1945 and comprised a series of battles. The Battle of Rimini was the critical engagement on the Gothic Line, lasting from August 25 to September 26,

---

221 Wikipedia, s.v. "Gothic Line," last modified September 1, 2023, https://en.wikipedia.org/wiki/Gothic_Line.

1944.[222] The Allied assault was on the Adriatic coastal plain, where the Polish II Corps and 1st Canadian Corps faced the German 10th Army, including Panzer Grenadier divisions 26, 29, and 90. The Battle of Rimini was one of the hardest engaged by the British Eighth Army, comparable to El Alamein and Monte Cassino. Two days after the Battle of Rimini, on September 28, 1944, Pawel Wojdak was captured by the Allies. Whether he was alone or part of a group is unknown. "Captured" is a euphemism for defection and probably took place at Rimini.

At the beginning of the Italian campaign, General Anders was asked by British command how the Polish Army in Italy could be reinforced in the event of heavy casualties—where could they draw reserves? Anders replied that reinforcements would join from the front lines; he explained that all Poles who had been conscripted by force into the German Army would come across the front lines as soon as they learned Polish soldiers were there for the Allies.[223] The Polish Army numbered 50 000 when they arrived in Italy but swelled to more than 100 000 by 1945.[224] Thousands more joined the Allies in the spring of 1945 after the liberation of POW and civilian prison camps in western Germany. In September 1944, Pawel Wojdak was among the first Poles to "come across."

Pawel Wojdak would have been relieved to join fellow Poles in Anders Army but anxious. Until he was questioned and determined not to be a German agent, he would be under guard. Would he be accepted and trusted by other soldiers? Would he feel relief or guilt and perhaps second-guess his decision?

Soldiers who defected to the Polish Army routinely were given the identity tag of a fallen soldier so that he would be spared the punishment of a deserter in the event he should be captured by the German Army. The only accurate information on the tag was his blood type. That is the reason Pawel Wojdak had the identity tag for Konstanty Mlotek. An inquiry to British Military Defence for Mlotek's military record was declined because I was not

222 Wikipedia, s.v. "Battle of Rimini," last modified May 3, 2023, https://en.wikipedia.org/wiki/Battle_of_Rimini_(1944).

223 Anders, *An Army in Exile*, 152–154.

224 Davies, *Trail of Hope*, 514–516.

a relative. However, the office confirmed that Konstanty Mlotek was born 1917, in Wilno, and served in the 7th Rifle Battalion of the 3rd Carpathian Infantry Division, not coincidentally the same unit as Pawel Wojdak.

Normally, military identity tags are separated into two parts: one-half to be used to notify next of kin and the other half to remain with the body. Perhaps the Polish Army knew Mlotek's family had died in Siberia, another reason not to follow the normal procedure. Konstanty Mlotek of Wilno is likely one of 1 072 Poles buried at Monte Cassino or at Rimini. Taking his place in the ranks of the 3rd Carpathian Rifle Division enabled Pawel Wojdak to fit seamlessly into the Polish Army. He turned away from a society that persecuted Poles and was losing the war and joined an army of his countrymen, soldiers who wanted to defeat Germany, free Poland, and return home. Crossing over was also a plunge into the unknown. It came eight months after his conscription, possibly his first opportunity to defect. A person's actions do not always derive from a logical progression of facts. Emotion is important in shaping our motives and guiding our decisions. Is it possible to know Pawel Wojdak's emotions?

Pawel Wojdak's new comrades in the 7th Rifle Battalion of the 3rd Carpathian Division would have told him their experiences in Siberia and their journey through Persia and Palestine. They would also talk about Konstanty Mlotek; perhaps Mlotek came to Palestine directly from Poland, assisted by partisans in the Balkans. Italian partisans assisted the Allies during the Italian campaign;[225] they may have assisted Polish defectors in the dangerous crossing between opposing armies. My father may have adopted Konstanty Mlotek's history as his own. His motives were probably multiple: the imperative to "fit in" with fellow Polish soldiers in battle; a need to forget discrimination as an *Untermensch*; and the guilt of deserting a spouse.

My father told me a curious war story, an intriguing event. He said that on a routine patrol, he and another soldier exchanged places. The other soldier was shot and killed by a sniper. This may have happened as he said,

---

225 Wikipedia, s.v. "Italian Resistance Movement," last modified November 1, 2023, https:// en.wikipedia.org/wiki/Italian_resistance_movement.

but now I understand it to be an allegory for changing places with Konstanty Mlotek. If so, it was the closest he came to telling me the real story.

It is sadly ironic that two Polish exiles to Siberia who travelled vastly different paths changed places in yet another foreign land. It is reminiscent of Jozef Pilsudski, who said it is the struggle, win or lose, that defines us— one of Pilsudski's famous quotations, "To be defeated and not submit, is victory."[226] Konstanty Mlotek lost his life, but his cause was not lost: another Pole took his place.

After losing the Battle of Rimini, the German Army fell back a short distance to the Senio River.[227] Crossing the Senio was one of the last great hurdles for the Allies before entering the expansive Po River plain; it was stubbornly defended by elite German troops. Pawel Wojdak participated in this hard-fought action between January 2 and April 8, 1945.

---

226 Wikipedia, s.v. "Jozef Pilsudski," last modified October 13, 2022, https://en.wikiquote.org/wiki/J%C3%B3zef_Pi%C5%82sudski#.

227 Wikipedia, s.v. "Senio," last modified September 8, 2022, https://en.wikipedia.org/wiki/Senio.

27.

No Freedom in Poland for the Polish II Corps

Two events in late 1944 that occurred far from the battle grounds of Italy crushed the morale of the Polish Army: the first reconfirmed Russian duplicity; the second revealed that the Western Allies would not stand by Poland.

In anticipation of the arrival of the liberating Red Army, the Polish Home Army, *Armia Krajowa*, rose against the German occupiers in Warsaw.[228] Instead of supporting the battle, the Russian Army stopped its advance thirty kilometres outside the city for two months. Pleas for assistance were ignored, allowing the Nazi Army to kill 16 000 resistance fighters and slaughter 150 000 to 200 000 civilians in public executions. It was the largest military effort undertaken by any national resistance during the War. Russia deliberately halted its forces, allowing Polish resistance to be crushed and the city of Warsaw to be destroyed. General Anders and his men knew the Russians to be treacherous, but in 1944, they were meant to be allies—yet another Russian act of bad faith left them disappointed and angry.

228 Wikipedia, s.v. "Warsaw Uprising," last modified September 10, 2023. https://en.wikipedia. org/wiki/Warsaw_Uprising.

The second event shocked the Polish Army; they were disappointed with their Western Allies, adding to their outrage. There was a secret agreement between Winston Churchill of Britain, Franklin Roosevelt of the United States, and Jozef Stalin of Russia about the post-war borders of Europe. Poland, France, and other nations were excluded from negotiations, and their interests were marginalized.[229] The secret deal was struck in November 1944 at a meeting between the Big Three, as they came to be known, and was made public in February 1945, at a conference in Yalta, a city on the Crimean Peninsula of the Black Sea. The eastern boundary of Poland would be the denounced Curzon Line. Poland was to gain territory in the west at the expense of Germany, including Silesia, where Pawel Wojdak lived in 1939.

The Kresy region that was to be excluded in the new map of Poland was home to most soldiers in the Polish Army, those deported to Russia in 1940; the 5th Kresowa Infantry Division of the Polish Army was named for the Kresy region. New lands in the west were poor compensation to these men faced with the loss of their homes, farms, and communities. Pawel Wojdak was not from Kresy, but he understood very well the harshness and suffering of Poles in Siberia. He probably confided some of his own experience there. If he did not fully understand the situation as a boy, other Siberian children would have explained that Russia was the cause of their misery.

General Anders met with Winston Churchill between the secret agreement in 1944 and the public disclosure in 1945 to express his disappointment and objections. Churchill assured Anders to "trust Great Britain who will never abandon you" and was not dissuaded; the agreement had been made. The entire conversation between Churchill and Anders was documented by Anders's secretary.[230] Anders understood Stalin better than Churchill and warned him that Russia, after the war, would maintain its armed forces of six million men and 70 000 aircraft, and it would look to expand further into Europe and threaten the West. Churchill rejected Anders's prediction, but

---

229 Wikipedia, s.v. "Yalta Conference," last modified September 9, 2023, https://en.wikipedia.org/wiki/Yalta_Conference.

230 Anders, *An Army in Exile*, 209–214.

it proved to be accurate: Russia maintained a strong military and the "arms race" became a central issue of the Cold War.

After Germany's unconditional surrender, the Yalta agreement was formalized at the Potsdam conference in Russian-occupied Germany.[231] The participants were Joseph Stalin for Russia, Winston Churchill for the United Kingdom, Harry Truman for the USA, and their respective foreign ministers. In arriving at their agreement on post-war Europe, each of the Big Three had their own priorities.[232] The United States's prime interest was Russian support in the war against Japan, including Russian participation in an invasion of Japan. For Britain, it was a guarantee of free elections and democratic governments in Eastern Europe, Poland in particular. Russia's chief concern was a sphere of political influence in Eastern Europe to guard against any future invasion. As a corollary, Russia insisted it retain eastern Poland, which it invaded in 1939. The Big Three agreed to divide Germany into four sectors: one each for themselves, plus a French sector. That was the only concession made by Stalin at the combined insistence of America and Britain. The creation of a United Nations was contemplated; Russia agreed to participate based on a secret understanding of a voting formula with a veto power for permanent members of the Security Council. This ensured Russia could block unwanted decisions.

As to the outcome of the Big Three's priorities at Yalta, Russia did not enter the Pacific War, but that did not matter after two atomic bombs brought Japan's surrender. Despite not participating in the Pacific War, Russia acquired the southern half of Sakhalin Island from Japan. Russia scored a resounding victory at Yalta because the United States and Britain conceded to Russian domination of Eastern Europe. Stalin had no intention of keeping his promise of free elections. Churchill famously said, "Poor Neville Chamberlain believed he could trust Hitler. He was wrong. But I don't think I am wrong about Stalin."[233]

---

231 Wikipedia, s.v. "Potsdam Conference," last modified October 22, 2023, https://en.wikipedia.org/wiki/Potsdam_Conference.

232 Wikipedia, s.v. "Western Betrayal," last modified August 22, 2023, https://en.wikipedia.org/wiki/Western_betrayal.

233 Simon Berthon and Joanna Potts, *Warlords: An Extraordinary Re-creation of World War II Through the Eyes and Minds of Hitler, Churchill, Roosevelt, and Stalin* (Boston: Da Capo

In fact, Churchill was wrong. It would take forty-six years for the empire Stalin created to begin to crumble with the teardown of the Berlin Wall. Finally, in 1989, there was a parliamentary election in Poland that was not entirely democratic but was a crucial step to overthrow communism and re-establish democracy in Poland.

The Polish Army in Italy was devastated to learn Winston Churchill's promise to stand by Polish interests was hollow; they were disinclined to continue fighting. The war was not over, and why should they lose their lives when their homes were already consigned to their false ally, Russia? General Anders threatened to withdraw the Polish Army prior to the Battle for Bologna, but British and American frontline commanders persuaded Anders that Polish troops were required because they had none to replace them.[234] And Polish honour was on the line.

The Battle of Bologna began in early April 1945 with a major bombardment. Pawel Wojdak said there was an occasion when the American Air Force bombed the wrong side of a river, killing Polish soldiers. In fact, this happened at the Senio River before the assault on Bologna: thirty-eight Polish soldiers were killed by "friendly fire" in the aerial bombardment prior to the battle.[235] In the ensuing ground battle, American and British ground forces occupied the German flanks while the Polish 3rd Carpathian and 5th Kresowa divisions fought their way up the middle in a series of advances. The Polish flag was raised in the Bologna town hall, and the inhabitants welcomed the Poles as liberators. The Polish II Corps suffered 234 dead and 1,228 wounded out of 55 780 front line personnel. Later, in April, the Polish Army was withdrawn from the front line; only mop-up actions remained as the German Army was in complete disarray.

Pawel Wojdak had a dozen wartime photos, all unlabelled, and he is recognizable in only three of them. They were taken in Italy, probably after hostilities had concluded. In photo 27.1, he stands with two other soldiers in front of a disabled fighter plane on an airstrip. It is a distinctive pose of my

---

Press, 2007), 209.

234 Anders, *An Army in Exile*, 251–252.

235 Wikipedia, s.v. "Battle of Bologna," last modified September 28, 2023, https://en.wikipedia.org/wiki/Battle_of_Bologna.

father; he often presented a profile in photographs, not looking directly at the camera. The other two photos show Italian civilians; in one, he is with a group of children who are eating ice cream perhaps purchased by Polish soldiers from the nearby vendor. These are my earliest photos of him; he was thirty-three or thirty-four years old.

Poland helped win the war but lost their country. In retrospect, we can speculate the reason the British sided with Russia in several major policy decisions. The Communist Party of Great Britain was founded in 1920 and, at its peak, in 1943, had 60 000 members.[236] Its focus was on domestic labour confrontations, but its international policies aligned with those of Russia. It denounced Britain's participation in World War II until Germany invaded Russia. The infamous Cambridge Five espionage ring began their treasonous activities in the United Kingdom in 1934. Kim Philby, Guy Burgess, Donald Maclean, Anthony Blunt, and John Cairncross attended Cambridge University together. They became convinced that communism was the best political system, in particular to counter the fascism that was on the rise at the time. They were recruited by Russian agents and, during their careers in various departments of the British government, supplied some 15 000 secret documents to their Russian "handler." These spies would not have set British policy, but they are indicative of extensive communist sympathies that influenced decision-makers.

---

236 Wikipedia, s.v. "Communist Party of Great Britain," last modified October 29, 2023, https://en.wikipedia.org/wiki/Communist_Party_of_Great_Britain.

Photo 27.1. Private Pawel Wojdak on the right, in Italy, with fellow soldiers on an airfield with disabled aircraft

28.

The Polish Resettlement Corps

The Polish Armed Forces fought with the Allies throughout World War II. Two Polish fighter squadrons distinguished themselves in the crucial aerial Battle of Britain in 1940. The Polish I Corps was based in Scotland for defence of Britain in case of German invasion and later fought in Europe. The 3rd Carpathian Rifle Division fought in North Africa. The Polish II Corps was instrumental in the Italian campaign, breaking German resistance at Monte Cassino. The Polish resistance was more active and effective than any other German-occupied country in Europe. They disrupted German supply lines to the Eastern Front by damaging or destroying one-eighth of all rail transport and provided almost half of all reports to British intelligence from occupied Europe. Despite Poland's strong role, the Allies ceased to recognize the Polish government-in-exile based in London. Instead, late in the war, the Allies acquiesced to Russia by acknowledging the Polish Committee of National Liberation, a Russian puppet government.

In March 1945, very late in the war, Russian General Ivanov invited Polish politicians in London and leaders of the disbanded Polish Home Army to Warsaw to discuss the new Polish government in an open dialogue. With their personal safety assured, participants included the Polish deputy prime minister from London, three Cabinet ministers still in Poland, nine members of political parties, a translator, and General Okulicki, the last commander of the Home Army. Okulicki had been part of General Anders's staff and volunteered to be dropped by parachute behind the German lines to lead the Home Army in the Warsaw Uprising. All fifteen were not heard of again until May, when, after persistent British and US inquiries, Russia revealed they had been arrested and charged with diversionary activities against the Red Army. Their show-trial is known as the Trial of the Sixteen.[237] Okulicki compared the Gestapo and Russian NKVD: "In comparison with the NKVD, the Gestapo methods are child's play."[238]

The Polish Army numbered 50 000 when they arrived in Italy from the Middle East but swelled to more than 100 000 by 1945. The British and Polish governments urged all Poles to return to Poland, -- Polish soldiers, prisoners of war, and those freed from German forced labour camps. They were told it was their patriotic duty and they should follow the example of Stanislaw Mikolajczyk, former prime minister of the government-in-exile, who had returned from London to join the new government. Polish soldiers with direct experience of Communist Russian malevolence and those who had been deported to Kazakhstan or Siberia were not convinced. They felt quite literally that it was worth their lives to return to Poland. They knew of the disappearance of those who returned to Poland and would soon learn more about the Trial of the Sixteen. This included Pawel Wojdak. In addition, Poles who had lost their homeland by annexation of Kresy to Belarus, Ukraine, and Lithuania had nowhere to return.

After World War II, there were more than forty million people displaced from their home countries; about eleven million of them were in Germany. Forced labourers in Germany who were from Poland and elsewhere in Eastern Europe were fearful of returning to homelands controlled by Russia. They became "displaced persons," or DPs, an acronym that became a derogatory slur throughout the Western world. In addition to displaced people, the Allies expelled twelve million Germans from Silesia in Poland,

---

237 Wikipedia, s.v. "Trial of the Sixteen," last modified July 14, 2023, https://en.wikipedia.org/wiki/Trial_of_the_Sixteen.

238 Wikipedia, s.v. "Leopold Okulicki," last modified August 31, 2023, https://en.wikipedia.org/wiki/Leopold_Okulicki.

the Sudetenland in Czechoslovakia and Hungary, and resettled them in a Germany that was reduced in size. Their intent was to avoid German ethnicity becoming an issue again in Central and Eastern Europe. The relocation of some fifty million people took five years.

Faced with a vast majority of Poles refusing to return, Britain established the Polish Resettlement Corps (PRC) in May 1946.[239, 240] Pawel Wojdak was one of 120 000 soldiers who enlisted. The troops were ferried by ship from Italy, but the ship manifests are incomplete: one listing Pawel Wojdak was not located. Polish soldiers were effectively displaced persons—people without a country, but without the DP acronym. They were entitled to national health services and had a clear path to British citizenship. Over a two-year period, they were meant to adapt to life in England by receiving language and skills training to integrate into the workforce.

Pawel Wojdak enlisted in the PRC on October 25, 1946. Members of the 3rd Carpathian Rifles Division were assigned to the Hodgemoor and Pipers Wood Camp 170,[241] near Amersham in Buckinghamshire (Bucks) Country, forty-five kilometres northwest of London. In total, there were 265 camps in England, Scotland, and Wales. The soldiers were joined by wives and dependents from refugee camps in Africa and India, bringing the total to about 249 000 people. Most camps were in the countryside, comprised of Nissen huts equipped with electricity, heating stoves, and crude plumbing facilities. Schooling was needed for young children as well as adults, and hospital facilities for the long-term war injured. Small Polish communities sprung up throughout rural England, Scotland, and Wales. A Polish culture website describes life and challenges in the camps.[242]

---

239 Agata Blaszczyk, "The Resettlement of Polish Refugees after the Second World War," *Forced Migration Review* 54 (2017). https://www.fmreview.org/resettlement/blaszczyk.

240 Wikipedia, s.v. "Polish Resettlement Corps," last modified July 18, 2023, https://en.wikipedia.org/wiki/Polish_Resettlement_Corps.

241 "List of Polish Resettlement Camps 1946-1948," Kresy Family website, https://www.polishresettlementcampsintheuk.co.uk/PRC/PRC.htm

242 Juliette Bretan, "Shelter and Community: Polish Post-War Resettlement Camps in the United Kingdom," *Polish Culture*, October 24, 2020, https://culture.pl/en/article/shelter-community-polish-post-war-resettlement-camps-in-the-united-kingdom.

Pawel Wojdak was at Pipers Wood (photos 28.1 and 28.2). He spoke well of his commanding officer, a colonel whom he served as an orderly or "batman." Apparently, the colonel came from a prominent family and was an excellent musical whistler. My father described to me that many soldiers in the camp were amputees and how remarkable it was to see a row of prostheses hung on hooks in the shower room. Today, the A413 Highway passes through the site of the Pipers Wood camp; not a trace remains.

Photos 28.1 and 28.2. Pawel Wojdak in the Polish Resettlement Corps at Pipers Wood Camp, as batman (orderly) he would deliver communications for the commanding officer by motorcycle

Pawel Wojdak was discharged on October 25, 1948, exactly two years after enlisting; his certificate of enlistment in 3rd Carpathian Rifle Division, 7th Battalion, is shown in photo 28.3. The road from Pipers Wood joins the road from Shardeloes in Amersham. During Pawel Wojdak's stay at Pipers Wood, he met a young woman from Amsterdam, perhaps walking on the road or at a social event in the town. Maria (Ricky) Versteeg worked as an attendant at Shardeloes Hospital, barely a kilometre across farm fields from

Pipers Wood. Ricky came to England in late 1946 or early 1947 to escape memories of famine and relationship breakdown caused by the war.

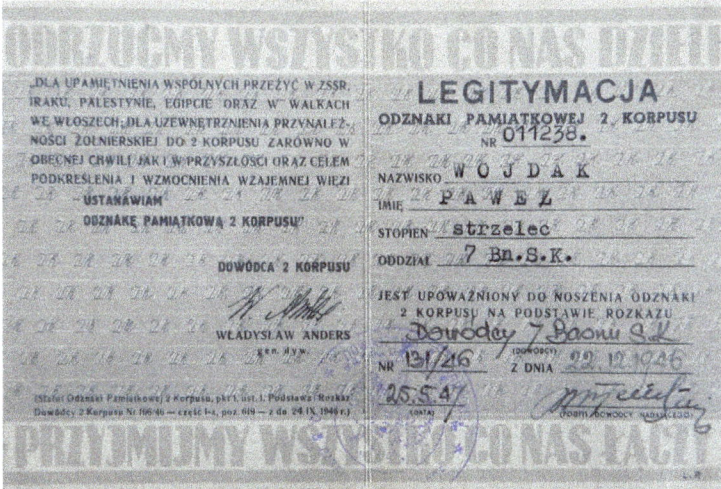

Photos 28.3 and 28.4. Certificates confirming Rifleman Pawel Wojdak's right to wear the badge of the Polish II Corps and that of the 3rd Carpathian Rifle Division

29.

Maria (Ricky) Versteeg
Comes to England

War can be at least as hard on civilians as it is on men-in-arms. Civilians may sustain physical injury from military action such as bombing, suffer from starvation or displacement as refugees, or dehumanization during occupation, such as from forced labour and racial or ethnic discrimination. My mother, Ricky Versteeg, experienced these directly or witnessed them happening to others. Pawel Wojdak suffered similarly, either in Siberia, Germany, or Italy.

The shoe store that employed Ricky in Amsterdam was owned by a family of German Jews, and most of the employees were Jewish. Ricky and her family were Catholic. Once Nazi German occupation was established, Jews had to wear a yellow star, and then they were not allowed on street cars. In protest, all Dutch people stopped using the street cars too. Jews began to disappear, taken away ultimately to death camps. Ricky's brother, Wim, was forced to work in Germany at the Messerschmitt production plant in Leipzig, leaving his wife, who was diabetic and asthmatic. Ricky still lived at home with her youngest sister but was engaged to be married to a member of the same family as her brother's wife.

Ricky and her fiancée decided to marry in the hope that might spare him from being forced to work in Germany too. That was not the case; he was sent to Karlsruhe, an industrial city on the Rhine River. When he came home after many months away, she found they had become strangers. She wanted to cancel the marriage plan, but there was family pressure, and in a Catholic family, she was obligated to proceed. They were married but did not live together: he went to live with his family, and Ricky lived alone in an apartment without heat or electricity, a virtual outcast from her family.

The family of Ricky's erstwhile husband was in disarray: the grandparents died, his mother suffered a nervous breakdown, an uncle was a Nazi sympathizer, and another was a socialist. Ricky's brother, married into the troubled family, felt compelled to escape from Leipzig in order to support his wife and his sister, Ricky. Wim was captured at the Dutch border, but luckily, he was put in a Dutch camp where he was able to escape again and come to Amsterdam. Unfortunately, without a ration card, he became a non-person in hiding. Wim described the forced labour camp to Ricky, how Jews and Poles received the worst treatment. In the Versteeg home, relationships were strained and conversations were guarded. One neighbour or another might be hiding Jews; no one wanted to accidentally give a clue that might be unknowingly passed on to an in-law Nazi sympathizer.

Ostracized by her family, Ricky transferred to work in the company's shoe store in The Hague; due to the steady disappearance of Jewish employees, the store was short-staffed. She commuted from Amsterdam, a forty-five-minute walk and one-hour trip by train. Returning one day to Amsterdam, the train was strafed by Allied planes. The train was disabled, and all the passengers, primarily Dutch civilians, ran to the nearest house for shelter overnight and came by another route the next day. Ricky's parents were worried; her father found her and asked her to return home to live. As a result, she went back to working at the shoe store in Amsterdam.

A German woman was installed as manager of the store, but when the Allies invaded France and it was evident Germany would lose the war, she and other German civilians left. Ricky became store manager. Coupons were dispensed for the Dutch to get shoes and clothes, although very little was available. One day, a German soldier came to the store and asked for shoes. Ricky was insolent; she asked if he had a coupon. Everyone knew a German soldier did not need a coupon. Then she told him, "Sorry, we have no shoes." In response to her being deliberately difficult, he took out his revolver and pulled boxes off the shelves; they were all empty. She felt threatened, and he might have shot her without consequence, but he turned and left.

Occasionally, the store received a small shipment of slippers made from carpet samples. Slippers were treasured by Dutch farmers, who wore wooden shoes in the soggy fields but had no footwear at home. At the shoe store, an overnight break-in was a regular occurrence and slippers were stolen. Ricky hid some slippers for herself where thieves could not find them, as they could be bartered for food. The slippers were loaded on a toboggan and covered, but the break-in and robbery had to be reported to the police, so she and her younger sister Jopie stopped at the police station. While Jopie waited outside, Ricky went into the station to report the theft. Years later, when she related this audacious event, she would always finish by saying, "And Jopie was so scared." What Ricky did not state was that it was she who was *not* afraid; I came to realize my mother was not intimidated by anyone.

As German fortunes in the war grew worse, civilians in occupied countries suffered more. In October 1944, the food ration decreased to 1 000 grams of potatoes and 400 grams of bread per week, which was insufficient to sustain life. People had to barter or beg for food from farmers in the countryside to survive during the unusually cold last winter of the war. Ricky would venture out of Amsterdam on her bike on her own with just a little bread for a week. All bikes by this stage of the war had non-inflatable tires made from old car tires. She traded slippers for pork chops and her watch for cabbages. She helped her family in other ways; she found a farm where her sister Tony and her daughter could stay in exchange for sewing work. Some trips to the countryside were with her brother Wim and a hand-drawn cart, which could carry more than a bike. Ricky was designated to knock on doors because people had more sympathy for a hungry woman than a man. Her father was able to smuggle a little coal from his job, which was used at home to cook sugar beets or, more rarely, carrots.

Twenty thousand Dutch civilians starved to death during the last months of the war. In late 1944, the Swedish Red Cross sent flour, powdered eggs, and margarine by ship and made arrangements with the German occupation for delivery using the ration system. For Ricky's family, this donation helped save lives. There was another food delivery by Allied air forces in the week immediately before the end of the war. Eastern Holland was liberated by Canadian forces in 1945, but Amsterdam and eastern Holland were occupied by Nazi Germany until their surrender on May 8. The Dutch still celebrate their appreciation toward Canadian troops for their liberation of the Netherlands.

Ricky formally ended her failed marriage by divorce on July 12, 1946. After six years of suppression and hardship, she and two friends went to England in 1946 to work as mother's helpers. On a night of indiscretion with a casual acquaintance, she became pregnant. She was very upset with herself. She spoke to another man she had met—Pawel Wojdak—and told him her situation and that she would return to Amsterdam. He suggested she stay in England together with him, that he would be the father of her child, and then they would have a family together.

30.

The New Wojdak Family

Pawel and Ricky came from much different backgrounds, but both experienced wartime trauma, which each recognized in the other and empathized. In that regard, Ricky and Pawel had a common past. For both, the war resulted in the end of a marriage; though the circumstances were quite different, the emotional hurt might be comparable. In England, they were unable to marry because Pawel had a wife in Poland; perhaps he did not know if she was still alive. Another question it is far too late to ask.

Shardeloes is notable for being the maternity hospital for London during the Blitz, the wartime bombing of London.[243] It was once part of an estate; the very large house was constructed about 1760 but became disused because it lacked central heating, plumbing, and electricity. It was requisitioned and converted to a fifty-five-bed birthing hospital. Shardeloes is now a Grade 1 listed building (photo 30.1). The Amersham Museum website lists some of the 5 000 babies born there; their individual stories of a mother and child lend a unique insight into women's lives during the war years.[244]

---

243 Wikipedia, s.v. "Shardeloes," last modified February 20, 2023, https://en.wikipedia.org/wiki/Shardeloes.

244 "Shardeloes Babies 1939–1948," *Amersham Museum*, accessed November 2, 2023, https://amershammuseum.org/history/shardeloes-babies/.

I was born in Shardeloes Hospital on January 4, 1948; the hospital closed two months later. I visited Shardeloes in 2014, to see where I was born. It is a grand building set on expansive grounds and overlooks a small man-made lake. It has been transformed into luxury apartments; a sign at the entrance gate reads, "Strictly private," and a plaque near the main entrance reads, "To commemorate cherished visits by H M Queen Elizabeth the Queen Mother."

When I was born, Pawel was adamant that my name would be Paul; he would consider nothing else. After my birth, my mother was required to have a hysterectomy due to a recurrence of uterine fibroids. Her inability to have other children was a great disappointment to my father. My mother said it was the only time she saw him cry. German was the only language they both spoke when they met, not the first language for either of them. Mother taught him English, and she was determined that English would be my first language. As part of that process, Pawel modified his name to the English equivalent of Paul.

Photo 30.1. Shardeloes was a maternity hospital during the
London Blitz; after the war, it was converted to luxury apartments.

Together, Pawel and Ricky were employed as domestic staff by Peter Caspari at Rock House, a prominent home fronting on Gold Hill Common in Chalfont St. Peter, seven kilometres south of Amersham.[245] My mother kept the house; my father looked after the garden and car. He was also employed at an automobile garage. Peter Caspari was a Jewish German architect of Hungarian descent. He escaped Europe before the war and, in England, designed houses and residential flats in London. In 1950, he emigrated to Canada, where he linked my father and mother to an employer for a similar domestic position in Port Credit, Ontario. In Canada, Peter Caspari had a distinguished architectural career.[246]

The book-cover image of Pawel Wojdak is a passport photo required for a trip to Amsterdam by the new Wojdak family in 1950 to connect with my mother's family. In the photo, he is thirty-eight years old. When I look into my father's face and step into my memory of him, I see strength but also apprehension, self-doubt and perhaps a fatalism to accept whatever comes next. There is a marked contrast with photos taken years later in Canada, where he looks confident, self-assured and, above all, happy. The background of chrysanthemums signifies his hidden memory of Japan.

By 1949, the Resettlement Corps had mostly ceased to function. About 150 000 Polish soldiers and their dependents settled in the United Kingdom, forming a significant Polish community. In March 1948, Polish ex-servicemen and other Poles were eligible to become British citizens. Their different culture and tradition, along with the shared traumatic wartime experience, slowly came to be seen as beneficial. As one local newspaper article of the time said, "Their assets and pastimes may differ, but that very difference is an asset to the joint community of the town."

Some of these Poles immigrated to America, Canada, Australia, Argentina, and Brazil; they are part of an extensive Polish diaspora around the Free World. Pawel, Ricky, and young Paul immigrated to Canada.

---

245 "Peter Caspari Fonds: Biographical Notes," *Canadian Centre of Architecture Archives*, accessed November 2, 2023, https://www.cca.qc.ca/en/archives/379560/peter-caspari-fonds.

246 Dave Leblanc, "Peter Caspari—A 'Bull' Who Helped Shape Toronto," *Globe and Mail*, December 4, 2014, https://www.theglobeandmail.com/life/home-and-garden/architecture/peter-caspari---a-bull-who-helped-shape-toronto/article21949216/.

31.

Pawel Wojdak Finds His Home in Canada

Pawel Wojdak was born in Russia, became an orphan in China, a refugee in Japan, a transient in America, a foster child and blacksmith in Poland, a migrant worker and conscript in Germany, a soldier in Italy, a displaced person in England, and, finally, a landed immigrant in Canada. In five years, he would become a Canadian citizen. Our family arrived by train to Toronto in mid-November 1952. We were met by Agar Rodney Adamson, usually called Rodney, and his wife, Cynthia. [247] Our small family was installed in a wing of their home on a wooded estate called "The Hogsback."

My first question immediately upon stepping out of the car was, "Where is the snow?" which was met with laughter. Our new residence was located outside of Port Credit, north of the Queen Elizabeth Highway. The name of the estate derives from its situation on a promontory overlooking the Credit River and was reached by a one-quarter-mile-long driveway. For me, soon to turn five years old, the house lay in the midst of a twenty-seven-acre forested playground simply called "the woods." Dad taught me to swim in

---

247 Wikipedia, s.v. "Agar Rodney Adamson," last modified August 21, 2023, https://en.wikipedia.org/wiki/Agar_Rodney_Adamson.

the Credit River, and in winter, the three of us skated two miles not quite to its mouth, because Lake Ontario was not frozen.

The Adamson family had a prominent Canadian military history and was linked by marriage with the wealthy Cawthra family, who owned extensive property west of Toronto. The Hogsback was one of those properties; another was on the shore of Lake Ontario, where Rodney's brother Anthony Adamson lived. Rodney Adamson was trained as a mining engineer, though I am doubtful he worked in that field. Anthony Adamson was an architect and associate professor of Town Planning at the University of Toronto. He shared an interest in urban development with an architect who newly arrived in Canada: Peter Caspari. Peter recommended the Wojdaks to Rodney Adamson and family for employment. My mother looked after the house, and my father tended the grounds: maintenance, mowing the large lawn, and other chores.

As a child, I had no thought of the immigration process, and now, it is too late to ask. I suppose we were sponsored by Rodney Adamson, meaning we were at the top of the queue of applicants to immigrate to Canada because my parents were assured of employment and would not be a burden to Canadian taxpayers. But as to who paid for our passage, I am uncertain. As a child, I thought we paid our own way.

Rodney Adamson was the Member of Parliament for York West. He and his wife, Cynthia, were in Ottawa much of the time, allowing relaxed work conditions for Paul and Ricky and few restrictions for me. Their son, Christopher, a year younger than me, was left at The Hogsback in the care of my parents. Christopher and I were natural playmates, with the closest neighbour being one-half kilometre away. My parents, especially my father, who loved children, were pleased to care for Christopher. When Rodney Adamson came home after a long absence, he was upset that Christopher was reluctant to approach him, going instead to my father.

Dad and I spent a lot of time together fishing from the riverbank below the house for bass and catfish but mainly catching suckers and carp. One day, I was startled while passing through the Adamsons' portion of the house to see a glossy, professionally made eight-by-ten photograph. It showed a beaming Rodney Adamson posed with one foot on a stack of firewood, his dress shirt off, and clad in an under-vest as though he had been hard at work. The image was so unlike him and remains clear in my mind. Years later, in mature hindsight, I realize the photograph was a publicity prop for an election campaign intended to connect Rodney Adamson to the working class. At the time, I simply saw it as false; my father would be the one to cut firewood.

Life for the Wojdak family took a dramatic turn on April 8, 1954, when Rodney and Cynthia Adamson died in a Trans-Canada Air Lines midair collision with an air force training plane over Moose Jaw, Saskatchewan.[248] Paul and Ricky were anxious about their future and greatly concerned for Christopher, who had become like a second son. They would have been happy to raise him. Christopher's uncle Anthony and aunt Augusta had fully-fledged children; they were like grandparents. The Adamsons consulted a psychologist, who recommended that Christopher live with them. Through the ensuing summer, we visited their estate on the lakeshore so Christopher and I could continue as playmates.

Happily, we were able to remain at The Hogsback. The house was rented by the Fogden family, and the previously unoccupied guest house was also rented to an American family who worked at the Toronto airport for the US government. We continued to live in our wing of the house, my parents in the same roles. The Fogdens had two sons—Mike and Pete, aged seventeen and fifteen—who were wild and irresponsible, at least in the view of our family with its European standards of behaviour. Perhaps they were normal Canadian teenagers. The Coblentzs had two young daughters close to my age. An austere man, Mr. Fogden was the president of Gilbey's Distillery, in nearby New Toronto. I rode in his black Buick each morning in complete silence to be dropped off on the shoulder of the Queen Elizabeth Highway, near my school. Mr. Fogden's wife was a warm person with a snazzy convertible. Home life became much different for us because the Fogdens were full-time residents. There was more washing and cleaning for my mother. The Hogsback was no longer our semi-private world, but Dad and I still managed to fish.

---

248 Wikipedia, s.v. "Trans-Canada Air Lines Flight 9," last modified August 21, 2022. https://en.wikipedia.org/wiki/Trans-Canada_Air_Lines_Flight_9.

Once, when Dad and I were quietly fishing from the riverbank, one of the Fogden boys came from around a bend in the river in a motorboat. At full speed, the motor roaring, he veered toward us, sending a wave against the shore as he passed close by. Probably, he thought it a harmless prank. But our fishing lines were cut, hooks and sinkers gone, and any fish scattered far from the disturbed water. My father was angry but said nothing; it was our employer's son and Dad's life had taught him to be silent and accept things.

My father worked one season for Lundy's Fence Company; hard work when post-holes were dug with hand tools. He was disgusted to be laid off at the end of the construction season, as seasonal work was an unfamiliar concept. Mr. Fogden helped him find a new job. There were two choices: the Ford Motor plant in Oakville, or the St. Lawrence Starch factory in Port Credit. Ricky recommended the latter because it would be more secure; she reckoned in difficult times, people might not buy a car, but they will buy groceries.

St. Lawrence Starch Company was structured to be a self-reliant factory. It produced its own power and drew its own water from Lake Ontario. The company employed about 300 people to process corn into food and industrial products. These included glucose, syrup, cooking and salad oil, and the principal product, a series of starches in 100-pound bags. They were for manufacturing paper and specialty starches for confectioners and brewers. The residual corn pulp was high-protein cattle feed. Consistent with a self-reliant model, the company made most of their mechanical replacement parts in an on-site machine shop.

Paul Wojdak began work in the coal-fired power plant and became a qualified stationary engineer, also called a power engineer. The job was a fair fit for a blacksmith trained to maintain a high-temperature furnace. Power generation was required twenty-four hours per day, seven days per week, which meant shift and weekend work. Home life, meals, and social events revolved around whether my father was working the day, evening, or night shift. His days off aligned with a weekend about once per month. As a child, I was very aware of our schedule for Christmas present opening and special meals.

The only unpleasant aspect of my father's job was the removal of coal ash ("clinkers"). This was done periodically and, to minimize downtime, was done while the furnace was still very warm. After a few years, a new oil-fired furnace was installed, complete with instrumentation (photo 31.1), and ash removal was eliminated. Paul Wojdak worked at St. Lawrence Starch for twenty-five years until retirement. I also worked at St. Lawrence Starch for four summers in my late teen years.

Photo 31.1 Paul Wojdak, stationary (power) engineer, about 1960

Paul and Ricky Wojdak were frugal and, by 1957, saved enough money for a down payment on a new house. It was located in Streetsville, a small town named after a land surveyor in pioneer days. The town was growing fast, on account of a booming aircraft manufacturing industry, which included the AVRO Arrow. New housing areas were popping up for skilled immigrants to build the new aircraft. Our house had been planned but was not built yet; in fact, there was not even a hole in the ground. We drove from The Hogsback once per week to view progress (photo 31.2).

We moved into our brand-new home in mid-summer 1957, and the next year, Mr. and Mrs. Pawel (Paul) Wojdak became Canadian citizens. A newspaper clipping lists the names of twenty-seven men and women who took the oath of allegiance on June 12, 1958, in Brampton, Ontario, presided by Judge Archibald Cochrane. This was a very important occasion; my presence was not required, but for my parents, it was more important for me to attend the ceremony than go to school that day. Pawel Wojdak had been in five orphanages, traversed three continents, and lived temporarily in nine countries until, finally, at 125 Fifth Line in Streetsville, he found a secure and permanent home.

Photo 31.2. The Wojdak family acquired a home of their own in 1957

Landscaping is an immediate requirement of a new home built on a barren site, a task that my father tackled vigorously. Flower beds, shrubs, and young trees were installed; some of the latter were transplanted from the thickly forested Hogsback and elsewhere. Closely spaced houses require lot boundaries be delineated. In Canada, this is normally done with fences, wooden or wire. Absolutely not for Paul Wojdak—it would be a hedge. One neighbour agreed, but the other was adamant it would be a fence, telling my father he would have a long beard before a hedge grew to a reasonable height. "Fine," said my father, "you build a fence and I will plant a hedge on my side." The privet hedge plants were indeed tiny when planted, but with new topsoil, a liberal application of fertilizer, including carp from the Credit River, and diligent care, it grew to more than six feet high and equally wide. Our neighbour's fence was overwhelmed. Flower gardens contained climbing roses and beds of tulips, dahlias, petunias, zinnias, marigolds, and cosmos.

My father had a rudimentary reading and writing ability; reading a newspaper was difficult for him. But his job as a stationary engineer required him to pass exams administered by a provincial association, initially a fourth-class ticket and later a third-class one. The latter was a great challenge for him; he failed his first attempt due to an inability to read, understand, and write the technical language of power generation: high-temperature boilers, high-pressure steam, turbines, and refrigeration. Ben Schultz was a German-speaking colleague and, later, his supervisor who came to our house as a patient teacher and friend. With his help, my father passed the third-class exam on his second attempt—an important achievement because it ensured job security.

Swear words give insight into a person's language familiarity. The strongest English swear words I had ever heard from my father were "damn" and "bloody." My mother told me that if he was more upset, the swear words were German, but if he was really angry, they were in Polish. Clearly, Polish, German, and finally English were my father's first, second, and third languages, respectively.

In the late 1950s, many young unemployed men came from the Maritime provinces to Ontario in search of better opportunities. A man from Nova Scotia found work alongside my father in the powerhouse at St. Lawrence Starch. Alf lived paycheque to paycheque and was a little on the wild side. One day after work and some hours at a tavern with fellow Maritimers, Alf had a traffic accident. Inebriated, he carried on to his boarding house; a policeman arrived soon after to arrest him. Alf became belligerent, and in the ensuing altercation, the policeman's arm was broken. Alf was charged with drunk driving, leaving an accident scene, resisting arrest, and assault; he was at risk of a substantial fine, a suspended driver's licence, and perhaps losing his job. My father and mother stood up for him in court, promising they would keep him on a better path by having him live with us. Alf stayed with us for at least a year and became a steady employee at St. Lawrence Starch. Alf, and later along with his wife, remained close friends of my father and mother.

Dad enjoyed owning a luxury car; he had a Chrysler and later a high-end Oldsmobile. It was well maintained, washed every few days and waxed regularly; on the road, it was in show-room condition. Everything he owned received similar treatment. In England, he would dismount from his bike in order to carry it across a puddle. In Canada, his home and yard, car, boat, and the rest were looked after carefully. He continued to enjoy growing flowers and fishing.

Every successful marriage is the outcome of a strong relationship, and my parents had that. They both worked hard and wanted the best for me; I was equally special to both of them. My father was loyal, honest, and loving; my mother was capable, strong-minded, and not intimidated by any situation. My father's symptoms of post-traumatic stress, the angry outbursts during my youth, became infrequent and disappeared without me realizing when they stopped. I suspect the events during World War II were the cause, but it may have been cumulative with events of his youth. My father became secure in his job, self-confident in his ability to communicate, and enjoyed a good social life—in short, he was content.

Immediately after we moved to our own home, my mother began a career of her own, more than happy to be finished with domestic work in someone else's house. She had a strong sense for business and had acquired basic office skills in the Netherlands. In Canada, she progressed through a succession of positions; her responsibilities increased to include all the functions of an accountant: processing accounts payable and accounts receivable, balancing the general ledger, and completing the payroll for about 100 employees. Later, she became an office manager in a law office. At work, she was respected and popular; at home, she ran a "tight ship" yet had a good sense of humour. Her favourite activities over many decades were solving a cryptic crossword and playing contract bridge.

Pawel and Ricky acquired a cottage in Muskoka, about an hour-and-a-half drive from their home, and spent most of their summer leisure time there and in the adjacent Severn River waterway (photo 31.3).

Photo 31.3. Pawel and Ricky at their cottage at Six Mile Lake in Muskoka

They travelled to the Netherlands and Australia to visit Ricky's family, to Hawaii, and to Vancouver to visit their son and grandchildren (photo 31.4).

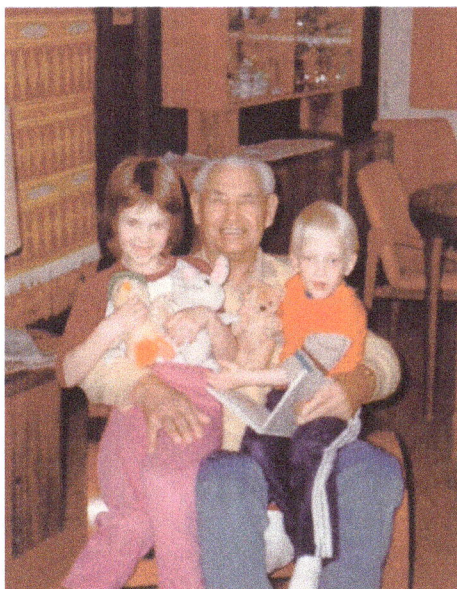

Photo 31.4. Pawel Wojdak with grandchildren Rachel and Graham in 1982

At age sixty-five, my father was reluctant to retire; working was a way of life. He and my mother were financially secure; she was eight years younger and enjoyed her job, and they would still have sufficient income for any unseen event. About the same time as retirement, hernia surgery prompted my father to quit smoking. For years, he spoke of quitting his lifelong habit but was reluctant to try, afraid he would not succeed. He rather surprised himself that due to the surgery, he successfully stopped smoking. He was pleased by how much better he felt for it.

By this time, I was married, raising children, dedicated to my job, and living in Vancouver. I was pleased to learn by telephone that he had retired in 1979 or 1980, and together, my parents enjoyed miles-long country walks. They were fit, healthy, and seemed ready to enjoy life for many years. My work focused on the summer season, so our face-to-face meetings happened about every second Christmas unless my parents were passing through Vancouver on their way to Australia or Hawaii.

Photo 31.5. Last summer at Six Mile Lake

Early in the 1980s, I was startled out of complacency by news that my father had lymphoma, cancer of the lymph system. My mother downplayed the issue, saying treatment was underway and the prognosis was good. Chemotherapy involved blood transfusions. Together with my wife and three children, we flew to Toronto to see Mom and Dad at their cottage at Six Mile Lake. I was alarmed to see my father, who had always been strong and robust, looking pale, thin, and weak (photo 31.5). Before we arrived, he insisted on a rock-work project to stabilize the shoreline, normally a task he would easily handle himself, but this time, he needed my mother's help.

Back in Vancouver, I kept in touch by phone and heard how much of a toll the transfusions continued to take. Still, it came as a shock when my mother called to say, "Come now." My mother was with him extensively when it was meaningful. She left it for me to be alone with Dad, but I ought to have been there sooner because he was heavily sedated. I am sure he knew when I entered his room and rushed to be by his side, but I doubt he was aware of much beyond those first moments. Nonetheless, I spoke continuously about our times together, events he knew about and those he did not. I told him of a summer afternoon at The Hogsback when I climbed a pine tree beside the road that he would drive past on his way home from work. I knew he would not see me, but I thought I could climb down, cut through the bush, and meet him on the driveway. I was too late then; he had passed by. And I was too late on his last day. My father passed away on November 12, 1984.

Not long after my father died, it became known that blood transfusions were contaminated with HIV, human immunodeficiency viruses. This results in the acquired immunodeficiency syndrome known as AIDS. The "tainted blood scandal" was at its peak in the early 1980s, exactly when my father was undergoing treatment. It is very likely AIDS caused my father's death, not lymphoma.

32.

Recapturing Memory

How does memory work? To a psychologist, memory is the term given to the structures and processes in the storage and subsequent retrieval of information.[249] Information that comes to us from sensory input is encoded in three ways: what we see, what we hear, and what it means. Psychologists have determined that short-term memory is retained by hearing, whereas long-term memory is principally retained by its meaning. Short-term memory is limited; most adults can store between five and nine items in short-term memory for up to thirty seconds. In contrast, long-term memory is thought to be unlimited and can last a lifetime. Long-term memory is stored and retrieved by association. The day Pawel Wojdak sang the Japanese anthem is a dramatic example of the recovery of a long-term memory by association, due to the presence and interaction with a Japanese person.

Memory is like a box of photographs. Each image shows a person, an event, and ourselves as we once were. It is like the box of photographs that I was shown by my mother of her family in the Netherlands and our beginnings in England. Memories of Japan were retained by Siberian children all their lives despite their brief time in the country, just two, three, or four

249 Saul McLeod, "Memory Stages: Encoding Storage and Retrieval," *Simply Psychology*, last modified June 16, 2023, https://www.simplypsychology.org/memory.html.

months. The kitchen drawer of Leopold Kulesza was a memory box containing not only paper maps, but also the Japanese songs, stories, and fragments of language that he treasured and thereby imparted to his daughter, Anna. Similarly, the postcard of Takao Atsumi was the key to Jan Samardakiewicz's treasured box of memories, and the ancient, creased photograph of Urszula Malewski's great-grandparents that her grandfather Innocenty Marszal carried nearly around the world connected her to a hidden past. During the difficult days of World War II, Antonina Liro recounted her memory, "I thought about Japan, I remembered they were so kind to us." There is no mistaking the delight of Henryk Sadowski's voice when the people of Tsuruga cheered, "Long live Poland and Polish children!" and later, how the children sang the anthems of both countries. Is it possible to separate good and bad memories, to keep them in separate drawers like photographs?

Leopold Kulesza, Jan Samardakiewicz, and Pawel Wojdak loved flowers and gardening. This trait in three Siberian children may derive from their time in Japan. Many Siberian children remarked on how impressed they were with the flowers in Japan. The floral and aesthetic beauty together with affection and kindness, was a beautiful image in their "box of photographs" that had a lifelong impact on each of them. My father planted vegetables but with nothing like the dedication he had for flowers—his true passion. In Japan, children are held in high regard; one of the Siberian children referred to Japanese society as the cult of the child.

Traumatic events experienced as a child can shape the processing of new information and leave marks lasting into adulthood, according to the Integrative Life Centre website.[250] Individuals who have experienced great stress at an early age sometimes suffer from memory loss, anxiety, and depression. Depending on the type of trauma, memory loss can be intentional or unintentional. Unintentional memory loss is also called dissociative amnesia.[251] It occurs when a person cannot remember key elements of their life and is, therefore, divorced from a full understanding of themselves

---

250 "Childhood Trauma and Memory Loss," Integrative Life Centre, last modified November 23, 2020, https://integrativelifecenter.com/childhood-trauma-memory-loss/#.

251 "Dissociative Amnesia," *Psychology Today*, last modified July 27, 2021, https://www.psychologytoday.com/us/conditions/dissociative-amnesia.

and their current state. It is not the same as forgetting; the memories are there but they cannot be accessed. [252] Their memory gap can significantly disrupt their lives because they may forget who they are and everything about themselves and their personal history. Pawel Wojdak's traumatic journey to Harbin, together with the death of his mother and father, may have caused him to forget his identity, even his own name. Instead of, or in addition to, dissociative amnesia, perhaps my father experienced elective mutism, the same condition as Antonina Liro. If he suffered a temporary loss of speech, he would have been unable to declare his name in Harbin or, later in, Japan. Accordingly, he was assigned the name of his father, Wladyslaw, and that stayed with him until St. Joseph Orphanage in Milwaukee. There, he began to assert his own name, confusing the orphanage record.

What Pawel Wojdak remembered about his past profoundly affected how he viewed himself, his identity. He had two types of suppressed memories. First, there were the horrifying events of his early life in Siberia, the desperate flight with his father and mother from Bolsheviks in the depth of winter. The circumstances of their death and the aftermath as an orphan were buried in his subconscious. Thirty-five years later, he was still physically unable to speak of them. We can imagine he was in emotional shock: his mind was numb; the world did not make sense. The result was a poor understanding of succeeding events, causing a disjointed memory. Singing the national anthem of Japan was a joyous memory that remained, though it, too, was somewhere below the surface and was only drawn out by the exceptional circumstance of meeting a Japanese person. Perhaps the beauty of yellow chrysanthemums was in the same category of memory.

The second type of Pawel Wojdak's suppressed memory relates to World War II, the preceding years and the war years. Pawel Wojdak said so little of his life on the Schulz farm that it is uncertain if he was happy or lonely. If some German people became his friends, their friendship was abruptly compromised when the war began. He went to work in Germany willingly, but life soon became very difficult for Poles. Reluctance to share unpleasant and violent events is common among war veterans. They are suppressed

---

252 "Dissociative Amnesia," Cleveland Clinic, https://my.clevelandclinic.org/health/diseases/9789-dissociative-amnesia

in the mind because of the strong emotions they can bring forth. Pawel Wojdak was one of many Poles conscripted by the Wehrmacht, and when he crossed over, he would have been welcomed by sympathetic Poles in the Polish Army. They would have understood he was powerless to protect his wife. But both topics would be uncomfortable to present in post-war England, along with speaking German fluently. Perhaps the conscious part of his mind found it convenient to suppress these memories, to consign them to another compartment like his lost memories. And it was easier to adopt Konstanty Mlotek's history of fighting in North Africa instead of a subhuman, an *Untermensch* in Germany.

Prosthetic memory refers to memories that a person did not experience. I was devastated to learn my father entered the German Army in 1944, and therefore could not have escaped Poland in 1939 and was not at the Battle of Tobruk in Libya. The memories he shared were false; were they lies? After gaining an appreciation of how the mind works, I am certain now this was a prosthetic memory. Events in Pawel Wojdak's life promoted this to happen. He was given the identity bracelet of Konstanty Mlotek and placed in the 7th Rifle Battalion, the same unit as Konstanty. Fellow soldiers had been Konstanty's friends and likely encouraged Pawel to imagine he was taking his place. Quite possibly, Konstanty Mlotek escaped from Poland through the Balkans and joined the Carpathian Brigade in Lebanon. Subsequently, he fought in Tobruk and may have died during the terrible Battle of Monte Cassino. Pawel Wojdak may or may not have been precisely at Monte Cassino; recall the front was 20 miles wide. "Adopting an observer-like perspective involves viewing the past in a novel way, which requires greater interaction among brain regions that support our ability to recall details of a memory and to recreate mental images in our mind's eye. Adopting an observer-like perspective may.... be an effective way of dealing with troubling memories by viewing the past from a distance and reducing the intensity of the emotions we feel."[253]

---

253 "Recalling Memories from a Third Person Perspective Changes How Our Brain Processes Them," Neuroscience News, https://neurosciencenews.com/third-person-memory-recall-16821/

Postmemory and cultural memory refers to memory we acquire from our parents, our relatives, our forebears. In postmemory, we absorb their experiences, be it hardship or accomplishment, so that it becomes part of our family identity. We only remember through their stories and images. Cultural memory is more than history; it involves the meaning of the past, how it is engrained in our conscience, and how we perceive the world. Cultural memory is preserved by institutions, not individuals. The institutions are countries, religious groups or international organizations. Cultural memory becomes ritualized; certain days become highly symbolic and marked by ceremonies.[254] Canada's observation of Remembrance Day is an example. The humanitarian rescue of the Siberian children is a Polish example. Knowing the story and keeping the memory alive enriches us by reminding us of the best values of humanity. Acclaimed Polish novelist Zofia Nalkowska wrote a short story titled "Bracia" ("Brothers") about Siberian children. In the 1930s, it was read in Polish schools so that new generations retained the cultural memory. After World War II, "Bracia" was removed from the curriculum because it was inconvenient for the Russian-backed administration. But the story of the Siberian children was not entirely forgotten. Gradually, since 1989, it has become well-known through the efforts of Teruo Matsumoto and Wieslaw Theiss, Fukudenkai, and the Port of Humanity Museum. In 2021, Polish media reported on a documentary film, *Andzia, The History of One Journey*, which tells the story of two-year-old Anna Wronska, the youngest of the Siberian children.[255] Notably, Anna Wronska was too young to remember her own story, in contrast to the children presented in this account.

Aneta Boldyrew explains the research of Wieslaw Theiss on war-damaged children.[256] Displaced or wandering children are deprived of being

254 "Memory: Types, Definitions," *The National Holocaust Centre and Museum*, https://www.holocaust.org.uk/memory.

255 Blanka Konopka, "Extraordinary Tale of Polish Orphans Saved from Siberia by Japan in 1920 Subject of New Documentary," *The First News*, April 20, 2021 https://www.thefirstnews.com/article/extraordinary-tale-of-polish-orphans-saved-from-siberia-by-japan-in-1920-subject-of-new-documentary-21387.

256 Boldyrew, "Education and Socialization."

fully aware of their roots, which is necessary to develop their identity. These roots constitute a cultural memory that precedes a person's individual life; it expands what one experiences in one's own life by opening the mind to identify with one's ancestors. These cultural memories incorporate an ancestral perspective and hierarchy of values. In Theiss's opinion, depriving Polish children in Russian care institutions of their memory and perspective of their culture is evidence of violence and was the tool used for indoctrination and denationalization.

A campaign to obliterate Polish culture began in the time of the czar and was reinstated during the Russian occupation of Poland during World War II, until glasnost and perestroika in the late 1980s. And it continues today, in Ukraine: it is a component of Russian aggression in occupied Ukraine. There are credible reports of children being deported into Russia to be indoctrinated into Russian culture, to destroy Ukrainian heritage. Similarly, in Canada, the system of residential schools was meant to distance Indigenous children from their cultural memory.

Wojtek Sawa, a bilingual Polish-American, produced an interactive multimedia exhibit called *The Wall Speaks: Voices of the Unheard* that "engages with the intricacies of remembering and forgetting."[257] Sawa interviewed many Polish children and teenagers who survived violence and dehumanization during World War II. In a radio interview on New Books Network, he describes the exhibit and its impact on participants and viewers. He was able to draw out suppressed traumatic memories and, surprisingly, humorous and positive ones. The exhibit resonates strongly with people today by enabling them to speak of their own much different hidden experiences, whether it is recent wartime violence, gender identity, or sexual violence.

Jonathan Durand is the Canadian grandson of a World War II *Sybirak*. Durand produced the film *Memory is Our Homeland*, about the discovery of his grandparents' home in the Kresy region of pre-war Poland.[258] Durand

---

257 Wojtek Sawa, "The Wall Speaks: Voices of the Unheard," National Center of Culture 2016, New Books Network, last modified June 5, 2018, https://newbooksnetwork.com/wojtek-sawa-the-wall-speaks-voices-of-the-unheard-national-center-of-culture-2016.

258 Jonathan Durand, *Memory is Our Homeland*, documentary film, 2018, video, 90:00, https://memoryisourhomeland.com/.

used family memories to locate the remains of the ancestral house in a tiny village that is now in Belarus and has a different name. Durand knew that his grandmother was in a Polish refugee camp in British East Africa during the war. He found film footage from a British documentary film project made during World War II. The project was not completed; the film lay in BBC archives for more than fifty years until he viewed it and, to his amazement, discovered images of his grandmother as a teenage girl! Truly a cultural memory. But Durand's story is more than the discovery of a cultural memory—it shows, once again, that loved ones may reach out across time to find us.

A survivor of emotional trauma once explained to me that when living with trauma, your heart is at first numb, but as love and kindness come into your life, the heart opens up, and traumatic memories recede. I now recognize that as a child, I could have asked different questions of my father. If I had inquired gently—"Tell me about Japan; what did their food taste like? Did you play games with someone in Milwaukee?"—instead of my harsh queries—"How did your mother die? What happened to your father? Why were you in Japan?"—those gentler questions may have elicited answers.

I have no insight into Pawel Wojdak's life in Germany during the early years of the war. He spoke nothing about this period. He and his wife may have been forced labourers and separated. It is entirely speculative but I can imagine there was pain and anguish and it became easier to adopt different memories. Once again, I ask, can we ever truly know the past? Facts may be plain on paper, but feelings and motives are in the mind and, therefore, obscure.

33.

Retrospective

Poland enjoyed freedom for twenty years between world wars. Russia and Germany sought revenge for the outcome of World War I by conquering and dividing Poland in 1939. The Siberian children were dispossessed again. Their families and careers were disrupted or lost, as were their homes and homeland; some lost their lives. Others became forced labourers and then refugees—displaced persons. They were scattered throughout the world: the United Kingdom, America, Australia, Argentina, New Zealand, and, for Pawel Wojdak and others, Canada.

Social media plays an important role in keeping them connected. On Facebook, the Kresy-Siberia Group has 2 600 members. There are 2 700 members in the Polish Resettlement Group, which is concerned with the lives of Polish soldiers and civilians who were displaced persons after the war and were accepted for resettlement in the United Kingdom. Family stories and photographs keep memories alive and, on rare occasions, connect family descendants who were separated eighty years ago.

Might history have been different if the Eastern European federation envisioned by Pilsudski became a reality? Could a cooperative of Poland-Ukraine-Lithuania-Latvia-Estonia-Finland-Czechoslovakia-Romania have withstood German and Russian aggression? Perhaps a formal cooperation will evolve soon as an outcome of the Ukraine War. Such an association of countries with their shared geography and history might be more functional in the region than NATO, with its far-flung membership.

Russia has been a recurring and ruthless enemy of Poland for more than 200 years. Profound change in the Russian government, from autocratic rule by the czar to autocratic rule by the leader of the Communist Party, has made no difference. Communist Russia incarcerated its own citizens in prisons and forced labour camps called gulags.[259] In 2023, Russia continues its aggression against Slavic people in Ukraine. Events that reflect poorly on Russia are suppressed from public scrutiny, historically with Siberian children and today in Ukraine. Poland and the Baltic countries know that if Russia were to succeed in occupying Ukraine, Russian aggression would turn next to them. After World War II, when Russia took control of Poland, the story of Siberian children in 1920–1921 was suppressed. It began to be told after Russia's grip on Poland weakened in 1990. The Social Welfare Corporation Fukudenkai recognizes the parallel of Russian aggression against Ukraine and is donating the equivalent of one million Canadian dollars for language and skills training for Ukrainian refugees in Poland.[260]

Many peoples and nationalities are widespread in the world; some have retained their culture, while others have not. One might reflect on the several reasons why. First, there are those who spread through imperialism—those nations who went forth to conquer Indigenous peoples and colonize new lands. These include the English, Spanish, French, Portuguese, and Dutch. Second, there are economic migrants—the impoverished who chose to find a better life in a foreign land. Prime examples are Chinese and Indian people, but also Italians and the Irish, in earlier times. Thirdly, there are those who were exploited—Black Africans brought to North and South America as slaves. Finally, there are those who move due to persecution—those forced from their homeland. This includes Poles, Jews, and other religious minorities; all were targets of deportation, exile (forced or

---

259 Avrahan Shifrin, *The First Guidebook to Prisons and Concentration Camps of the Soviet Union* (Toronto, ON: Bantam Books, 1982).

260 Takaaki Ohta, President of Corporation Fukudenkai, announcement on September 26, 2023, in Warsaw.

self-imposed), and genocide. The first two groups—colonists and economic migrants—brought their culture with them. Slaves and exiles are in grave danger of losing their cultural memory.

The issue of compensation for war crimes has been pursued in recent years. Germany is to be commended for stating that crimes were committed, accepting collective guilt, and paying compensation to those who were wronged. The monetary repayment is not as important as the principle of confession and sincere apology. A monetary value cannot be calculated, except for expropriated property. For war crimes—physical and mental anguish, lost years, and lost lives—the value cannot be measured. Germany has paid substantial money to a great many people, and that adds weight to their sincerity.[261] Having done so, there is a way to move forward, as demonstrated in Western Europe today.

In contrast, Russia has never admitted to war crimes against Poles, or even crimes against its own citizens. With the Gulag system, the Russian government has essentially waged war on its own people ever since it replaced the czar. Russia does not recognize the human rights of anyone, or the rights of citizenship of its own people. Revenge is a powerful motive for Russia. Yevgeny Miller was commander of the White Army in the Archangel region during the civil war and escaped to France in 1920.[262] In 1937 he was kidnapped by Soviet NKVD agents, drugged, and smuggled in a steamer trunk to Moscow, where he was tortured and executed. Such is the far-reaching determination of Soviet revenge.

Miller and Grigori Semyonov were guilty of multiple murders in Siberia and ought to face justice, but their illegal extraction by Russian agents from France and China sixteen and twenty-three years after the fact shows complete disregard for international borders. Both Miller and Semyonov were not tried in court; they were tortured for a lengthy period before

261 Germany Federal Ministry of Finance, *Wiedergutmachung: Provisions Relating to Compensation for National Social Injustice* (Berlin: German Federal Ministry of Finance, 2018), https://www.bundesfinanzministerium.de/Content/EN/Standardartikel/ Press_Room/Publications/Brochures/2018-08-15-entschaedigung-ns-unrecht-engl. pdf?__blob=publicationFile&v=8.

262 Wikipedia, s.v. "Yevgeny Miller," last modified October 15, 2023, https://en.wikipedia.org/ wiki/Yevgeny_Miller

being executed. Today, Russia has no qualms concerning execution, by any means, of citizens who are outspoken critics of its leadership: journalists, human rights lawyers, public figures, or civil servants.[263] Recent killings include Alexander Litvinenko, Vitaly Shishov, Natalie Estemirova, Boris Nemstov, Darya Dugina, Stanislaw Markelov, and the attempted murder of Sergei Skripal and his daughter, Yulia. And, as with Miller and Semyonov, Russia will send its agents into any sovereign nation to carry out an execution, seeming to relish flaunting its power and impunity.

The strength and duration of the Polish national struggle are remarkable—more than 200 years from the first partition in 1795 to 2023, as shown by the Kresy Family website.[264] Why? Polish men were rebels and soldiers. It was Polish women, whether in subjugated Poland or in remote Siberia, who instilled their children with Polish language, culture, and values to guarantee the next generation of patriots. This Polish identity or nationalism was the current in the stream that carried the Siberian children across two oceans and a continent to a homeland where they had never been. Pawel Wojdak did not have a strong Polish identity—the force that bound members of the Resettlement Corps together in the United Kingdom and continues to bind the Kresy-Siberia Group today. Probably, if he had attended Wejherowo instead of living on the Schulz farm on the border with Germany, he would have become more nationalistic.

This book deals with history from a personal perspective, and with the struggle of a child to reach across the divide of trauma and silence to understand their parent.

As I learned my father's history, a friend said, "He was a hero!" I consider "survivor" to be a more accurate characterization. My father experienced poverty that went far beyond hunger and not having money. The greatest form of poverty is to lose your family and home, your language and culture, your past and your own history. Due to the traumas he experienced at such a young age, my father struggled for much of his life with the aftereffects of

---

263 Wikipedia, s.v. "List of Assassinations in Europe," Wikipedia, last modified September 2, 2023, https://en.wikipedia.org/wiki/List_of_assassinations_in_Europe#Russia.

264 "Kresy Family: Polish WWII History Group," accessed November 2, 2023, https://www.kresyfamily.com/.

being an orphan in Siberia. He did not become bitter or hateful; he developed positive values: love of home and family, loyalty to friends, dedication to hard work, respectfulness, and a love of children and flowers. Learning my father's life story, as incomplete and uncertain as it is, is hugely important to me. My only regret is that it came too late to share it with him.

I have known since forever that my father was not my biological father. I knew by a sort of emotional remote sensing when I was young, a perception enhanced as I grew older by our very different appearance. The adage "blood is thicker than water" is thought-provoking for me. The saying suggests that an association of unrelated people is not as strong as a biological link. That may be true for some relationships, but by no means all. I know for certain that a bond of love is the strongest and most enduring of all relationships. I am my father's son—I buy flowers regularly for my wife.

BIBLIOGRAPHY

Anders, Wladyslaw. *An Army in Exile: The Story of the Second Polish Corps."* London, EK: MacMillan & Co. Ltd., 1949.

Amersham Museum. "Shardeloes Babies 1939–1948." Accessed November 2, 2023. https://amershammuseum.org/history/shardeloes-babies/.

Archives Unbound. "Russian Civil War and American Expeditionary Forces in Siberia, 1918–1920." US National Archives Historical Files M-917, 1920. https://www.gale.com/binaries/content/assets/gale-us-en/primary-sources/archives-unbound/primary-sources_archives-unbound_russian-civil-war-and-american-expeditionary-forces-in-siberia-1918-20.pdf.

ASAGAO. "Where Japan and Poland Meet." Accessed October 31, 2023. https://asagao-pl.translate.goog/?_x_tr_sl=ja&_x_tr_tl=en&_x_tr_hl=en&_x_tr_pto=sc

Beevor, Antony. *Russia, Revolution and Civil War, 1917–1922.* New York, NY: Viking Press, 2022.

Berthon, Simon, and Joanna Potts. *Warlords: An Extraordinary Re-creation of World War II Through the Eyes and Minds of Hitler, Churchill, Roosevelt, and Stalin.* Boston, MA: Da Capo Press, Boston, 2007.

Birth Record, Wladyslaw Wojdak. https://metryki.genealodzy.pl/index.php?op=pg&ar=21&zs=0180d&se=&sy=1891&kt=1&plik=144-145.jpg&x=0&y=350&zoom=2.600297176820208.

Blaszczyk, Agata. "The Resettlement of Polish Refugees after the Second World War." *Forced Migration Review* 54 (2017). https://www.fmreview.org/resettlement/blaszczyk#.

Boldyrew, Aneta. "Education and Socialization of Polish Children During World War II: Sources, Methods and the Areas of Activity of the Historians of Education." *Piotrkowski Zeszyty Historyczne* 14 (2013): 163–182.

Borysiewicz, Mariusz. "Polish Settlement in Manchuria (1898–1950): A Brief Historical Survey." *Studia Polonijne* 39 (2018): 125–166. https://doi.org/10.18290/sp.2018.6.

Bretan, Juliette. "Shelter and Community: Polish Post-War Resettlement Camps in the United Kingdom." *Polish Culture*, October 24, 2020. https://culture.pl/en/article/shelter-community-polish-post-war-resettlement-camps-in-the-united-kingdom.

Canadian Centre of Architecture Archives. "Peter Caspari Fonds: Biographical Notes." Accessed November 2, 2023. https://www.cca.qc.ca/en/archives/379560/peter-caspari-fonds.

Charzynska, Katarzyna, M. Anczewska, and P. Switaj. "A Brief Overview of the History of Education in Poland." 93. https://files.eric.ed.gov/fulltext/ED567110.pdf

Cleveland Clinic. "Dissociative Amnesia." https://my.clevelandclinic.org/health/diseases/9789-dissociative-amnesia.

Cotnam, Hallie. "Polish Seafaring Yarn Gets Canadian Reboot." *CBC*, February 24, 2020. https://www.cbc.ca/news/canada/ottawa/sailing-adventure-polish-hero-autobiography-translation-history-1.5449662.

Davies, Norman. *Trail of Hope: The Anders Army, An Odyssey Across Three Continents*. Oxford, UK: Osprey Publishing, 2015.

Domaradzka, Anna. "Stories of Rescued Children." Oral presentation at Siberian Children conference, Wejherowo Special Needs Education School Complex, Poland, September 25, 2019.

Durand, Jonathan Kolodziej. *Memory is Our Homeland.* Documentary film, 2018. Video, 90:00. https://memoryisourhomeland.com/.

"Extermination of Polish Nobles, Landowners, etc. by Russia." *Morning Post,* September 1, 1863, 2. https://www.newspapers.com/image/396231435/?fcfToken=eyJhbGciOiJIUzI1NiIsInR5cCI6IkpXVCJ9.eyJmcmVlLXZpZXctaWQiOjM5NjIzMTQzNSwiaWFoIjoxNjgxOTM3ODc2LCJleHAiOjE2ODIwMjQyNzZ9.R-VuiEfMA_BRhKDDsyEJ6kWvRT1Dm78QNo3LlHsZUWQ.

Gentes, Andrew A. "Siberian Exile and the 1863 Polish Insurrectionists According to Russian Sources." *Jahrbücher Für Geschichte Osteuropas* 51, no. 2 (2003): 197–217. www.jstor.org/stable/41051062.

Geoportal, Poland Head Office of Geodesy and Cartography, accessed July 2023, https://www.gov.pl/web/gugik-en/geoportal

Germany Federal Ministry of Finance. *Wiedergutmachung: Provisions Relating to Compensation for National Social Injustice.* Berlin: German Federal Ministry of Finance, 2018. https://www.bundesfinanzministerium.de/Content/EN/Standardartikel/Press_Room/Publications/Brochures/2018-08-15-entschaedigung-ns-unrecht-engl.pdf?__blob=publicationFile&v=8.

GoodTherapy. "Psychogenic Mutism." Last modified August 18, 2015. https://www.goodtherapy.org/blog/psychpedia/psychogenic-mutism.

Hetherington, Peter. *Unvanquished: Joseph Pilsudski, Resurrected Poland and the Struggle for Eastern Europe.* Houston: Pingora Press, 2012.

Humphrey, Grace. *Pilsudski: Builder of Poland.* New York, NY: Scott and More, 1936.

Inoue, Kazihiko. "Poland Is One of the Most Pro-Japanese Nations: Here's Why." *Japan Forward*, October 18, 2019. https://japan-forward.com/poland-is-one-of-the-most-pro-japanese-nations-heres-why/.

Integrative Life Centre. "Childhood Trauma and Memory Loss." Last modified November 23, 2020. https://integrativelifecenter.com/childhood-trauma-memory-loss/#.

Isitt, Benjamin. *From Victoria to Vladivostok: Canada's Siberian Expedition, 1917–1919.* Vancouver, BC: UBC Press, 2010.

Japan-Poland Youth Association. Accessed October 31, 2023. https//jpya.or.jp/.

Jedras, Stanislaw. *Miastro I Gmina Bojanowo.* Nakladem Gminy Bojanowo. Leszno, Poland, 2005.

Kharghani, Narges. *Madame: One of the Last Polish Refugees in Iran.* Documentary film, 2017, video, 70:00. https://www.youtube.com/watch?v=F-1PqmZvS_g.

Konopka, Blanka. "Extraordinary tale of Polish orphans saved from Siberia by Japan in 1920 subject of new documentary." The First News, April 20, 2021. https:// www.thefirstnews.com/article/extraordinary-tale-of-polish-orphans-saved-from-siberia-by-japan-in-1920-subject-of-new-documentary-21387.

Kresy Family: Polish WWII History Group. Accessed November 2, 2023. https://www.kresyfamily.com/

Kresy Siberia Virtual Museum. "Pavel Wojdak: Wall of Tribute, List of 3rd Carpathian Rifle Division." Accessed November 2, 2023. https://kresy-siberia.org/list-3rd-carpathian-rifle-division/?pagenum=160.

Language Disorder Australia. "What is Language Disorder?" https://languagedisorder.org.au/what-is-language-disorder/?gad=1&gclid=CjwKCAiA3aeqBhBzEiwAxFiOBg5CMINnyHhZJvFMQby72tWcsK2ldVRh7xmWOK9bXXWkuS7TtF_ULRoCUHYQAvD_BwE

Leblanc, Dave. "Peter Caspari—a 'Bull' Who Helped Shape Toronto." *Globe and Mail*, December 4, 2014. https://www.theglobeandmail.com/life/home-and-garden/architecture/peter-caspari---a-bull-who-helped-shape-toronto/article21949216/.

Leslie, R. F. "The Emergence of an Independent Polish State." In *The History of Poland Since 1863*, edited by R. F. Leslie, 112–138. Cambridge, UK: Cambridge University Press, 1980.

Libicki, Piotr, and Marcin Libicki. *Dwory i pałac wiejskie na Mazowszu* (*Country Manors and Palaces in Masovia, Palace in Lochow*). (Rebis Publishing House, 2013).

Manghaa Museum. Accessed November 20, 2003. https://manghaa.pl/en/

Matsumoto, Teruo, and Wieslaw Theiss. *Siberian Children: Japan's Aid for Polish Children, 1919–1922*. Warsaw: Wydawnictwo Sejmowe, 2018.

McLeod, Saul. "Memory Stages: Encoding Storage and Retrieval." *Simply Psychology*. Last modified June 16, 2023. https://www.simplypsychology.org/memory.html.

Misiewicz, Ewa. *Siberian Dreams* (*Sybery Jskie Sny*). Documentary film, 2001. Video, 52:25. https://www.youtube.com/watch?v=p7zbIogBdbs.

Natural Earth. Free vector and raster map data at 1:10m, 1:50m and 1:110 scales. https://www.naturalearthdata.com.

Neuroscience News. "Recalling Memories from a Third Person Perspective Changes How Our Brain Processes Them." https://neurosciencenews.com/third-person-memory-recall-16821/.

O'Callaghan, Tommy. "8 Mind-Blowing Facts about Harbin, the Chinese City Built by the Russians." *Russia Beyond*, August 19, 2018. https://www.rbth.com/history/328985-harbin-russian.

Online Coin Club. "Poland, Russian Mikolaj I (Emperor Nicholas I of Russia, King of Poland." Accessed November 2, 2023. https://onlinecoin.club/Info/Reigns/Poland_Russian/King_Nicholas_I/.

Polish Rescue Committee. "Wrocily dzieci polskie z Syberji do Ojczyzny" ("Polish Children from Siberia Returned to Their Homeland"). In *Echo z Dalekiego Wschodu*, edited by Piotrowski Wienczyslaw, 7–44. Tokyo: Anna Bielkiewicz, 1924.

Popova, Zhanna. "The Two Tales of Forced Labour: Katorga and Reformed Prison in Imperial Russia (1879–1905)." *Almanack*, no. 14 (2016): 91–117. https://www.scielo.br/j/alm/a/GySfYqMB6HgDNBQgQqNJXRK/?lang=en&format=pdf.

Psychology Today. "Dissociative Amnesia." Last modified July 27, 2021. https://www.psychologytoday.com/us/conditions/dissociative-amnesia.

Rayfield, Donald. *Anton Chekhov: A Life*. London, UK: Harper Collins, 1997.

Sakamoto, Pamela Rotner. *Japanese Diplomats and Jewish Refugees: A World War II Dilemma.* New York, NY: Praeger, 1998.

Sawa, Wojtek. "The Wall Speaks: Voices of the Unheard." National Center of Culture, New Books Network, 2016. Last modified June 5, 2018. https://newbooksnetwork.com/wojtek-sawa-the-wall-speaks-voices-of-the-unheard-national-center-of-culture-2016

Shifrin, Avraham. *The First Guidebook to Prisons and Concentration Camps of the Soviet Union.* Translated from Russian. Toronto, ON: Bantam Books, 1982. https://vtoraya-literatura.com/pdf/shifrin_the_first_guidebiik_to_prisons_and_concentrations_camps_of_soviet_union_1982__ocr.pdf.

Sinelschikova, Yekaterina. "Why Did Vladimir Lenin Adopt the Name Lenin?" *Russia Beyond,* October 9, 2020. https://www.rbth.com/history/332831-vladimir-lenin-nickname.

Smith Archive. *Gold Mine in Lena Prior to the Lena Massacre.* Stock Photograph, Alamy, 191. https://www.alamy.com/stock-photo/lena-russia.html?blackwhite=1&sortBy=relevant.

Social Welfare Corporation Fukudenkai. "Interview with Slawomir Samardakiewicz." *Siberian Children,* August 2, 2021. https://siberianchildren.pl/en/slawomir-samardakiewicz-en/.

———. "Lukasz Grabowski." *Siberian Children,* October 25, 2020. https://siberianchildren.pl/en/interview-lukasz-grabowski-en/.

———. "History." *Siberian Children.* Accessed September 11, 2023. https://siberianchildren.pl/en/historia-dzieci-syberyjskich/.

———. "On the Meeting of Descendants of Siberian Children." Unpublished paper, Warsaw, October 7, 2022. 39-46

Stone, Norman. *The Eastern Front 1914–1917.* London, UK: Hodder & Stoughton, 1975.

Szarejko, Sylwia. "Polskie dzieci w Kraju Kwitnacej Wisni" [Polish children in the Land of the Rising Sun]. Siberia Memorial Museum, 2023.

Theiss, Wieslaw. *Dzieci Syberyjskie 1919–2019: Z Syberyii Przez Japonie I Stany Zjednoczone do Polski* [*Siberian Children 1919–2019: From Siberia through Japan and the United States to Poland*], second edition. Krakow: Manggha Museum of Japanese Art and Technology, 2020, 43.

———. "Help, Care and Rescue of Children in Poland in the War and Occupation Period (1939–1945). An Outline." *Social Work in Poland,* no. 1 (2018): 4–20.

———. Personal letter to author, 2019.

———. "Siberian Children – Two Meetings," Unpublished speaking notes of an address in Warsaw, September 26, 2023.

———. "Sieroctwo Wojenne Polskich Dzieci (1939–1945). Zarys Problematyki" ["The War Orphanhood of Polish Children (1939–1945). An Outline"]. *Przeglad Pedagogiczny*, no. 1 (2012): 79–95.

———. *Zniewolone Dziecinstwo: Socjalizacja w Skrajnych Warunkach Spoleczno-Politycznych* [*Enslaved Childhood: Socialization in Extreme Socio-Political Conditions*]. Warsaw: Zak Academic Publishing House, 1996.

The National Holocaust Centre and Museum. "Memory: Types, Definitions." https://holocaust.org.uk/memory.

Tsuruga Tourism Association. "Tsuruga Guide, Port of Humanity Museum." Accessed October 10, 2021. https://www.turuga.org/en/museum/museum.html. [broken URL; no archived version available]

Wandycz, Piotr S. "Soviet-Polish Relations 1917–1921." Cambridge, MA: Harvard University Press, 1969.

Wienczyslaw, Piotrowski, ed. *Echo z Dalekiego Wschodu* [*Echo of the Far East*]. Tokyo: Anna Bielkiewiczowa, 1921–1929. https://mbc-cyfrowemazowsze-pl.translate.goog/dlibra/doccontent?id=54000&_x_tr_sch=http&_x_tr_sl=pl&_x_tr_tl=en&_x_tr_hl=en&_x_tr_pto=sc.

———. *Echo z Dalekiego Wschodu* [*Echo of the Far East*]. Tokyo: "Drama of Children in Siberia, Memoirs of a 16 year old Boy," as related to Maria Brant. 7 (1922) 13-14, and 8 (1922) 11-12.

"Why Is Mikolaj the Polish Reflex of Nicholas?" Stack Exchange: Linguistics, last modified January 15, 2014. https://linguistics.stackexchange.com/questions/6193/why-is-miko%C5%82aj-the-polish-reflex-of-nicholas.

Wikipedia. "1900 Amur Anti-Chinese Pogroms." Last modified October 19, 2023. https://en.wikipedia.org/wiki/1900_Amur_anti-Chinese_pogroms.

———. "5th Rifle Division (Poland)." Last modified July 6, 2023. https://en.wikipedia.org/wiki/5th_Rifle_Division_(Poland)#History.

———. "Agar Rodney Adamson." Last modified August 21, 2023. https://en.wikipedia.org/wiki/Agar_Rodney_Adamson.

———. "Alexander Kolchak." Last modified October 29, 2023. https://en.wikipedia.org/wiki/Alexander_Kolchak.

———. "Allied Intervention in the Russian Civil War." Last modified October 30, 2023. https://en.wikipedia.org/wiki/Allied_intervention_in_the_Russian_Civil_War.

———. "American Expeditionary Force, Siberia." Last modified October 23, 2023. https://en.wikipedia.org/wiki/American_Expeditionary_Force,_Siberia

———. "Amur Annexation." Last modified October 6, 2023. https://en.wikipedia.org/wiki/Amur_Annexation.

———. "Anna Bielkiewicz." Last modified July 28, 2022. https://pl-m-wikipedia-org.translate.goog/wiki/Anna_Bielkiewicz?_x_tr_sl=pl&_x_tr_tl=en&_x_tr_hl=en&_x_tr_pto=sc.

———. "Battle of Bologna." Last modified August 16, 2023. https://en.wikipedia.org/wiki/Battle_of_Bologna.

———. "Battle of Lake Baikal." Last modified September 28, 2023. https://en.wikipedia.org/wiki/Battle_of_Lake_Baikal.

———. "Battle of Monte Cassino." Last modified October 31, 2023. https://en.wikipedia.org/wiki/Battle_of_Monte_Cassino

———. "Battle of Rimini." Last modified May 3, 2023. https://en.wikipedia.org/wiki/Battle_of_Rimini_(1944).

———. "Bezdany Raid." Last modified September 6, 2022. https://en.wikipedia.org/wiki/Bezdany_raid.

———. "Bronislaw Pilsudski." Last modified October 29, 2023. https://en.wikipedia.org/wiki/Bronisław_Piłsudski.

———. "Casimir Gzowski." Last modified August 5, 2023. https://en.wikipedia.org/wiki/Casimir_Gzowski.

———. "Chinese Eastern Railway." Last modified July 9, 2023. https://en.wikipedia.org/wiki/Chinese_Eastern_Railway.

———. "Chiune Sugihara." Last modified October 13, 2023. https://en.wikipedia.org/wiki/Chiune_Sugihara.

———. "Combat Organization of the Polish Socialist Party." Last modified March 17, 2023. https://en.wikipedia.org/wiki/Combat_Organization_of_the_Polish_Socialist_Party.

———. "Communist Party of Great Britain." Last modified October 29, 2023. https://en.wikipedia.org/wiki/Communist_Party_of_Great_Britain.

———. "Czechoslovak Legion." Last modified October 12, 2023. https://en.wikipedia.org/wiki/Czechoslovak_Legion.

———. "Eastern Front (World War I)." Last modified October 29, 2023. https://en.wikipedia.org/wiki/Eastern_Front_(World_War_I).

———. "Far Eastern Republic." Last modified September 19, 2023. https://en.wikipedia.org/wiki/Far_Eastern_Republic.

———. "Forced Labour Under German Rule During World War II." Last modified October 29, 2023. https://en.wikipedia.org/wiki/Forced_labour_under_German_rule_during_World_War_II.

———. "Free City Incident." Last modified November 23, 2023. https://en.wikipedia.org/wiki/ Free_City_Incident#:~:text=The%20Free%20City%20Incident%20was,the%20Pro%2DRussian%20resistance%20groups.

———. "Gothic Line." Last modified September 1, 2023. https://en.wikipedia.org/wiki/Gothic_Line.

———. "Grigory Mikhaylovich Semyonov." Last modified October 30, 2023. https://en.wikipedia.org/wiki/ Grigory_Mikhaylovich_Semyonov.

———. "Harbin." Last modified October 25, 2023. https://en.wikipedia.org/wiki/Harbin

———. "History of Poland." Lasted modified September 21, 2023. https://en.wikipedia.org/wiki/History_of_Poland.

———. "Ignacy Paderewski." Last modified October 29, 2023. https://en.wikipedia.org/wiki/Ignacy_Jan_Paderewski.

———. "Italian Resistance Movement." Last modified November 1, 2023. https://en.wikipedia.org/wiki/Italian_resistance_movement.

———. "Jan Zwartendijk." Last modified September 4, 2023. https://en.wikipedia.org/wiki/Jan_Zwartendijk.

———. "Jozef Haller." Last modified October 29, 2023. https://en.wikipedia.org/wiki/J%C3%B3zef_Haller

———. "Jozef Jakobkiewicz." Last modified July 3, 2022. https://translate.google.ca/translate?hl=en&sl=pl&u=https://pl.wikipedia.org/wiki/J%25C3%25B3zef_Jak%25C3%25B3bkiewicz&prev=search&pto=aue.

———. "Jozef Pilsudski." Last modified October 13, 2022. https://en.wikiquote.org/wiki/J%C3%B3zef_Pi%C5%82sudski#.

———. "Jozef Pilsudski." Last modified October 24, 2023. https://en.wikipedia.org/wiki/Józef_Piłsudski.

———. "Katorga." Last modified August 23, 2023. https://en.wikipedia.org/wiki/Katorga.

———. "Kresy." Last modified October 30, 2023. https://en.wikipedia.org/wiki/Kresy.

———. "Lena Gold Mining Partnership." March 15, 2023. https://en.wikipedia.org/wiki/Lena_Gold_Mining_Partnership

———. "Lena Massacre." Last modified July 5, 2023. https://en.wikipedia.org/wiki/Lena_massacre.

———. "Leopold Okulicki." Last modified August 31, 2023. https://en.wikipedia.org/wiki/Leopold_Okulicki.

———. "List of Assassinations in Europe." Last modified September 2, 2023. https://en.wikipedia.org/wiki/List_of_assassinations_in_Europe#Russia.

———. "Massacre of Svobodny." Last modified July 28, 2023. https://en.wikipedia.org/wiki/Massacre_of_Svobodny. [page deleted; archived version at https://web.archive.org/web/20230319093319/https://en.wikipedia.org/wiki/Massacre_of_Svobodny].

———. "Medard Downarowicz." Last modified October 24, 2023. https://pl.wikipedia.org/wiki/Medard_Downarowicz.

———. "Molotov-Ribbentrop Pact." Last modified October 30, 2023. https://en.wikipedia.org/wiki/Molotov%E2%80%93Ribbentrop_Pact.

———. "Nikolayevsk Incident." Last modified July 30, 2023. https://en.wikipedia.org/wiki/Nikolayevsk_incident.

———. "Novosibirsk." Last modified September 3, 2023. https://en.wikipedia.org/wiki/Novosibirsk.

———. "Olesnica." Last modified February 9, 2023. https://en.wikipedia.org/wiki/Ole%C5%9Bnica#cite_note-12.

———. "Panzergrenadier." Last modified August 30, 2023. https://en.wikipedia.org/wiki/Panzergrenadier.

———. "Partitions of Poland." Last modified October 25, 2023. https://en.wikipedia.org/wiki/Partitions_of_Poland.

———. "Peace of Riga." Last modified October 27, 2023. https://en.wikipedia.org/wiki/Peace_of_Riga.

———. "Poles in the Wehrmacht." Last modified July 20, 2023. https://en.wikipedia.org/wiki/Poles_in_the_Wehrmacht.

———. "Polish Armed Forces in the East (1914–1920)." Last modified September 18, 2021. https://en.wikipedia.org/wiki/ Polish_Armed_Forces_in_the_East_(1914%E2%80%931920).

———. "Polish Armed Forces in the West." Last modified August 29, 2023. https://en.wikipedia.org/wiki/ Polish_Armed_Forces_in_the_West.

———. "Polish I Corps in Russia." Last modified September 2, 2021. https://en.wikipedia.org/wiki/Polish_I_Corps_in_Russia.

———. "Polish Independent Carpathian Rifle Brigade." Last modified December 15, 2022. https://en.wikipedia.org/wiki/ Polish_Independent_Carpathian_Rifle_Brigade.

———. "Polish Resettlement Corps." Last modified July 18, 2023. https://en.wikipedia.org/wiki/Polish_Resettlement_Corps.

———. "Potsdam Conference." Last modified October 22, 2023. https://en.wikipedia.org/wiki/Potsdam_Conference.

———. "Revolution in the Kingdom of Poland 1905–1907." Last modified August 20, 2023. https://en.wikipedia.org/wiki/ Revolution_in_the_Kingdom_of_Poland_(1905%E2%80%931907).

———. "Russian Revolution." Last modified October 15, 2023. https://en.wikipedia.org/wiki/Russian_Revolution.

———. "Russo-Japanese War." Last modified October 30, 2023. https://en.wikipedia.org/wiki/Russo-Japanese_War.

———. "Senio." Last modified September 8, 2022. https://en.wikipedia.org/wiki/Senio.

———. "Shardeloes." Last modified February 20, 2023. https://en.wikipedia.org/wiki/Shardeloes.

———. "Svobodny." Last modified October 20, 2023. https://en.wikipedia.org/wiki/Svobodny,_Amur_Oblast.

———. "Sybirak." Last modified April 4, 2023. https://en.wikipedia.org/wiki/Sybirak.

———. "Tadeusz Kosciuszko Camp." Last modified June 15, 2022. https://pl.wikipedia.org/wiki/Tadeusz_Kosciuszko_Camp.

———. "The Curzon Line." Last modified October 20, 2023. https://en.wikipedia.org/wiki/Curzon_Line.

———. "Trans-Canada Air Lines Flight 9." Last modified August 21, 2022. https://en.wikipedia.org/wiki/ Trans-Canada_Air_Lines_Flight_9.

———. "Trans-Siberian Railway, Construction." Last modified October 14, 2023. https://en.wikipedia.org/wiki/Trans-Siberian_Railway#Construction.

———. "Trial of the Sixteen." Last modified July 14, 2023. https://en.wikipedia.org/wiki/Trial_of_the_Sixteen.

———. "USS *Princess Matoika*." Last modified June 9, 2023. https://en.wikipedia.org/wiki/USS_Princess_Matoika.

———. "Volksdeutsche." Last modified October 31, 2023. https://en.wikipedia.org/wiki/Volksdeutsche.

———. "Volksgrenadier." Last modified May 31, 2023. https://en.wikipedia.org/wiki/Volksgrenadier.

———. "Warsaw Uprising." Last modified September 10, 2023. https://en.wikipedia.org/wiki/Warsaw_Uprising.

———. "Warthegau." Last modified September 28, 2023. https://en.wikipedia.org/wiki/Reichsgau_Wartheland.

———. "Wehrmacht Foreign Volunteers and Conscripts." Last modified October 17, 2023. https://en.wikipedia.org/wiki/Wehrmacht_foreign_volunteers_and_conscripts.

———. "Western Betrayal." Last modified August 22, 2023. https://en.wikipedia.org/wiki/Western_betrayal.

———. "Yakov Tryapitsyn." Last modified September 5, 2023. https://en.wikipedia.org/wiki/Yakov_Tryapitsyn.

———. "Yalta Conference." Last modified September 9, 2023. https://en.wikipedia.org/wiki/Yalta_Conference.

———. "Yevgeny Miller." Last modified October 15, 2023. https://en.wikipedia.org/wiki/Yevgeny_Miller.

———. "Zaamurets." Last modified July 19, 2023. https://en.wikipedia.org/wiki/Zaamurets.

———. "Zamoyski Family." Last modified October 12, 2023. https://en.wikipedia.org/wiki/Zamoyski_family.

APPENDICES

Appendix 1

POLISH SIBERIAN CHILDREN OF THE
FIRST RESCUE MISSION, BOYS, 1920–1921

Names and Parental Status;
P – parents alive, M – mother only, F – father only, O – orphan

LIST OF BOYS

	Name of Child	Age	Where Found	P	M	F	O	USA Location
1	Andrzejewski, Piotr	15	Nikolajewsk na Amur		√			Cambridge Springs, PA
2	Andrzejewski, Wiktor	16	Nikolajewsk na Amur		√			Cambridge Springs, PA
3	Andrzejewski, Wsiewolod	10	Nikolajewsk na Amur		√			Cambridge Springs, PA
4	Aniskowicz, Pawel		Okieanskaja		√			Emsworth, PA
5	Aniskowicz, Piotr		Okieanskaja		√			Emsworth, PA
6	Arendt, Alfred	10	Nikolsk, Buryatia		√			Niles, IL
7	Arendt, Edmunt	12	Nikolsk, Buryatia		√			Niles, IL
8	Arendt, Henryk	5	Nikolsk, Buryatia		√			Niles, IL
9	Bertulis, Boleslaw	13	Charbin				√	Polonia, WI
10	Bertulis, Jan	11	Charbin				√	Polonia, WI
11	Bertulis, Jozef	7	Charbin				√	Polonia, WI
12	Bielicki, Ignacy	7	Czyta	√				Niles, IL

13	Bielicki, Pawel	16	Czyta	√				Cambridge Springs, PA
14	Boginski, Edward	14	Charbin		√			Orchard Lake, MI
15	Boginski, Walerjan	15	Charbin		√			Orchard Lake, MI
16	Bohdanowicz, Walerjan	5	Wladywostok		√			Emsworth, PA
17	Bohdaowski, Adam	7	Konstantyn		√			Emsworth, PA
18	Bolubojarski, Wiktor	12	Wladywostok				√	Emsworth, PA
19	Brzosko, Konstanty	9	Aleksiejewsk	√				Manitowoc, WI
20	Brzosko, Wlodzimierz	10	Aleksiejewsk	√				Manitowoc, WI
21	Budzinowski, Wilhelm	11	Nikolsk, Buryatia	√				Cambridge Springs, PA
22	Ciechanowicz, Jan	12	Charbin				√	Cambridge Springs, PA
23	Ciepiel, Piotr	5	Chabarowsk				√	Emsworth, PA
24	Choderski, Aleksander	9	Charbin		√			Manitowoc, WI
25	Choderski, Konstanty	10	Charbin		√			Manitowoc, WI
26	Cytowicz, Eugeniusz	11	Chabarowsk		√			Niles, IL
27	Czuryllo, Jan	13	Charbin				√	Polonia, WI
28	Daniuk, Karoll	14	Charbin		√			Cambridge Springs, PA
29	Dabrowski, Stanislaw	13	Charbin	√				Cambridge Springs, PA
30	Dreiski, Aleksander	8	Chabarowsk		√			Niles, IL
31	Dreiski, Leon	4	Chabarowsk		√			Niles, IL
32	Dreiski, Piotr	6	Chabarowsk		√			Niles, IL
33	Drogoszewski, Boleslaw	13	Wladywostok				√	Cambridge Springs, PA

34	Dudowicz, Adam	14	Chabarowsk	√				Cambridge Springs, PA
35	Dudowicz, Stanislaw	12	Chabarowsk	√				Emsworth, PA
36	Dudzki, Bolesaw	14	Chabarowsk	√				Cambridge Springs, PA
37	Dudzki, Jozef	9	Chabarowsk	√				Emsworth, PA
38	Dudzki, Wladyslaw	12	Chabarowsk	√				Emsworth, PA
39	Erdman, Anatol	8	Kniewiczy				√	Emsworth, PA
40	Faltyn, Bronislaw	13	Charbin		√			Cambridge Springs, PA
41	Fuks, Henryk	12	Wladywostok	√				Polonia, WI
42	Fuks, Wladyslaw	9	Wladywostok	√				Polonia, WI
43	Gadomski, Marcin	10	Wladywostok		√			Cambridge Springs, PA
44	Galat, Feliks	10	Chabarowsk		√			Emsworth, PA
45	Galat, Kazimierz	6	Chabarowsk		√			Emsworth, PA
46	Galczynski, Edward	11	Wladywostok		√			Niles, IL
47	Galczynski, Waclaw	9	Wladywostok		√			Niles, IL
48	Gierwatowski, Henryk	9	Charbin		√			Niles, IL
49	Gorski, Wladyslaw	12	Wladywostok	√				Polonia, WI
50	Gryszkus, Jozef	7	Czyta			√		Milwaukee, WI
51	Gryszkus, Kazimierz	4	Czyta			√		Milwaukee, WI
52	Gryszkus, Jan	11	Czyta			√		Milwaukee, WI
53	Grzegorzewski, Wiktor	8	Czyta		√			Milwaukee, WI
54	Halaburda, Piotr	5	Czyta		√			Cambridge Springs, PA
55	Hulewicz, Eljasz	9	Aleksiejewsk				√	Polonia, WI
56	Hulewicz, Kuzma	11	Aleksiejewsk				√	Polonia, WI

57	Hulewicz, Jan	12	Aleksiejewsk			√	Polonia, WI
58	Hulewicz, Piotr	5	Aleksiejewsk			√	Polonia, WI
59	Jablonski, Eugenjusz	11	Chabarowsk			√	Emsworth, PA
60	Jablonski, Henryk	7	Chabarowsk			√	Emsworth, PA
61	Jablonski, Leon	13	Chabarowsk			√	Emsworth, PA
62	Jablonski, Romuald	5	Chabarowsk			√	Emsworth, PA
63	Jackowski, Mieczyslaw	10	Blagowieszczen		√		
64	Jadykin, Aleksander	11	Chabarowsk	√			Polonia, WI
65	Jadykin, Mikolaj	7	Chabarowsk	√			Polonia, WI
66	Jermolenek, Wlodzimierz	9	Chabarowsk	√			Emsworth, PA
67	Jewpak, Jan	11	Konstantyn			√	Emsworth, PA
68	Jewpak, Jan	8	Konstantyn			√	Emsworth, PA
69	Krylow, Wadim	8	Wladywostok				Emsworth, PA
70	Kairski, Borys	7	Aleksiejewsk			√	New Britain, CT
71	Kamienski, Alfred	13	Charbin	√			New Britain, CT
72	Kamienski, Telesfor	12	Charbin	√			New Britain, CT
73	Kanczus-Bajton, August	10	Czyta	√			New Britain, CT
74	Kapelusznik, Bazyli	10	Chabarowsk			√	Emsworth, PA
75	Karbowiak, Zygmunt	9	Charbin			√	New Britain, CT
76	Kasperowicz, Aleksander	15	Wladywostok			√	Emsworth, PA
77	Kazimierski, Michal	11	Charbin			√	Niles, IL
78	Kazimierski, Walenty	15	Charbin			√	Niles, IL
79	Kogutnicki, Wladyslaw	5	Wladywostok			√	Conshohecken, PA

80	Kiewra, Jan	9	Aleksiejewsk		√			Conshohecken, PA
81	Kowalski, Edward	11	Wladywostok	√				Polonia, WI
82	Kot, Stanislaw	11	Charbin			√		Polonia, WI
83	Kozlowski, Jan	15	Charbin			√		Polonia, WI
84	Krol, Feliks	16	Chabarowsk		√			Cambridge Springs, PA
85	Kawecki, Wiktor	10	Wladywostok	√				Conshohecken, PA
86	Kubis, Antoni	9	Blagowieszczensk			√		Conshohecken, PA
87	Kuczynski, Piotr	10	Blagowieszczensk		√			Conshohecken, PA
88	Kuczynski, Stanislaw	15	Blagowieszczensk		√			Conshohecken, PA
89	Kujawa, Aleksander	12	Chabarowsk			√		Emsworth, PA
90	Kulczycki, Czeslaw	8	Charbin			√		Emsworth, PA
91	Kulczycki, Kazimierz	10	Charbin			√		Emsworth, PA
92	Kulesza, Leopold	12	Blagowieszczensk	√				New Britain, CT
93	Kulczycki, Leon	12	Charbin			√		Emsworth, PA
94	Kulesza, Stanislaw	8	Charbin				√	Polonia, WI
95	Kosik, Bohdan	7	Charbin				√	Conshohecken, PA
96	Lachowski, Adam	10	Wladywostok		√			Polonia, WI
97	Lachowski, Wiktor	6	Wladywostok		√			Polonia, WI
98	Lachowski, Wladyslaw	6	Wladywostok		√			Polonia, WI
99	Lebida, Leon	8	Nikolajewsk na Amur			√		Niles, IL
100	Leonowicz, Wiktor	5	Wladywostok					Conshohecken, PA

101	Lesniewski, Romuald	11	Charbin		√			Emsworth, PA
102	Lipinski, Henryk	7	Wladywostok		√			Emsworth, PA
103	Lipinski, Leopold	9	Wladywostok		√			Polonia, WI
104	Lapinski, Stanislaw	14	Nowokijewsk		√			Cambridge Springs, PA
105	Lawrynowicz, Edward	12	Wladywostok			√		Cambridge Springs, PA
106	Lawrynowicz, Waclaw	14	Wladywostok			√		Cambridge Springs, PA
107	Lukomski, Zygmunt	15	Blagowieszczensk	√				Cambridge Springs, PA
108	Maciejewicz, Radoslaw	6	Chabarowsk		√			Emsworth, PA
109	Majsak, Antoni	13	Aleksiejewsk	√				Cambridge Springs, PA
110	Majsak, Ignacy	11	Aleksiejewsk	√				New Britain, CT
111	Markowski, Aleksander	16	Charbin				√	Cambridge Springs, PA
112	Markowski, Wladyslaw	12	Charbin				√	Niles, IL
113	Marszal, Inocenty	12	Czyta		√			Milwaukee, WI
114	Marszal, Ludwik	3	Czyta		√			Milwaukee, WI
115	Mazur, Leonard	7	Chabarowsk	√				Emsworth, PA
116	Michalowski, Stanislaw	8	Wladywostok		√			Emsworth, PA
117	Michniewicz, Konstanty	12	Chabarowsk			√		Emsworth, PA
118	Michniewicz, Stanislaw	5	Chabarowsk			√		Emsworth, PA
119	Michniewicz, Wladyslaw	14	Chabarowsk			√		Cambridge Springs, PA
120	Mielnik, Jozef		Chabarowsk		√			Emsworth, PA
121	Mielnik, Walenty		Chabarowsk		√			Emsworth, PA
122	Mietek, Wladyslaw	9	Nowokijewsk		√			Niles, IL

123	Mularczyk, Zygmunt	9	Wladywostok			√		Cambridge Springs, PA
124	Niewinowski, Edward	15	Wladywostok			√		Cambridge Springs, PA
125	Nowakowski, Edmund	8	Chabarowsk			√		Niles, IL
126	Nowakowski, Henryk	16	Chabarowsk			√		Cambridge Springs, PA
127	Oleszczuk, Antoni	11	Kamieniec Podolski				√	Emsworth, PA
128	Otocki, Stanislaw	7	Chabarowsk			√		Niles, IL
129	Pancerzynski, Jozef	14	Blagowieszczensk		√			Cambridge Springs, PA
130	Pancerzynski, Kazimierz	10	Blagowieszczensk	√				Manitowoc, WI
131	Pierzchala, Stanislaw	14	Chabarowsk		√			Cambridge Springs, PA
132	Poliszczuk-Cecyluk, Aleksander	12	Wladywostok		√			Cambridge Springs, PA
133	Polubianko, Czeslaw	14	Chabarowsk		√			Emsworth, PA
134	Poponczyk, Jan	15	Wladywostok		√			Cambridge Springs, PA
135	Romanowski, Feliks	16	Blagowieszczensk				√	Cambridge Springs, PA
136	Rudzienski, Leon	9	Chabarowsk		√			Emsworth, PA
137	Rudzki, Apolinary	8	Aleksiejewsk	√				Emsworth, PA
138	Rudzki, Leon	14	Aleksiejewsk	√				New Britain, CT
139	Rudzki, Piotr	5	Aleksiejewsk	√				Emsworth, PA
140	Rymkiewicz, Edward	14	Czyta	√				Niles, IL
141	Sadkowski, Antoni	9	Charbin		√			Conshohecken, PA
142	Sadkowski, Kazimierz	13	Charbin		√			Conshohecken, PA

143	Sadkowski, Wladyslaw	10	Charbin		√			Conshohecken, PA
144	Samardakiewicz, Antoni	9	Charbin		√			Niles, IL
145	Samardakiewicz, Jan	10	Charbin		√			Niles, IL
146	Samojlis, Aleksander	11	Chabarowsk		√			Niles, IL
147	Samojlis, Wladyslaw	13	Chabarowsk		√			Cambridge Springs, PA
148	Sandro, Piotr	7	Chabarowsk				√	Emsworth, PA
149	Stapien, Wladyslaw	12	Chabarowsk			√		Emsworth, PA
150	Sierota, Jan	13	Chabarowsk				√	Niles, IL
151	Sierota, Stefan	6	Chabarowsk				√	Niles, IL
152	Sierota	12	Wladywostok				√	Niles, IL
153	Sikorski, Andrzej	11	Blagowieszczensk			√		New Britain, CT
154	Siwek, Henryk	5	Razdolnoje	√				Manitowoc, WI
155	Siwek, Leon	9	Razdolnoje	√				Manitowoc, WI
156	Skapski, Henryk	9	Blagowieszczensk			√		New Britain, CT
157	Skapski, Kazimierz	7	Blagowieszczensk	√				Emsworth, PA
158	Sledzinski, Zenon	9	Aleksiejewsk	√				Emsworth, PA
159	Smaga, Wiktor	10	Chabarowsk	√				Cambridge Springs, PA
160	Sobystjanski, Benedykt	6	Konstantynopol				√	Niles, IL
161	Sokolowski, Boleslaw	3	Charbin	√				Niles, IL
162	Stanecki, Piotr	7	Aleksiejewsk	√				Niles, IL
163	Stanecki, Wladyslaw	12	Aleksiejewsk	√				Manitowoc, WI
164	Staszak, Filip	15	Blagowieszczensk				·√	Cambridge Springs, PA
165	Stoczynski, Leon	16	Wladywostok				√	Cambridge Springs, PA

166	Swidarski, Boleslaw	15	Blagowieszczensk		√			Cambridge Springs, PA
167	Szaltenis, Stanislaw	10	Blagowieszczensk				√	Emsworth, PA
168	Szaltenis, Stefan	11	Blagowieszczensk				√	New Britain, CT
169	Szpinda, Emil	14	Chabarowsk				√	Cambridge Springs, PA
170	Szpinda, Jan	10	Chabarowsk				√	Niles, IL
171	Szurkus, Jerzy	9	Charbin				√	Milwaukee, WI
172	Szurkus, Jozef	11	Chabarowsk				√	Polonia, WI
173	Szurkus, Stanislaw	6	Charbin				√	Polonia, WI
174	Szydlowski, Jozef	10	Wladywostok		√			
175	Szylwian, Zygmunt	14	Charbin			√		Cambridge Springs, PA
176	Traczynski, Jan	5	Sierebranka			√		
177	Ubars, Adolf	8	Wladywostok		√			Manitowoc, WI
178	Ubars, Edwin	7	Wladywostok		√			Manitowoc, WI
179	Walewicz, Mikolaj		Chabarowsk				√	Emsworth, PA
180	Wedzik, Wladyslaw	6	Wladywostok		√			Milwaukee, WI
181	Widero, Edward	9	Okieanskaja		√			Polonia, WI
182	Wisniewski, Stanislaw	13	Charbin				√	Cambridge Springs, PA
183	Wiszniewski, Bronislaw	13	Charbin		√			Cambridge Springs, PA
184	Wieckowski, Edmund	7	Charbin		√			Emsworth, PA
185	Wojcieszak, Aleksander	15	Czyta				√	Cambridge Springs, PA
186	Wojdak, Wladyslaw	7	Charbin				√	Milwaukee, WI
187	Wolanski, Antoni	14	Wladywostok	√				Cambridge Springs, PA
188	Wolanski, Mieczyslaw	15	Wladywostok	√				Niles, IL

189	Wolikowski, Jozef	11	Wladywostok		√			Niles, IL
190	Wolikowski, Ludoslaw	8	Wladywostok		√			Niles, IL
191	Wojcik, Feliks	13	Chabarowsk	√				Emsworth, PA
192	Wojcik, Karol	12	Chabarowsk	√				Emsworth, PA
193	Wojcik, Waclaw	15	Chabarowsk	√				Cambridge Springs, PA
194	Voigt, Andrzej	10	Wladywostok	√				Emsworth, PA
195	Voigt, Wiktor	13	Wladywostok	√				
196	Zalewski, Aleksander	15	Charbin	√				Cambridge Springs, PA
197	Zanierczyk, Antoni	11	Chabarowsk				√	Cambridge Springs, PA
198	Zapolski, Jan	12	Wladywostok	√				Niles, IL
199	Zawadzki, Leon	12	Wladywostok	√				Cambridge Springs, PA
200	Zolotarewicz, Dymitr	4	Chabarowsk	√				Cambridge Springs, PA
201	Zolotarewicz, Jan	15	Chabarowsk	√				Cambridge Springs, PA
202	Zolotarewicz, Piotr	9	Chabarowsk	√				Emsworth, PA
203	Zurszel, Aleksander	8	Chabarowsk		√			Emsworth, PA
204	Zurszel, Mokalaj	9	Chabarowsk				√	Emsworth, PA
205	Zygrykalis, Antoni	9	Charbin				√	Emsworth, PA
206	Zygrykalis, Kazimierz	13	Charbin				√	Emsworth, PA

POLISH SIBERIAN CHILDREN OF THE
FIRST RESCUE MISSION, GIRLS, 1920–1921

Names and Parental Status;
P – parents alive, M – mother only, F – father only, O – orphan

LIST OF GIRLS

	Name of Child	Age	Where Found	P	M	F	O	USA Location
1	Aniskowicz, Aniela	10	Okleanskaja		√			
2	Brauer, Antonina	7	Wladywostok					Emsworth, PA
3	Bazar, Maria	12	Wladywostok				√	Detroit, MI
4	Badzynska, Helena	9	Chabarowsk			√		Niles, IL
5	Badzynska, Irena	11	Wladywostok			√		Emsworth, PA
6	Brauer, Marja	12	Wladywostok					Emsworth, PA
7	Bielecka, Helena	8	Wladywostok		√			Niles, IL
8	Birzanska, Helena	11	Wladywostok		√			Reading, PA
9	Brzanska, Marja	11	Wladywostok		√			Reading, PA
10	Bogdanowicz, Genowefa	3	Wladywostok		√			Emsworth, PA
11	Bohdanowska, Marja	4	Chabarowsk		√			Emsworth, PA
12	Bowszyc, Walerja	11	Wladywostok		√			Reading, PA
13	Brant, Joanna	2	Wladywostok	√				
14	Brzosko, Wiktoria	10	Aleksiejewsk	√				Reading, PA
15	Brzosko, Zofia	6	Aleksiejewsk	√				Reading, PA
16	Choderska, Katarzyna	12	Charbin		√			Reading, PA

17	Ciepel, Aleksandra	7	Chabarowsk				√	Emsworth, PA
18	Cypian (Cynin), Antonina	12	Czyta	√				Detroit, MI
19	Cypian (Cynin), Ewa	14	Czyta	√				Detroit, MI
20	Cytowicz, Luba		Chabarowsk	√				Niles, IL
21	Cytowicz, Nadzieja		Chabarowsk	√				Niles, IL
22	Cytowicz, Wiera		Chabarowsk	√				Niles, IL
23	Czesnlewska, Antonina		Chabarowsk				√	Niles, IL
24	Czesnlewska, Helena		Chabarowsk				√	Niles, IL
25	Czesnlewska, Valentyna		Chabarowsk				√	Niles, IL
26	Erdman, Antonina		Okleanskaja				√	Emsworth, PA
27	Erdman, Halina	9	Okleanskaja				√	Emsworth, PA
28	Fuks, Janina	7	Wladywostok	√				Reading, PA
29	Fuks, Regina	5	Wladywostok	√				Reading, PA
30	Calczynska, Jadwiga	8	Wladywostok		√			Niles, IL
31	Gersz, Antonina	3	Wladywostok				√	Detroit, MI
32	Gotowicka, Adela	9	Wladywostok	√				Reading, PA
33	Gotowicka, Genowefa	10	Wladywostok	√				Reading, PA
34	Grzegorzewska, Bronislawa	11	Czyta		√			Milwaukee, WI
35	Halaburda, Anastazja	8	Czyta		√			Emsworth, PA
36	Halaburda, Elzbieta	6	Czyta		√			Emsworth, PA

37	Halaburda, Marja	14	Czyta		√		Emsworth, PA
38	Hulewicz, Katarzyna	6	Aleksiejewsk			√	Emsworth, PA
39	Jackowska, Janina	12	Blagowieszczensk	√			Emsworth, PA
40	Jackowska, Natalia	7	Blagowieszczensk	√			Emsworth, PA
41	Janiszewska, Aleksandra	11	Wladywostok		√		Detroit, MI
42	Janiszewska, Katarzyna	6	Wladywostok		√		Detroit, MI
43	Janiszewska, Tatjana	15	Wladywostok		√		Detroit, MI
44	Jazina-Jazick, Weronika	10	Chabarowsk			√	Niles, IL
45	Jermolenok, Amelja	3	Chabarowsk		√		Emsworth, PA
46	Jermolenok, Anna	10	Chabarowsk		√		Emsworth, PA
47	Jermolenok, Michalina	13	Chabarowsk		√		Emsworth, PA
48	Jewpak, Krystyna	10	Konstantyn		√		Emsworth, PA
49	Kanczus-Bajton, Flora	14	Czyta		√		Emsworth, PA
50	Krylowa, Tamara	9	Wladywostok		√		Emsworth, PA
51	Kapelusznik, Aleksandra	13	Chabarowsk			√	Emsworth, PA
52	Kotlarz, Klaudyna	8	Chabarowsk			√	Emsworth, PA
53	Kotlarz, Serafina	6	Chabarowsk			√	Emsworth, PA
54	Kowtun, Albina	10	Aleksiejewsk		√		Emsworth, PA
55	Krajewska, Eugenia	7	Charbin			√	Detroit, MI
56	Krauze, Izabela	10	Chabarowsk	√			Detroit, MI

57	Krauze, Olga	13	Chabarowsk	√				Detroit, MI
58	Kujawa, Antonina	9	Chabarowsk		√			Emsworth, PA
59	Kujawa, Wiera	8	Chabarowsk		√			Emsworth, PA
60	Kulczycka, Jadwiga	13	Charbin			√		Emsworth, PA
61	Kulczycka, Marja	6	Charbin			√		Emsworth, PA
62	Kulczycka, Zofja	4	Charbin			√		Emsworth, PA
63	Kulesza, Felicja	14	Blagowieszczensk	√				Reading, PA
64	Kulesza, Lucja	15	Blagowieszczensk	√				Reading, PA
65	Krzywicka, Bronislawa	15	Wladywostok			√		Reading, PA
66	Leonowicz, Antonina	10	Wladywostok	√				Reading, PA
67	Leonowicz, Olga	7	Wladywostok	√				Reading, PA
68	Lewinska, Eugienia	11	Charbin		√			Emsworth, PA
69	Luginiec, Eudokja	10	Chabarowsk			√		Emsworth, PA
70	Maciejewicz, Janina	9	Chabarowsk		√			
71	Marszal, Anna	4	Czyta		√			Detroit, MI
72	Marszal, Helena	8	Czyta		√			Detroit, MI
73	Mazur, Janina	11	Chabarowsk	√				Emsworth, PA
74	Mazur, Wladyslawa	7	Chabarowsk	√				Emsworth, PA
75	Michniewicz, Zofja	9	Chabarowsk				√	Emsworth, PA
76	Mielnik, Ludmila	13	Chabarowsk		√			Emsworth, PA

77	Milachowska, Antonina	10	Wladywostok	√				Reading, PA
78	Milachowska, Stanislawa	9	Wladywostok	√				Reading, PA
79	Mularczyk, Antonina	6	Wladywostok			√		Emsworth, PA
80	Mularczyk, Kazimiera	11	Wladywostok			√		Emsworth, PA
81	Mularczyk, Helena	10	Wladywostok			√		Emsworth, PA
82	Mularczyk, Wladyslawa	8	Wladywostok			√		Emsworth, PA
83	Myczkiewicz, Bronislawa	8	Chabarowsk		√			Emsworth, PA
84	Mietek, Janina	12	Nowokijewsk		√			Niles, IL
85	Niewiadomska, Marja	5	Charbin				√	Niles, IL
86	Niewiadomska, Janina	8	Wladywostok			√		Emsworth, PA
87	Niewiadomska, Julja	13	Wladywostok			√		Emsworth, PA
88	Niewiadomska, Marja	5	Wladywostok			√		Emsworth, PA
89	Niewiadomska, Zofja	11	Wladywostok			√		Emsworth, PA
90	Nowajczuk, Marja	12	Carowka				√	Niles, IL
91	Nowakowska, Janine	13	Chabarowsk	√				Niles, IL
92	Nowicka, Natalja	13	Chabarowsk	√				Niles, IL
93	Oleszczuk, Adela	7	Kamieniec Podolski				√	Emsworth, PA
94	Otocka, Franciszka	11	Chabarowsk	√				Niles, IL
95	Pawlowska, Katarzyna	10	Chabarowsk				√	Niles, IL

96	Pawlowska, Konstancja	16	Czyta				√	[pursued education]
97	Paszkiewicz, Antonina	6	Charbin		√			Detroit, MI
98	Paszkiewicz, Brontislawa	9	Charbin		√			Detroit, MI
99	Paszkiewicz, Irena	13	Charbin		√			Detroit, MI
100	Pieczajka, Karolina	6	Mandzurja		√			Detroit, MI
101	Pierzchala, Jadwiga	13	Chabarowsk		√			[at mother's]
102	Poliszczuk-Cecyluk, Anaztazja	8	Wladywostok		√			Emsworth, PA
103	Poliszczuk-Cecyluk, Helena	10	Wladywostok		√			Emsworth, PA
104	Polublanko, Bronislawa	14	Chabarowsk				√	Emsworth, PA
105	Ratajska, Janina	13	Chabarowsk				√	Detroit, MI
106	Roszkowska, Anna	13	Charbin				√	Emsworth, PA
107	Rudzianska, Julja	7	Chabarowsk			√		Emsworth, PA
108	Rudzianska, Marja	11	Chabarowsk			√		Emsworth, PA
109	Rudzianska, Marja	11	Chabarowsk		√			Emsworth, PA
110	Rudzka, Leonarda	11	Aleksiejewsk	√				Emsworth, PA
111	Ryga, Anaa	7	Chabarowsk				√	Emsworth, PA
112	Ryga, Eudokja	6	Chabarowsk				√	Emsworth, PA
113	Sapierzynska, Regina	16	Charbin				√	Milwaukee, WI

114	Sierota, Paulina	12	Wladywostok			√	Emsworth, PA
115	Siwek, Eugenja	11	Razoolnoje	√			Reading, PA
116	Skapska, Nadzieja	13	Blagowieszczensk		√		Emsworth, PA
117	Sledzinska, Janina	11	Aleksiejewsk	√			Emsworth, PA
118	Smaga, Genowefa	11	Chabarowsk	√			Emsworth, PA
119	Smaga, Walenty	9	Chabarowsk	√			Emsworth, PA
120	Stanecka, Bronislawa	11	Aleksiejewsk	√			Emsworth, PA
121	Stanecka, Julja	9	Aleksiejewsk	√			Emsworth, PA
122	Stepien, Aniela	14	Chabarowsk			√	Emsworth, PA
123	Superska, Aniela	10	Konstantynow		√		Niles IL
124	Superska, Franciszka	6	Konstantynow		√		Niles IL
125	Szeptycka, Nadzieja	7	Chabarowsk			√	Niles IL
126	Szerejko, Anastazja	9	Chabarowsk			√	Niles IL
127	Szkuropadzka, Jadwiga	6	Aleksiejewsk		√		Niles IL
128	Szydlowska, Marja	12	Wladywostok		√		Reading, PA
129	Szyszkarewska, Aleksandra	6	Chabarowsk			√	Niles IL
130	Szyszkarewska, Halina	7	Chabarowsk			√	Niles IL
131	Szydlowska, Antonina	7	Wladywostok		√		Reading, PA
132	Szydlowska, Marja	12	Wladywostok		√		Reading, PA
133	Szylwian, Wilhelmina	11	Charbin		√		Emsworth, PA

134	Traczynska, Antonina	7	Rogaczewska		√		Reading, PA
135	Traczynska, Jozefa	12	Aleksiejewsk		√		Reading, PA
136	Traczynska, Marjanna	10	Rogaczewska		√		Reading, PA
137	Traczynska, Rozalja	6	Rogaczewska		√		Reading, PA
138	Tysmieniecka, Ludmila	13	Chabarowsk	√			Emsworth, PA
139	Urbanowicz, Janina	10	Chabarowsk	√			Emsworth, PA
140	Urbars, Leonora	7	Chabarowsk	√			Emsworth, PA
141	Urbanowicz, Ludmila	5	Chabarowsk	√			Emsworth, PA
142	Urbanowicz, Tamara		Chabarowsk	√			Emsworth, PA
143	Wasilewska, Aniela	11	Carowka	√			Niles IL
144	Wasilewska, Apolonja	9	Chabarowsk	√			Niles IL
145	Wasilewska, Leonarda	5	Chabarowsk	√			Niles IL
146	Wasilewska, Marja	9	Chabarowsk	√			Niles IL
147	Wasilewska, Wiktoria	7	Chabarowsk	√			Niles IL
148	Wasilewska, Marja	14	Wladywostok			√	Niles IL
149	Wedzik, Marja	14	Wladywostok	√			Detroit, MI
150	Wilczynska-Simonowicz, Teofila	9	Wladywostok			√	Emsworth, PA
151	Wieckowska, Helena	9	Charbin	√			Emsworth, PA

152	Wieckowska, Wanda	8	Charbin		√			Emsworth, PA
153	Wojcik, Helena	7	Chabarowsk				√	Emsworth, PA
154	Wojcik, Stanislawa	10	Chabarowsk	√				Emsworth, PA
155	Wronska, Anna	2	Charbin				√	Emsworth, PA
156	Wroblewska, Helena	9	Wladywostok				√	Detroit, MI
157	Wroblewska, Zofja	14	Wladywostok				√	Detroit, MI
158	Wysocka, Ksenja	13	Chabarowsk				√	Niles, IL
159	Zielinska, Bronislawa	14	Wladywostok		√			Reading, PA
160	Zielinska, Katarzyna	9	Wladywostok		√			Reading, PA
161	Zielinska, Regina	9	Charbin		√			Reading, PA
162	Zielinska, Stanislawa	13	Wladywostok		√			Reading, PA
163	Zielinska, Zofja	5	Wladywostok		√			Reading, PA
164	Zolotarewicz, Katarzyna	12	Chabarowsk	√				Emsworth, PA
165	Zukowska, Antonina	14	Czyta				√	Emsworth, PA
166	Zurawel, Eugenja	6	Chabarowsk		√			Emsworth, PA

Appendix 2

POLISH SIBERIAN CHILDREN OF THE
SECOND RESCUE MISSION, 1922

LIST OF BOYS

	Name of Child	Age	Where Found
1	Baranowski, Wladyslaw	10	Harbin
2	Bednarczyk, Stanislaw	2	Czyta
3	Bem, Jerzy	4	Mandzuria
4	Bem, Stanislaw	1	Mandzuria
5	Bielicki, Stanislaw	10	Nik. Ussuryjski
6	Bielicki, Zygmunt	6	Nik. Ussuryjski
7	Bielawski, Teodor	13	Blagowieszczensk
8	Bielewicz, Bronislaw	6	Chabarowsk
9	Bielewicz, Stanislaw	12	Chabarowsk
10	Bejtman, Jozef	16	Chabarowsk
11	Bejtman, Kazimierz	11	Chabarowsk
12	Bejtman, Wincenty	12	Chabarowsk
13	Bitner, Tadeusz	15	Czyta
14	Blizinski, Stanislaw	7	Wierchnieudzinsk
15	Bogucki, Alfons	14	Wierchnieudzinsk
16	Brestowski, Bronislaw	8	Harbin
17	Budzinski, Michal	9	Chabarowsk
18	Buglewski, Wladyslaw	2	Blagowieszczensk
19	Burdziuk, Wladyslaw	9	Blagowieszczensk
20	Choroszewicz, Pawel	13	Harbin
21	Chryzan Zelinski, Leon	13	Blagowieszczensk
22	Cymek, Stanislaw	5	Harbin
23	Cymek, Wladyslaw	7	Harbin
24	Cymek, Bazyli	12	Harbin

25	Czamlaj, Pawel	11	Blagowieszczensk
26	Czuryllo, Kazimierz	5	Blagowieszczensk
27	Dajkowski, Kazimierz	11	Blagowieszczensk
28	Dajkowski,Wladyslaw	14	Blagowieszczensk
29	Danilewicz, Waclaw	12	Blagowieszczensk
30	Danilewicz, Wilhelm	14	Blagowieszczensk
31	Danilewicz, Wincenty	9	Blagowieszczensk
32	Dauter, Bronislaw	10	Aleksiejewsk
33	Dauter, Witold	3	Aleksiejewsk
34	Dabrowski, Feliks	8	Chabarowsk
35	Domalanus, Feliks	16	Chabarowsk
36	Draganski, Leopold	12	Chabarowsk
37	Druksziejn, Jan	9	Chabarowsk
38	Druksziejn, Henryk	10	Chabarowsk
39	Dryzalowski, Zygmunt	10	Chabarowsk
40	Ertner, Kazimierz	15	Chabarowsk
41	Fik, Bazyli	10	Harbin
42	Fedorczuk, Eugienjusz	8	Harbin
43	Fedorczuk, Stanislaw	12	Harbin
44	Fedorczuk, Wladyslaw	15	Harbin
45	Fedorowicz, Franciszek	5	Harbin
46	Fedorowicz, Jozef	11	Harbin
47	Gajewski, Boleslaw	7	Blagowieszczensk
48	Godlewski, Albin	12	Chabarowsk
49	Grabarczyk, Rafal-Tadeusz	12	Blagowieszczensk
50	Grocholski, Anatol	3	Blagowieszczensk
51	Grudzinski, Aleksander	12	Blagowieszczensk
52	Grudzinski, Henryk	10	Blagowieszczensk
53	Horoszewicz, Konstanty	7	Blagowieszczensk
54	Huwald, Witold	12	Blagowieszczensk
55	Hulewicz, Florjan	3	Aleksiejewsk

56	Hulewicz, Jozef	8	Aleksiejewsk
57	Hulewicz, Piotr	10	Aleksiejewsk
58	Hyba, Eugienjusz	9	Aleksiejewsk
59	Jackowski, Jozef	4	Blagowieszczensk
60	Jackowski, Kazimierz	6	Blagowieszczensk
61	Jaklinski, Szczepan	14	Blagowieszczensk
62	Janczarek, Franciszek	14	Blagowieszczensk
63	Janczarek, Zygmunt	6	Blagowieszczensk
64	Jaltuchowski, Jozef	11	Blagowieszczensk
65	Jankowski, Czeslaw	10	Blagowieszczensk
66	Jankowski, Jan	8	Blagowieszczensk
67	Jankowski, Stanislaw	11	Blagowieszczensk
68	Kaminski, Mieczyslaw	8	Blagowieszczensk
69	Kanonik, Antoni	12	Blagowieszczensk
70	Kanonik, Mikolaj	14	Blagowieszczensk
71	Karasinski, Stanislaw	11	Blagowieszczensk
72	Karasinski, Bonawentura	15	Wladywostok
73	Kisiel, Mikolaj	9	Wladywostok
74	Koczerowski, Mikolaj	10	Wladywostok
75	Kongel, Ludwik	10	Chabarowsk
76	Kongel, Pius	14	Chabarowsk
77	Kongel, Wiktor	12	Chabarowsk
78	Konopka, Edmund	12	Blagowieszczensk
79	Konopka, Waclaw	14	Blagowieszczensk
80	Korzec, Aleksander	6	Blagowieszczensk
81	Korzec, Franciszek	13	Blagowieszczensk
82	Kozer, Zygmunt	14	Blagowieszczensk
83	Kot, Zygmunt	16	Blagowieszczensk
84	Kot-Kotkowicz, Antoni	7	Blagowieszczensk
85	Kot-Kotkowicz, Kazimierz	9	Blagowieszczensk
86	Kot-Kotkowicz, Stanislaw	4	Blagowieszczensk

87	Kotynski, Bronislaw	15	Blagowieszczensk
88	Kotynski, Cezary	7	Blagowieszczensk
89	Kotynski, Franciszek	12	Blagowieszczensk
90	Kotynski, Leonard	16	Blagowieszczensk
91	Kowalski, Aleksander	11	Charbarowsk
92	Krajsberg, Mikolaj	14	Blagowieszczensk
93	Krzyszczuk, Bonifacy	11	Wladywostok
94	Krzyszczuk, Dominik	7	Wladywostok
95	Krzyszczuk, Piotr	13	Wladywostok
96	Kuczkowski, Wladyslaw	2	Mandzurja
97	Kunko, Wladyslaw	11	Chilok
98	Kusznierow,Francixzek	8	Charbarowsk
99	Kusznierow, Konstanty	12	Charbarowsk
100	Lewkowicz, Henryk	10	Charbarowsk
101	Lewkowicz, Wladyslaw	14	Charbarowsk
102	Lipski, Aleksander	12	Blagowieszczensk
103	Labanski, Grzegorz	12	Blagowieszczensk
104	Latkowski, Aleksy	13	Blagowieszczensk
105	Luzowski, Wladyslaw	10	Chabarowsk
106	Luczynski, Stanislaw	11	Blagowieszczensk
107	Lugowski, Juljusz	8	Blagowieszczensk
108	Lugowski, Stefan	15	Blagowieszczensk
109	Lugowski, Pawel	12	Blagowieszczensk
110	Lukojaniuk, Jan	8	Blagowieszczensk
111	Majewski, Bronislaw	14	Blagowieszczensk
112	Major, Konstanty	8	Blagowieszczensk
113	Malunowicz, Antoni	10	Blagowieszczensk
114	Marszal, Benjamin	11	Blagowieszczensk
115	Mazur-Galuszynski, Augustyn	12	Aleksiejewsk
116	Mazur-Galuszynski, Jan	6	Aleksiejewsk
117	Mazur-Galuszynski,Piotr	10	Aleksiejewsk

118	Mazurkiewicz,Miroslaw	8	Chabarowsk
119	Mickiewicz, Jan	10	Blagowieszczensk
120	Mlynarczyk,Aleksander	6	Blagowieszczensk
121	Muczynski, Marjan Konstanty	4	Blagowieszczensk
122	Musial, Stanislaw-Andrzej	11	Blagowieszczensk
123	Niedzialowski, Michal	8	Wladyvostok
124	Noga, Bronislaw	4	Blagowieszczensk
125	Nosowicz, Franciszek	6	Blagowieszczensk
126	Oborski, Wladyslaw	11	Wladyvostok
127	Oligorski, Aleksander	12	Chabarowsk
128	Oligorski, Wladyslaw	10	Chabarowsk
129	Ospiacz, Aleksander	12	Chabarowsk
130	Pastuch, Aleksander	10	Blagowieszczensk
131	Pastuch, Mikolaj	12	Blagowieszczensk
132	Pietrzyk, Aleksander	9	Blagowieszczensk
133	Pietrzyk, Bogdan	12	Blagowieszczensk
134	Pietrzak, Edward	10	Blagowieszczensk
135	Pietrzak, Marjan	14	Blagowieszczensk
136	Piotuch, Antoni	16	Blagowieszczensk
137	Piotuch, Jan	18	Blagowieszczensk
138	Piotrowski, Waclaw	15	Czyta
139	Ploszajski, Jerzy	12	Charbin
140	Ploszajski, Tadeusz	4	Nikolsk Ussuryjski
141	Powierza, Waclaw	6	Nikolsk Ussuryjski
142	Pomian, Dymitr	12	Nikolsk Ussuryjski
143	Pomian, Jakob	6	Nikolsk Ussuryjski
144	Protalinski, Innocenty	14	Blagowieszczensk
145	Rodzewicz, Romuald	9	Cycykar
146	Rodzewicz, Tadeusz	11	Blagowieszczensk
147	Romanowski, Leon	9	Blagowieszczensk
148	Romejko, Stanislaw	10	Chabarowsk

149	Sadowski, Henryk	11	Blagowieszczensk
150	Sadowski, Wladyslaw	7	Blagowieszczensk
151	Samojlis, Henryk	6	Blagowieszczensk
152	Sciezko, Walenty	8	Blagowieszczensk
153	Sielski, Antoni	13	Cyzta
154	Sielski, Wladyslaw	11	Czyta
155	Sikorski, Aleksander	15	Blagowieszczensk
156	Skrotski, Pawel	9	Blagowieszczensk
157	Skowera, Genadjusz	12	Blagowieszczensk
158	Skowera, Wlodzimierz	10	Blagowieszczensk
159	Slizin, Wiktor	4	Blagowieszczensk
160	Stepnicki, Aleksander	4	Wladywostok
161	Stepnicki, Jerzy	14	Wladywostok
162	Stepanow, Ryszard	14	Wladywostok
163	Sobczynski, Donat	6	Wladywostok
164	Sobczynski, Kazimierz	15	Wladywostok
165	Solomianko, Jozef	6	Wladywostok
166	Sulimirski, Stefan	13	Blagowieszczensk
167	Szantyr, Jerzy	13	Blagowieszczensk
168	Szopa, Jozef	13	Blagowieszczensk
169	Szczesnowicz, Marjan	9	Imanpo
170	Szczesnowicz, Waclaw	4	Imanpo
171	Szemlowski, Aleksander	7	Blagowieszczensk
172	Szemlowski, Stanislaw	13	Blagowieszczensk
173	Szuk, Oleg	6	Chabarowsk
174	Szychalewski, Michal	6	Czyta
175	Szydlowski, Pawel	6	Wladywostok
176	Trzesniewski, Roman	14	Chabarowsk
177	Trzinski, Eugienjusz	11	Chabarowsk
178	Turowicz, Wladyslaw	12	Chabarowsk
179	Twarynowicz, Bazyli	14	Chabarowsk

180	Urban, Wladyslaw	14	Chabarowsk
181	Wachonin, Stanislaw	14	Chabarowsk
182	Wachonin, Wiktor	9	Chabarowsk
183	Wasiewicz, Adolf	14	Chabarowsk
184	Wasiewicz, Leon	10	Chabarowsk
185	Weber, Wiktor	14	Blagowieszczensk
186	Wisniewski, Wiktor	7	Harbin
187	Wisniewski, Henryk	2	Harbin
188	Wisniewski, Kazimierz	4	Harbin
189	Wisniewski, Witold	8	Harbin
190	Wojtulewicz, Wiktor	9	Wladywostok
191	Wojtulewicz,Wladyslaw	7	Wladywostok
192	Woloncaj, Wiktor	11	Wladywostok
193	Woloncaj, Eugenjusz	13	Wladywostok
194	Woronko, Stanislaw	10	Blagowieszczensk
195	Wolczynski, Wladyslaw	15	Blagowieszczensk
196	Wroblewski, Bronislaw	12	Blagowieszczensk
197	Wroblewski,Mieczyslaw	15	Blagowieszczensk
198	Wroblewski, Wladyslaw	15	Blagowieszczensk
199	Zapolski, Teofil	10	Blagowieszczensk
200	Zawadzki, Stanislaw	14	Czyta
201	Zawadzki, Wladyslaw	14	Czyta
202	Zawadzki, Mieczyslaw	16	Czyta
203	Zawadzki, Wladyslaw	16	Czyta
204	Zielinski, Adolf	13	Chajlar
205	Zielinski, Bronislaw	8	Chajlar
206	Zielinski, Feliks	15	Chajlar
207	Ziolkowski, Karol	11	Aleksiejewsk
208	Zwolski, Mamert	9	Aleksiejewsk
209	Zak, Borys	16	Aleksiejewsk
210	Zak, Mikolaj	14	Aleksiejewsk

LIST OF GIRLS

	Name of Child	Age	Where Found
1	Agejewa, Eugenja	3	Blagowieszczensk
2	Baranowska, Janina	7	Harbin
3	Bem, Danuta	12	Mandzurja
4	Bem, Janina	11	Mandzurja
5	Bem, Halina	10	Mandzurja
6	Bejtman, Jadwiga	14	Blagowieszczensk
7	Bejtman, Marja	8	Blagowieszczensk
8	Blizinska, Alicja	6	Wierchnieudzinsk
9	Bogucka, Eleonora	10	Wierchnieudzinsk
10	Bogdan, Eugenja	15	Harbin
11	Brestowska, Petronela	9	Harbin
12	Budzynska, Genowefa	9	Chabarowsk
13	Burdziuk, Irena	9	Blagowieszczensk
14	Chorzelska, Janina	14	Harbin
15	Chorzelska, Marja	17	Harbin
16	Choroszkiewicz, Eugenja	2	Harbin
17	Choroszkiewicz, Helena	10	Harbin
18	Cieslikowska, Wanda	12	Blagowieszczensk
19	Cudzinska, Lucja	10	Blagowieszczensk
20	Cymek, Marja	10	Harbin
21	Dajkowska, Stefanja	10	Blagowieszczensk
22	Danilewicz	15	Blagowieszczensk
23	Dauter, Eleonora	11	Blagowieszczensk
24	Dabrowska, Janina	12	Chabarowsk
25	Draganska, Irena	10	Chabarowsk
26	Drzyzelowska, Marja	10	Chabarowsk
27	Falkowska, Aniela	14	Chabarowsk
28	Fik, Eugenja	9	Harbin
29	Fedorczuk, Felicja	15	Harbin

30	Golik, Marja	9	Harbin
31	Grabarczy, Walentyna	12	Blagowieszczensk
32	Grabarczyk, Wanda	8	Blagowieszczensk
33	Herman, Helena	7	Blagowieszczensk
34	Hulewicz, Feliksa	5	Aleksiejewsk
35	Jackowska, Zofia	15	Blagowieszczensk
36	Jadykina, Aleksandra	8	Chabarowsk
37	Jadykina, Klaudja	11	Chabarowsk
38	Janczarek, Antonina	10	Blagowieszczensk
39	Janczarek, Stanislawa	12	Blagowieszczensk
40	Jankowska, Helena	9	Blagowieszczensk
41	Jankowska, Wanda	8	Blagowieszczensk
42	Jezykowska, Antonina	6	Aleksiejewsk
43	Jezykowska, Apolonja	10	Aleksiejewsk
44	Jezykowska, Stanislawa	8	Aleksiejewsk
45	Kalinowska, Leokadja	9	Aleksiejewsk
46	Kesik, Zofia	7	Blagowieszczensk
47	Kesik, Slawa	11	Blagowieszczensk
48	Kisiel, Tatjana	6	Wladywostok
49	Kolowska, Bronislawa	6	Wladywostok
50	Kongiel, Stanislawa	8	Chabarowsk
51	Konczewska, Helena	15	Blagowieszczensk
52	Korkuc, Antonina	5	Blagowieszczensk
53	Korkuc, Helena	14	Blagowieszczensk
54	Koronowska, Janina	14	Blagowieszczensk
55	Kot Kotkiewicz, Marja	12	Blagowieszczensk
56	Kowalska, Walentyna	8	Chabarowsk
57	Kowalska, Zenajda	6	Chabarowsk
58	Kowzan, Jadwiga	15	Chabarowsk
59	Kowzan, Stanislawa	9	Chabarowsk
60	Krauze, Jadwiga	9	Chabarowsk

61	Krzysztofik, Anna	15	Chabarowsk
62	Krzysztofik, Anna	12	Chabarowsk
63	Krzyszczuk, Aniela	10	Wladywostok
64	Krzyszczuk, Marja	8	Wladywostok
65	Kuczkowska, Jadwiga	1	Mandzurja
66	Kusznierow,Katarzyna	10	Chabarowsk
67	Lasocka, Sabina	10	Chabarowsk
68	Lipska, Marja	13	Blagowieszczensk
69	Lipska, Karolina	11	Blagowieszczensk
70	Liszkowska, Teodora	14	Blagowieszczensk
71	Lukomsak,Aleksandra	7	Blagowieszczensk
72	Luczynska, Zofia	14	Blagowieszczensk
73	Lukojaniuk, Ksenia	12	Blagowieszczensk
74	Lukojaniuk, Matrona	14	Blagowieszczensk
75	Maciejewska,Czeslawa	8	Blagowieszczensk
76	Maciejewska, Marja	2	Blagowieszczensk
77	Majewska, Halina	13	Blagowieszczensk
78	Majewska, Jadwiga	15	Blagowieszczensk
79	Malunowicz, Jadwiga	7	Blagowieszczensk
80	Matusiewicz,Aleksandra	7	Wladywostok
81	Matusiewicz, Jadwiga	8	Wladywostok
82	Matusiewicz,Stanislawa	9	Wladywostok
83	Matusiewicz, Regina	11	Harbin
84	Macewicz, Marja	15	Harbin
85	Mazurkiewicz, Halina	12	Harbin
86	Mazurkiewicz, Marja	14	Harbin
87	Mazurkiewicz, Zofia	8	Harbin
88	Mejers, Jadwiga	14	Czyta
89	Merkowska, Marja	15	Blagowieszczensk
90	Mickiewicz, Nadzieja	8	Blagowieszczensk
91	Mlynarczyk, Helena	3	Blagowieszczensk

92	Modzelewska, Eugenja	11	Blagowieszczensk
93	Muczynska, Marja	10	Blagowieszczensk
94	Napiorkowska, Balbina	13	Charbin
95	Napiorkowska, Irena	7	Charbin
96	Napiorkowska, Janina	11	Charbin
97	Napiorkowska,Genowefa	9	Charbin
98	Nasikowska, Elzbieta	11	Aleksiejewsk
99	Nasikowska, Genowefa	14	Aleksiejewsk
100	Nasikowska, Janina	7	Aleksiejewsk
101	Nasikowska, Karolina	9	Aleksiejewsk
102	Niewinowska, Marja	7	Wladywostok
103	Niedzialkowska, Helena	10	Wladywostok
104	Niedzialkowska, Janina	9	Wladywostok
105	Nosowicz, Antonina	12	Blagowieszczensk
106	Nosowicz, Jadwiga	11	Blagowieszczensk
107	Oligorska, Wiera	15	Chabarowsk
108	Otocka, Antonina	7	Chabarowsk
109	Ostrowska, Marja	6	Chabarowsk
110	Poniznik, Antonina	9	Blagowieszczensk
111	Poniznik, Julja	12	Blagowieszczensk
112	Pancerzynska, Marja	10	Blagowieszczensk
113	Piatkowska, Eugenia	12	Blagowieszczensk
114	Piatkowska, Julja	5	Blagowieszczensk
115	Piatkowska, Walentyna	13	Blagowieszczensk
116	Pietrzyk, Barbara	8	Blagowieszczensk
117	Piotrowska, Natalja	10	Nik. Ussuuryjski
118	Ploszasjka, Marja	14	Nik. Ussuuryjski
119	Powierza, Honorata	10	Nik. Ussuuryjski
120	Polonska, Wladyslawa	14	Nik. Ussuuryjski
121	Powierza, Jkzefa	9	Nik. Ussuuryjski
122	Retunska, Olga	13	Blagowieszczensk

123	Rodzewicz, Zofia	13	Cycykar
124	Romejko, Marja	9	Chabarowsk
125	Romejko, Regina	6	Chabarowsk
126	Romejko, Zofia	5	Chabarowsk
127	Rosowieecka,Stanislawa	14	Blagowieszczensk
128	Rudzinska, Zofia	1	Blagowieszczensk
129	Rymsza, Eleonora	11	Blagowieszczensk
130	Rymsza, Regina	8	Blagowieszczensk
131	Rysjaniec, Isabella	5	Blagowieszczensk
132	Sysjanjec, Zofia	4	Blagowieszczensk
133	Samojlis, Anna	10	Blagowieszczensk
134	Skrotcka, Antonina	6	Blagowieszczensk
135	Slizin, Emilja	10	Blagowieszczensk
136	Slizin, Halina	12	Blagowieszczensk
137	Slizin, Lucja	6	Blagowieszczensk
138	Slupecka, Helena	7	Wladywostok
139	Stepnicka, Aleksandra	9	Wladywostok
140	Stepnicka, Barbara	7	Wladywostok
141	Sobczynska, Cecylja	14	Wladywostok
142	Sobczynska, Helena	10	Wladywostok
143	Sobczynska, Jadwiga	8	Wladywostok
144	Solomianko, Halina	2	Wladywostok
145	Solomianko, Karolina	8	Wladywostok
146	Solomianko,Wladyslawa	14	Wladywostok
147	Sroczynska, Wanda	9	Wladywostok
148	Sulimirska, Stanislawa	15	Blagowieszczensk
149	Sulimirska, Zofia	12	Blagowieszczensk
150	Swiderska, Eleonora	14	Blagowieszczensk
151	Szymczyk, Janina	8	Blagowieszczensk
152	Szymczyk, Walerja	4	Blagowieszczensk
153	Szymczyk, Zofia	15	Blagowieszczensk

154	Szczesnowicz, Anna	6	Imanpo
155	Szczesnowicz,Genowefa	9	Imanpo
156	Szuk, Alla	12	Chabarowsk
157	Szuk, Luba	12	Chabarowsk
158	Szychalewska, Marja	2	Czyta
159	Troll, Anna	14	Wladywostok
160	Trzesniewska, Genowefa	11	Chabarowsk
161	Trzcinska, Stanislawa	13	Chabarowsk
162	Wachonina, Anna	6	Chabarowsk
163	Wachonina, Bronislawa	11	Chabarowsk
164	Wachonina, Irena	8	Chabarowsk
165	Wachonina, Weronika	13	Chabarowsk
166	Wolontaj, Walerja	9	Wladywostok
167	Wojcik, Zofja	7	Blagowieszczensk
168	Woronka, Jadwiga	12	Blagowieszczensk
169	Wroblewsla, Jenina	14	Blagowieszczensk
170	Zadwornych, Katarzyna	10	Blagowieszczensk
171	Zakoscielna, Katarzyna	12	Blagowieszczensk
172	Zapolska, Elonora	7	Blagowieszczensk
173	Zawadzka, Felicja	4	Czyta
174	Zawadzka, Marja	9	Czyta
175	Zielinska, Janina	15	Chajlar
176	Zielinska, Zofia	10	Chajlar
177	Zwolska, Eugenja	15	Aleksiejewsk
178	Zwolska, Marja	14	Aleksiejewsk
179	Zaluk, Walerja	8	Aleksiejewsk
180	Zak, Anna	12	Aleksiejewsk
181	Zak, Helena	4	Aleksiejewsk

Appendix 3

SIBERIAN CHILDREN REGISTERED AT ST. HEDWIG'S AND TRANSFERRED TO ST. JOSEPH ORPHANAGE

(Registration of Wladyslaw Wojdak shown in Figure 30, 31)

Gryszkus, Jan (John)
Gryszkus, Jozef (Joseph)
Gryszkus, Kazimiera (Casimiera)
Grzegorzewska, Regina (Bronis)
Grzegorzewski, Wiktor (Victor)
Kanezus-Bajlon, August
Kanezus-Bajlon, Flora
Marszal, Anna,
Marszal, Helena
Marszal, Inocenty (Innocent)
Marszal, Ludwik (Louis)
Sapierzynska, Regina (Benigna)
Szurkus, Jerzy (George)
Wedzik, Marja (Mary)
Wedzik, Wladyslaw (Ladislaus)

Gryszkus, Jan (John)

POLISH SIBERIAN WAR CHILDREN
UNDER THE CARE OF
THE NATIONAL POLISH COMMITTEE OF AMERICA
CHICAGO, ILL.

HISTORY

Name of Child ..Gryszkus..John.........Age...... Born 1909 years on...................19...

Admitted.18.. day of..October......................1920

Name of Parish ....Baptized in ....Parish

Address .... City of..... Janiszki .... State..............

Father's name ..Bonifacy....................... Nationality...................

Father's occupation and income ....

           Address ..Czyta I Tatarska 14 d.Dorofejewa..........

Mother's name .... Nationality ....

Mother's occupation and income ....

           Address .Dead..............................

Father's creed .........R.C..................Mother's creed ......R.C...

Is father living?...... Mental or Physical condition ....

Is mother living?...... Mental or Physical condition ....

Is father dead?...... Cause of death .... Date ....

Is mother dead?...... Cause of death .... Date ....

Particulars ..Father.does.not.care.for.him..Aunt.living.in.Konwieńskiej

....

....

....

....

....

....

Gryszkus, Jozef (Joseph)

POLISH SIBERIAN WAR CHILDREN
UNDER THE CARE OF
THE NATIONAL POLISH COMMITTEE OF AMERICA
CHICAGO, ILL.

HISTORY

Gryszkus Joseph   Born 1913.

Name of Child ....Age...... years on...................19...

b 16   October

Admitted...... day of................................1920

Name of Parish ....Baptized in ....Parish

Janiszki

Address .... City of..................... State.............

Bonifacy

Father's name .... Nationality.................

Father's occupation and income ....

Uzyta I Tatarska 14 d.Dorofejewa

Address ....

Mother's name .... Nationality ....

Mother's occupation and income ....

Dead

Address ....

R.C.   R.C.

Father's creed ....Mother's creed ....

Is father living?...... Mental or Physical condition ....

Is mother living?...... Mental or Physical condition ....

Is father dead?...... Cause of death .... Date ....

Is mother dead?...... Cause of death .... Date ....

Particulars ....

Father does not care for him. Aunt living in Konwiskiej.

....

....

....

....

....

Gryszkus, Kazimiera (Casimiera)

POLISH SIBERIAN WAR CHILDREN
UNDER THE CARE OF
THE NATIONAL POLISH COMMITTEE OF AMERICA
CHICAGO, ILL.

HISTORY

Name of Child .....Gryszkus Kazimiera ..... Born 1906. ..... Age..... years on.....19...

Admitted 26... day of. October 1920

Name of Parish ..... Baptized in ..... Parish

Address .....Konwieńkiej ..... City of..... State.............

Father's name .....Bonifacy ..... Nationality.................

Father's occupation and income .....Laborer ....

Address .....uzyta I Tatarska 14 d.Dorofejewa ....

Mother's name ..... Nationality ....

Mother's occupation and income ....

Address .....Dead ....

Father's creed .....R.C. ..... Mother's creed .....R.C. ....

Is father living?...... Mental or Physical condition ....

Is mother living?...... Mental or Physical condition ....

Is father dead?...... Cause of death ..... Date ....

Is mother dead?...... Cause of death ..... Date ....

Particulars .....Father does not care for her. Aunt living in Konwieńskiej. ....

....

....

....

....

....

....

Grzegorzewska, Regina (Bronis)

POLISH SIBERIAN WAR CHILDREN
UNDER THE CARE OF
THE NATIONAL POLISH COMMITTEE OF AMERICA
CHICAGO, ILL.

HISTORY

Name of Child ...Grzegorzewska Bronislaia.... Age...Born 1909 years on...................19...

Admitted...16 day of...October...................1920

Name of Parish ...Bujwidzkiej........... Baptized in ....Parish

Address .... City of.................... State.............

Father's name ...Joseph.................. Nationality...Polish.........

Father's occupation and income ....

Address .Dead.................................

Mother's name .....Josephine.................. Nationality .....Polish.......

Mother's occupation and income ..Polish Army...................

Address .Czyta II Angarska róg Irkutskiej ul....................

Father's creed .....R.C................ Mother's creed ......R.C.........

Is father living?...... Mental or Physical condition ....

Is mother living?...... Mental or Physical condition ....

Is father dead?...... Cause of death .... Date ....

Is mother dead?...... Cause of death .... Date ....

Particulars ....
.........Parents formerly lived in Wileńskiej, gub. w Bujwidzkiej parafii
...Brothers: Felix, Ignatius, Adam..............................
....
....
....
....
....

Grzegorzewski, Wiktor (Victor)

POLISH SIBERIAN WAR CHILDREN
UNDER THE CARE OF
THE NATIONAL POLISH COMMITTEE OF AMERICA
CHICAGO, ILL.

HISTORY

Name of Child Grzegorzewski Wiktor ..... Age. 8 ... years on....... 1920 ....19...

Admitted. 16. . day of. October......................1920

Name of Parish .... Baptized in Blagowieszozyńłk .....Parish

Address .... City of...................... State...............

Father's name .Joseph........................... Nationality... Polish...........

Father's occupation and income ....

Address ..Dead..

Mother's name .. Josephine .... Nationality ... Polish ....

Mother's occupation and income ... Polish Army...............................

Address .Ozyta II Angarska róg Irkutskiej ul.

Father's creed .....R.C,.................... Mother's creed .....R.C,.............

Is father living?...... Mental or Physical condition ....

Is mother living?...... Mental or Physical condition ....

Is father dead?...... Cause of death .... Date ....

Is mother dead?...... Cause of death .... Date ....

Particulars ..Parents.lived.formerly.in.Wileńskiej.gub,.w.sujwidzkiej..

...........parafii,..

Brothers: Felix,Ignatius,Adam

....

....

....

....

....

Kanezus-Bajlon, August

POLISH SIBERIAN WAR CHILDREN
UNDER THE CARE OF
THE NATIONAL POLISH COMMITTEE OF AMERICA
CHICAGO, ILL.

———

HISTORY

Name of Child Kanczus - Bajlon August Born 1910 Age...... years on...................19...

Admitted..16.. day of...October.......................1920

Name of Parish .... Baptized in ..Czyta................Parish

Address .... City of...................... State.............

Father's name .John............................. Nationality......................

Father's occupation and income ....

        Address ..Dead...

Mother's name ..Helen......................... Nationality......................

Mother's occupation and income ....

        Address .Czyta Bulwarna ul.....................................

Father's creed .........R.C................Mother's creed ..R.C.................

Is father living?...... Mental or Physical condition ....

Is mother living?...... Mental or Physical condition .Deaf and Dumb..............

Is father dead?...... Cause of death .... Date ....

Is mother dead?...... Cause of death .... Date ....

Particulars Own a house in Czyta Bulwarna ul.................................

    Sister and grandfather living in Czyta.

....

....

....

....

....

....

Kanezus-Bajlon, Flora

POLISH SIBERIAN WAR CHILDREN
UNDER THE CARE OF
THE NATIONAL POLISH COMMITTEE OF AMERICA
CHICAGO, ILL.

HISTORY

Name of Child ....Kanczus - Bajlon Flora.... Age..... years on...............19... Born 1906

Admitted......16 day of....October............................1920

Name of Parish .... Baptized in ....Czyta..............Parish

Address .... City of...................... State..............

Father's name ....John....................:.............. Nationality....................

Father's occupation and income ....

Address ....Dead..

Mother's name ....Helen................................ Nationality ....

Mother's occupation and income ....

Address ....Czyta Bulwarna ul.................................

Father's creed ....R.C.................. Mother's creed ....R.C.................

Is father living?...... Mental or Physical condition ....

Is mother living?...... Mental or Physical condition ....Deaf and dumb..........

Is father dead?...... Cause of death .... Date ....

Is mother dead?...... Cause of death .... Date ....

Particulars ....
....Own a house in Czyta Bulwarna ul.....................
....Sister and grandfather living in Czyta................
....
....
....
....

Marszal, Anna

POLISH SIBERIAN WAR CHILDREN
UNDER THE CARE OF
THE NATIONAL POLISH COMMITTEE OF AMERICA
CHICAGO, ILL.

HISTORY

Name of Child ....Marszal Anna........ Age.6... years on...August.15....19.20

Admitted:16.... day of..October....................1920

Name of Parish ....Baptized in Sacred.Heart.of.JesusParish

Address Azabu-Tokyo-Japan... City of.................... State.............

Father's name ....Casimir.................... Nationality....................

Father's occupation and income ....

Address .Dead......................

Mother's name ....Antonia.................... Nationality ....

Mother's occupation and income ....

Address ....Czyta II Korotkowska,d.Szerygowa..............

Father's creed ....R.C....................Mother's creed .........R.C...........

Is father living?..no.. Mental or Physical condition ....

Is mother living?..yes. Mental or Physical condition ....

Is father dead?...... Cause of death .... Date ....

Is mother dead?...... Cause of death .... Date ....

Particulars ......Benjamin.and.Victor,brothers,live.with.mother:..........

..........Father's.brothers.and.grandmother.living.near.Warsaw........

....Mother.does.not.care.for.Anna.................

....

....

....

....

Marszal, Helena

POLISH SIBERIAN WAR CHILDREN
UNDER THE CARE OF
THE NATIONAL POLISH COMMITTEE OF AMERICA
CHICAGO, ILL.

HISTORY

Name of Child ...Marszal Helena............ Age...... years on...Born 1912...........19...

Admitted...26... day of...October......................1920

Name of Parish .... Baptized in ....Parish

Address .... City of...Bodajbo near Mandhuria.......... State...............

Father's name ...Casimir............... Nationality....................

Father's occupation and income ....

Address ...Dead...

Mother's name ...Antonia.............. Nationality ....

Mother's occupation and income ....

Address ...Uzyta II Korotkowska,d.Szerygowa.

Father's creed ...R.C.................... Mother's creed ...R.C...........

Is father living?...dead... Mental or Physical condition ....

Is mother living?...yes... Mental or Physical condition ....

Is father dead?...... Cause of death .... Date ....

Is mother dead?...... Cause of death .... Date ....

Particulars ...Benjamin and victor-brothers with mother.Father's brothers and grandmother are living near Warsaw.

...Mother does not care for Helen.

Marszal, Innocenty (Innocent)

POLISH SIBERIAN WAR CHILDREN
UNDER THE CARE OF
THE NATIONAL POLISH COMMITTEE OF AMERICA
CHICAGO, ILL.

HISTORY

Name of Child .....Marszal Innocent...... Born 1908 Age...... years on................19...

Admitted...... 16 day of ....October....................1920

Name of Parish .... Baptized in ....Parish

Address .... City of.....uspieńsk,Siberia.. State..............

Father's name .....Casimir.................... Nationality..................

Father's occupation and income ....

Address .....Dead..

Mother's name ......Antonia.................... Nationality ....

Mother's occupation and income ....

Address .....Uzyta II Korotkowska,d.Szerygowa.......

Father's creed .....R.C.................. Mother's creed .R.C.................

Is father living?...... Mental or Physical condition ....

Is mother living?...... Mental or Physical condition ....

Is father dead?...... Cause of death .... Date ....

Is mother dead?...... Cause of death .... Date ....

Particulars ....Benjamin and victor with mother.Father's brothers and....

grandmother live near Warsaw..

.........Mother does not care for Innocent...........................

Marszal, Ludwik (Louis)

POLISH SIBERIAN WAR CHILDREN
UNDER THE CARE OF
THE NATIONAL POLISH COMMITTEE OF AMERICA
CHICAGO, ILL.

HISTORY

Name of Child ..Marszal Ludwik.......Age..Born 1917 years on.................19...

Admitted..16.. day of..October......................1920

Name of Parish ....Baptized in ....Parish

Address .... City of...Czyta............. State..............

Father's name ..Casimir......................... Nationality....................

Father's occupation and income ....

Address .Dead..

Mother's name .Antonia.................... Nationality ....

Mother's occupation and income ....

Address ..Czyta II Korotkowska,d.Szerygowa..................

Father's creed ..........R.C............. Mother's creed .........R.C................

Is father living?...... Mental or Physical condition ....

Is mother living?...... Mental or Physical condition ....

Is father dead?...... Cause of death .... Date ....

Is mother dead?...... Cause of death .... Date ....

Particulars ....Benjamin and Victor with mother...Father's brothers....

.... and grandmother living near Warsaw..............................

.................Mother does not care for Ludwik..............

....

....

....

....

Sapierzynska, Regina (Benigna)

POLISH SIBERIAN WAR CHILDREN
UNDER THE CARE OF
THE NATIONAL POLISH COMMITTEE OF AMERICA
CHICAGO, ILL.

HISTORY

Name of Child Sapieżynska Benigna Age 17 years on August 23 19 20

Admitted 16 day of October 1920

Name of Parish Baptized in Parish

Address City of Warsaw State

Father's name John Nationality

Father's occupation and income

Address Ufy, Tujnary.

Mother's name Frances Nationality

Mother's occupation and income

Address Ufy, Tujnary.

Father's creed R.C. Mother's creed R.C.

Is father living? Mental or Physical condition

Is mother living? Mental or Physical condition

Is father dead? Cause of death Date

Is mother dead? Cause of death Date

Particulars Parents remained near Ufy, Tujnary.

Aunt, Malgorzata Sapieżynska living in Czerczanowie near Warsaw.

Szurkus, Jerzy (George)

POLISH SIBERIAN WAR CHILDREN
UNDER THE CARE OF
THE NATIONAL POLISH COMMITTEE OF AMERICA
CHICAGO, ILL.

HISTORY

Born 1911

Name of Child ...Szurkus George......Age...... years on...................19...

Admitted...16. day of...October.....................1920

Name of Parish ....Baptized in ....Parish

Address .... City of..................... State.............

Father's name ....Anton............................ Nationality...................

Father's occupation and income ....

Address ...Dead..

Mother's name ..Martha............................ Nationality ....

Mother's occupation and income ..Służy u księdza w Nowo- Nikołajewsku........

Address ....

Father's creed ....Mother's creed ....R.C.................

Is father living?...... Mental or Physical condition ....

Is mother living?...... Mental or Physical condition ....

Is father dead?...... Cause of death .... Date ....

Is mother dead?...... Cause of death .... Date ....

Particulars

...........Wzięty z ochronki przy kościele w Charbinie.............

....

....

....

....

....

Wedzik, Marja (Mary)

POLISH SIBERIAN WAR CHILDREN
UNDER THE CARE OF
THE NATIONAL POLISH COMMITTEE OF AMERICA
CHICAGO, ILL.

HISTORY

Name of Child .Wedzik.Mary............. Age...... Born 1916 years on................. .19...

Admitted... 16 day of...October.....................1920

Name of Parish .... Baptized in ....Parish

Address .... City of..................... State.............

Father's name .... Nationality.....................

Father's occupation and income ....

       Address ....

Mother's name .... Frances.................. Nationality .... Polish.....

Mother's occupation and income ....

       Address ... Wladywostok. 10.Robocza.N.9....................

Father's creed .... Mother's creed ....

Is father living?...... Mental or Physical condition ....

Is mother living?...... Mental or Physical condition ....

Is father dead?...... Cause of death .... Date ....

Is mother dead?...... Cause of death .... Date ....

Particulars ....

....

....

....

....

....

....

Wedzik, Wladyslaw (Ladislaus)

POLISH SIBERIAN WAR CHILDREN
UNDER THE CARE OF
THE NATIONAL POLISH COMMITTEE OF AMERICA
CHICAGO, ILL.

HISTORY

Name of Child Wedzik Ladislaus ....Age...... years on...................19...   Born 1910

Admitted...... day of.................................1920

Name of Parish ....Baptized in R.C. ....Parish

Address .... City of..................... State.............

Father's name .... Nationality.....................

Father's occupation and income ....

Address ....

Mother's name Frances .... Nationality ....

Mother's occupation and income ....

Address Wladywostok 10 Robocza N 0 ....

Father's creed .... Mother's creed ....

Is father living?...... Mental or Physical condition ....

Is mother living?...... Mental or Physical condition ....

Is father dead?...... Cause of death .... Date ....

Is mother dead?...... Cause of death .... Date ....

Particulars ....

....

....

....

....

....

....

ABOUT THE AUTHOR

Paul Wojdak

Before retiring in 2011, Paul Wojdak worked as a professional geologist for forty years. A boyhood passion for stamp collecting led to an adult interest in history, foreign cultures and travelling the world. He currently lives with his wife, Teresa, on Tyhee Lake, in British Columbia, in a home they built together.

Printed in the USA
CPSIA information can be obtained
at www.ICGtesting.com
JSHW070222141024
71552JS00004B/9

9 781039 196865